Constructing Hornbeck

Constructing Hornbeck

Dayton Lummis

iUniverse, Inc.
New York Lincoln Shanghai

Constructing Hornbeck

iUniverse books may be ordered through booksellers or by contacting:

iUniverse
2021 Pine Lake Road, Suite 100
Lincoln, NE 68512
www.iuniverse.com
1-800-Authors (1-800-288-4677)

Because of the dynamic nature of the Internet, any Web addresses or links contained in this book may have changed since publication and may no longer be valid.

The views expressed in this work are solely those of the author and do not necessarily reflect the views of the publisher, and the publisher hereby disclaims any responsibility for them.

Cover photograph of author by Meredith Jennings

Rear cover photograph of Hornbeck by Michael Vann Moore, East Mojave, 1967

Rear cover photograph of Dayton Lummis by Meredith Jennings, NYC, January 2007

ISBN: 978-0-595-44306-2 (pbk)
ISBN: 978-0-595-88635-7 (ebk)

Printed in the United States of America

For Hornbeck

Who got an early start
killing time …

Contents

PROLOGUE

Doctor Avis called the other night from Watertown up in Connecticut. After some rambling conversation he suddenly asked, out of nowhere:

"Do you remember Hornbeck? That crazy fellow from North Beach, the one who used to sit at our table at Vesuvio in 'the old days?' Told weird stories. I half-believed most of them. He called Bill Howarth 'the lanky Bolshevik?' That was good! Remember, he disappeared, no one knew where? Well, an old friend from North Beach called the other night, said he thought he had seen Hornbeck on Upper Grant Avenue. That special way of walking he had, like a sailor's gait. He called, 'Hey, Hornbeck!' The man paused, turned, and then was gone, around a corner and into the fog …"

◆　　◆　　◆

"Dayton, you really should give up this Hornbeck thing, let it go. It is not at all healthy for you, especially at your age. I tell this to you as your friend, college roommate, and as a medical doctor. Let it go!"

—J.E.O. Hughes, M.D.

INTRODUCTION

It was Doctor Avis who first met Hornbeck, one night in Spec's in North Beach. He got talking to some guy about Captain Jennings, the chance of getting a job on his tugboat. The guy said to the Doctor, "I'm Hornbeck, National Maritime Union. You got papers, or are you just another intellectual posing as a working man?"

Hornbeck was in Spec's and Vesuvio a lot, and he often joined us. Then, he was suddenly gone—no one knew where. That happened often in North Beach.

I remember after Hornbeck disappeared going with Doctor Avis to the apartment in the Haight-Ashbury where he had lived. There was, as usual, a bunch of hippies sitting around drinking beer and smoking dope. It was not a productive atmosphere. A few of them knew that we had known Hornbeck. I asked if the man had left anything behind. "Not much." one of the hippies said. "A bunch of old, worn out clothes and a falling apart briefcase stuffed with papers, from San Francisco State classes probably." We asked if we could see the briefcase. Sure, one said, and retrieved it from another room. It was indeed falling apart, and was stuffed with papers. We asked if we could have it. The hippie said sure, they were just going to toss it.

So, the Doctor and I took that briefcase back to 1922 Larkin and that night over Rainier Ale examined the contents. A treasure trove of notes, observations, philosophic meanderings, poetry and short fiction pieces. Why had Hornbeck left that stuff behind? Who knows ...

The briefcase went out for the scavengers, but all the papers, notes, etc., went into a secure box that I have kept over all these years, moving around the country from one place to another. I used to think about Hornbeck, discuss him from time to time with the Doctor. Had he gone to Oregon? Fallen under a freight train in Northern California? Gone to Mexico, or back East where some said he was from, many years ago? Recently, in my mind I began to construct Hornbeck, who he had been, who he might have become, might be now. Something like that. A book began to take shape in my mind. Constructing Hornbeck ...

This is going to be a strange book. It is loosely organized, if organized at all. At times it may not seem to be making much sense, but there is a structure, and eventually things will fall into place—if you have the imagination and intuition to allow them to do so. A sense will emerge—the sort of sense wherein two plus two makes one …

There is a chronology, leading up to Hornbeck's "disappearance" from North Beach. From the face of the earth, if you will. Then a series of impressionistic pieces about Santa Fe, followed by more contemporary descriptive pieces that have to with travels both in the United States and in Europe. The scene shifts largely to the East Coast, and brings us up to almost this very moment. At least to this year. A very different sort of character emerges, someone who has formerly lived many different lives, but is now merging them into one, the mystic past and the very real present. A contemporary man …

◆   ◆   ◆

This is perhaps—probably—a strange and somewhat confused book. I think I know what I have been trying to present here, and what the conclusion is. But I may not have succeeded—I don't know. It is up to the you, the reader, to make that judgement.

Sometimes, as I often did years ago on Mount Tamalpais in Marin County north of San Francisco, one wanders in a fog, sort of "feeling one's way" for familiar terrain and finally achieving it, emerging at the place where one set out, thankfully. A victory of sorts, if a small one. A sort of salvation—redemption, if you will.

And so it is with our wanderings in the natural/psychic world. We often set out not knowing our route or the destination. We stumble, get disoriented, lose the way in fogs. And finally emerge in some sunlit place, wondering at the strangeness of it all.

The journey, half-remembered, sets the course onward, to the present. The future cannot be accurately known, only guessed at, often with unease. We mark certain points in our journey, like blazes on trees, thinking we might retrace our steps and start over. But we often find the blazes gone, or we cannot find them. Seeking to start over at some point, we once again lose our way, stumble around, then find ourselves on the same path as before. There is no going back and starting over. The path and the journey are rigid, leading only to the present as before. There is no changing things, no re-defining …

We emerge from a forest of doubt—both reasonable and unreasonable—but once in the place of bright sunlight we feel that we are saved. That there is a definition that can be understood, shared.

Back in the safe confines of our abodes, where we have hung "our many hats," we seek to put things together, to match things up, to explain the many parts of the journey. To inject meaning into many things that perhaps have none, perhaps were not ever meant to have any.

That is what we do—what I have done. Retrace steps, and attempt the trail again. Put things together and try to look at them in new ways. To attempt construction ...

PART ONE

FORMATIVE

Hornbeck fired the shotgun into the ceiling of the supermarket—KABOOM!

He always did that when knocking over a place. He loved the loud sound, the ceiling tiles and plaster exploding, dust everywhere. And the muthafuckers crouching down, wild-eyed with fear. Others running for cover. Yeah, Hornbeck thought, THAT DOES GET THEIR ATTENTION! And the RESPECT! that he deserved. Man with the gun, and BIG BOOM—HE THE BOSS! Yeah.

◆   ◆   ◆

Hornbeck, struggling for control …

Come on, come on, let's go, baby, take me by the hand and shake like this—never mind who I am or where we are, let's go, whether you know me or not I am not drunk just turned on for this wild ride in the runaway night of drunken moons struggling to rise over too many lost peaks, this night that flashes by in a thousand images, men stumbling in the fog trying to find their way in the hills, shadows in silent dumbstruck remoteness forms lurching among trees looking up hoping for stars this big bike hums and surges in this too fast night the wind tearing pieces off us and hurling them away into this all too real racial polyglot world full of dangerous and violent thoughts impulses acts, hang on, the career is a hanging on. Beyond the river and the shadows is the future, promise beyond the time that pursues us, clings to us, is always there dragging, clutching, no wall can end this trip you don't fool me time the time is now, always now …

Gives us Barabbas!

Some black man behind me in the crowded bar mumbling to himself, "That's Sonny Rawlins blowin' now. Sonny, he's a Rosicrucian, like me. Nobody know that …" I guess when you come from a pine board shack in the Mississippi Delta everything seems big time different.

And this girl at a party: "I really dig Castro—he's so SEXUAL." She is trying to warm herself over an old cast iron radiator.

There is a crudely printed graffiti in the men's room, right above the urinal—you can't miss it—which reads "Ginsberg is a neo-classicist." All vacant peasant faces here tonight, no uprising or peasant revolution out of this crowd! They are in thrall of the sign above the bar: "Avoid the Christmas rush—drink early!"

I have been all over town tonight looking for an old friend. That's OK—I have a man coming later with a jug of wine. Dr. Cribari. These people don't know what they are waiting for. Some don't even know if it's day or night. Know what I mean?

♦   ♦   ♦

THE ASTRAL TRAVEL OF HORNBECK

The beach seemed to shimmer—Hornbeck guessed that was the right word—in the mid-day heat, a thin mist or haze rising from the area where the spent waves rolled up on the flat sand and reflecting the sun shining down out of a cloudless sky. Sky—SPACE, he thought—endless, timeless, devoid of any life probably—we ARE alone. He mused on SPACE, thought of giant, massive, huge—what words?—things, aren't they?—moving, drifting, hurtling—again, what words?—through SPACE. He imagined that there were sometimes great explosions in SPACE, deafening. But who was there to hear? No one. The objects in SPACE, they were all round, were they not? He thought they must be round. Yes, everything in SPACE is ROUND! He tried to imagine himself drifting in SPACE. Would he be ROUND? He would drift in silence, in cold darkness. Where would he get a beer? No beer in SPACE. He felt uneasy. No women in SPACE. He would be alone, terribly alone. Forever.

He finished his beer, stood up and walked toward the water. He wondered if the water was like SPACE. He thought of those things that lived in the water, of sea-snakes, of octopuses, of sandpaper-skin sharks. Mermaids, too, he thought of those.

Hornbeck later sat in a bar talking to a girl. There was music playing, and he felt amused. The girl seemed to find him beautiful. "You are a beautiful man," she said, pulling on his finger. He looked at the girl. She seemed like a child, a young and playful child, as she pulled on his finger. "What do you think of SPACE?" he asked her suddenly. She laughed, and said, "I don't …"

He felt a sudden need to fly, to be high above everything, soaring and dipping. He told the girl, "I need to fly." She stopped pulling on his finger and looked at him strangely. He smiled and put his finger to her lips. "Don't say anything. There are swamps in Africa, vast swamps." he told her, still holding his finger to her lips.

"You are a very strange man," she said, "a strange and beautiful man. I have waited a long time to meet you." "Yes," he said, talking his finger from her lips, "but there is no time in SPACE." The girl leaned forward and kissed him on the forehead. He stared into her tank top, at her breasts, as she lingered with her lips on his forehead. The SPACE, he thought, between her breasts, a tunnel through time, beyond time into darkness. He pulled back and looked at the girl. She had her eyes closed and she still seemed like a child—a mermaid perhaps, he mused. The girl opened her eyes and smiled. "Iodine," he said, "you smell of iodine." He took her hands. "Your hands smell like those of a doctor I knew when I was five."

he said. "Iodine." The girl looked puzzled, and said, "Iodine. That's what you put on cuts." "Yes," he said, "and much more. There is smell to the sea, but no smell to SPACE." He drew a circle in the air with his finger, then said, "I must go now, forever, but remember that I have been your friend. Remember that." The girl reached for her drink and looked at him, pleading in her eyes. "Don't go, please don't go," she said. But he was already gone.

Later Hornbeck was in his truck driving north along the rugged and empty coast. He saw jet contrails in the sky, and thought again of flying. Of sailing through canyons, rising on thermal updrafts, of diving like a bullet toward the sea. He thought of being suspended in the sea, far down where rays of light do not reach, of dozing weightless and inert in the darkness, then darting powerfully ahead with a swipe of his tail, phosphorescent bubbles breaking wildly in the water. He smiled as he sped in his truck along the cliffs above the sea. He imagined driving a SPACE SHIP somewhere so distant it could not be calculated, and he wondered about the immense surges of strange energy that would propel him farther and farther from that tiny speck called by some "earth." "Am I insane?" he wondered, as he pulled the truck into a deserted campground. Mountains rose up out of the sea and stretched away to the north. There was no one around, no one at all. He looked around and thought, "I have been here before, many times, during different stages of my existence, of my journey through SPACE." He remembered the times he had camped along this coast, his clothing all red and black, his long hair blowing in the wind, times when his mind was unsettled. He specifically remembered a piece of lasagna he had consumed at campground here, warmed in tinfoil over a fire, washed down with much beer. He thought of walking the ridges above the sea with Parkhurst, who was oblivious to earth as he talked of stars and the universe. And of Cristina Iversen, who was perhaps still walking beside the still waters of the world holding her blue flower. He drank beer and ate a sandwich, listening to the fierce wind and waves crashing below in the growing darkness. It was like CORNWALL, he thought, reaching far into the past. He smiled, drank more beer and then lay back in the bed of the truck and slept.

The girl came toward him, out of the mist, smiling, he thought. But when she came near he saw that she was not smiling but grimacing, and that she was not as young as she appeared. "Don't reject me," she said, pleadingly, "please." She stood in the cold mist before him, with her hand outstretched and her face contorted, as if in pain. He looked at her and said softly, "No, never, but remember that it was you who abandoned me so me so many centuries ago." He reached to take her hand, but she was suddenly not there, gone! He heard the sea crashing wildly on rocks below. A storm, shouts, the sounds of a ship breaking up. He watched helplessly as the ship and its crew disappeared into the frothing waters. It was disturbing. "A dream," he thought, sitting bolt upright. "Several dreams—I have had too much beer, and my mind is not right, not RIGHT!" He fell back in the truck bead and slept again. Until the sun came up bright and strong over the steep, smoothly rounded mountains that rose from the sea. He awoke feeling rested and refreshed. Strong! He no longer felt insane. He was ready to deal with things, to take charge. Of WHAT? He felt ready to deal with SPACE! To fly, to soar, not drifting inertly deep in the water, waiting. No need to wait!

That night Hornbeck was sitting in a bar in North Beach in San Francisco, listening to jazz and drinking a dark beer. A girl sat at the table with him, her hand resting on his arm. "You are an interesting man," she said, "but you are insane ..." He looked at her, surprised, then laughed. And laughed. The girl withdrew her hand from his arm and stared at him. After a bit he stopped laughing and looked at her, deeply, saying, "I have come all this way, I have found you among all the billions of people on this planet to be told that I am insane? I have known that throughout SPACE! You need not be afraid, I am your friend, now and forever." They both laughed, sat there laughing while jazz played. They laughed wildly, and bumped heads as they leaned toward each other to kiss, until there was no SPACE between them.

Hornbeck was still laughing as he signed his name on some form—"Edward," no last name. Last names did not matter in SPACE. And then they laughed as they ascended on bubbles over the Bay, high above the Bay Bridge, and drifted on thermal currents over the Central Valley, over the crest of the Sierra. They laughed as they rose higher over the Great Basin, over the tiny dots of light called Colorado towns. They laughed as they cart-wheeled through the sky, through SPACE, happy and childish as their tears of laughter blended and drifted into mists that diffused the rays of stars and distant unknown suns.

And Amydon, great King of the Sythians, astronomer and knower of secrets, the all powerful and the all merciful one, watched with his telescope from his golden couch, amused as the glowing pinpoints of light moved across the sky, across SPACE. And as he watched he thought of a name for what seemed to him a golden couple tumbling forever in SPACE. To the assembled sages he announced, "I have seen the STAR SCREWERS." The sages all nodded and looked at one another. One sage whispered, "The King is insane ..." "No," said another, "he is just drunk." "Perhaps," said a third, "but sometimes I believe he sees things we cannot."

The sages withdrew, to fiddle with their potions and tablets. King Amydon stretched on his golden couch, drank deep of his wine, smiled and slipped into sleep. And in his dreams he drove a metallic chariot that moved without beasts. He listened to strange music and felt his finger pulled. He camped beside frothing seas in strange land, and heard himself called a strange name—"EDWARD," it sounded like. He awoke, smiled and breathed deeply. "I have seen the STAR SCREWERS," he said to himself, and smiled again. He dozed, and his goblet fell against his chest, the wine spilling in a widening dark stain across his velvet tunic. "Hornbeck," he mumbled softly. The sages watched from the dark recesses of the Kings chamber, and they were afraid ...

◆   ◆   ◆

One evening while Hoffman and I were sitting in the kitchen in St. David's we got to talking about direction, purpose in life, in our own. Or, perhaps, the lack of it. In response to some question that I have forgotten I told Hoffman, "I always felt, believed, from a very early age that anything that could go wrong in (my) life would go wrong." He answered, "That is pretty pessimistic, particularly at a very early age." I agreed that it was but to a large extent that attitude has defined my life. How so? We talked about that ...

Why this deeply ingrained pessimism? Where did it come from? One might presume, that a certain amount of it was inherited from my father, a deeply pessimistic man. When did I first become aware of this thinking, believe in it? In college, I think. The study of existentialism. That existential stuff of the 1950s, being and nothingness, did not help. Hoffman agreed, "Sure didn't." Events beyond individual control. Blown like leaves in a winter wind, pointlessly. A sense of "helplessness, meaninglessness." Fashionable—yes, at the time, in the bohemia of Greenwich Village and such places. But deeply disturbing.

A gnawing fear of death, an early death, sudden, unexpected. I remember riding from New Haven with classmates to various women's colleges for "fun and adventure," fearing crushing auto accidents, an early death, nothingness. I sank into a depression, could see no meaningful future in life. I just wanted the "here and now" to go on forever. I knew it couldn't but wanted it to. An immature irresponsibility.

I thought of all the people slaughtered in wars throughout history, people whose lives were taken from them for nothing that they had anything to do with. It all seemed so unjust. Nothingness. A sense of hopelessness. No beliefs or religious system could either explain or justify any of that. A growing sense of atheism. No God in heaven to take refuge in. A world of idealistic dreams, disconnected from any reality, one that could not be dashed to pieces. A sense that it will all be as if it had never been ...

◆   ◆   ◆

Article from the *Yale Daily News*, spring 1959:

LONELINESS, DEATH FORM LIFE'S BASIS, BROMBERT AFFIRMS

Insisting that "death and isolation are the basic facts of man's condition," Victor H. Brombert, associate professor of French, discussed the novels of Andre Malraux in a Trumbull College night lecture yesterday.

In all of Malraux's novels there is a deep conviction "that if there is any-thing through which man can conquer (his fate), it is through the attitudes in which he succeeds in negating his nothingness," Mr. Brombert said. Since loneliness is a basis of human life, Mr. Brombert stated that the one thing men do share is the "anguish of loneliness." Malraux realized that man does not know himself as he knows others, and consequently there is a divorce between the inner and outer worlds.

Even the "sexual act is seen as a lonely exercise … in which the body of another is used as a solitary vice," Mr. Brombert said. He continued: "No matter where we turn, man's lot in an absurd universe is death and loneliness."

Commenting on style, Mr. Brombert said that what the reader sees is a series of movements which are not for their own sake, but are to emphasize the tragic elements of Malraux's workers.

◆   ◆   ◆

"… in the darkest depths of our nihilism I have sought only the means of transcending it."

—Albert Camus

◆   ◆   ◆

These are complicated matters, and even the "dance of little heels" on our backs can do little to help us transcend nihilism or conquer our fate. But I must suppose that such a "dance" helps. It's like Frank Sinatra said, "I'm for anything that gets you through the night, booze or religion."

◆   ◆   ◆

I'll throw on other quote in here, since it may have some relevance:

"Man is by nature polygamic whereas woman as a rule is monogamic and polyandrous only when tired of her lover. For the man, as has been truly said, loves the woman, but the love of the woman is for the love of the man."

—Sir Richard Burton, *Arabian Nights*

◆   ◆   ◆

I do not look back on my childhood as a particularly happy time, but neither do I look upon it as a vale of unhappiness and suffering. There were incidents that were troubling, and I suppose that I was thought "difficult." Living as a single child with a divorced mother in the house of elderly grandparents, albeit well-off ones, was not an optimum situation. I just think of those times as being when I was a child, knowing little or nothing of the world or its implications. I did not quite understand that actions have consequences. What might be called happiness or unhappiness were simply brief periods when things were going or not going to my satisfaction. Evaluation of "the pursuit of happiness," one might say. In the simplistic language of our day, it was period when a child "did his thing," and in as much as this was unobstructed the child was happy. Or so it was thought. But, it would be incorrect to assume that a simple time was a happy time; it would be the most superficial of longings to deduce that in retrospect. Childhood is, probably, a sort of limbo, where the winds may blow either hot or cold.

I have read that by the time one is seven or eight years old one is either an optimist or a pessimist. That may be so, but how does it come about? What forces or experiences? Or something that grows from within? Perhaps the proverbial "all of the above." It seems harshly deterministic that one's life be laid out and formed at such an early age. It gives credence to the theory that "nothing is anyone's fault." It would seem that "a happy childhood" would not play a part in such determination, because of primeval forces lurking in the psyche. All riches and blessings could be showered on the child, who still would grow up to be a gloomy, negative individual. Not a happy thought.

The passage of time tends to make one look back at childhood with nostalgia and fondness, as the mind filters away any negative or unpleasant thoughts—unless, of course, they are extreme. The freshness of finding the world "just as it is," and not having to worry about how things have changes for the worse. Not the world as it should be, but with all things possible. This dissipates with time, as one grows more aware that the world and life very well may not be to one's liking or satisfaction. All relative to chance, the role of the individual and the conditions in which he finds himself.

Camus said, "In this world you are either an executioner or a victim. And the choice is entirely yours ..."

◆   ◆   ◆

When I was about twelve years old my mother decided I should have some sort of "counseling" to put me on the right path in life. I think she was concerned that I had drifted away from any such—but what should one expect at age twelve? It was arranged for me to attend sessions at something in Philadelphia connected with the University of Pennsylvania called "The Child Guidance Clinic." I was driven to a series of sessions there, in a somewhat shabby office building near the campus, linoleum floors, institutional furniture, old fashioned office doors with etched glass, faint disinfectant smell. It was not forbidding, but far from cheerful. The psychologist I met with was "from central casting." Middle aged, balding, dressed in rumpled tweed coat, pipe smoking. I remember very well the pipe smoke smell of his office. But, he seemed kind and interested. That was his job.

There was a series of sessions, maybe half a dozen, consisting of interviews, IQ and aptitude tests, the works. I found it tiresome and boring. As a bribe my mother would stop in a neighborhood bakery on the way home and buy some hot cross buns. They were delicious, and somewhat compensated for the boring sessions I had to endure. We would come out from town on Lancaster Avenue, even in those days considered not exactly safe—colored people! I was admonished to "Lock your door!" Something we never did around Strafford in the suburbs.

In retrospect I suppose my mother was doing a wise thing in seeking help in my upbringing. I think I was more than she could handle and she was worried. Perhaps she had every right to be. Anyway, after the interview, aptitude tests and some other evaluation stuff my mother was called for a summation and a report. I remember her and my grandfather talking seriously about "the report," but nothing it seems was much acted on. Why not, I don't know.

Over the years I began to learn the gist of the results of the evaluation and the suggestions in the report. They were roughly as follows, highly summarized: that I was imaginative, creative, very bright but highly strung and undisciplined. A procrastinator (it did not to my knowledge say anything about optimism or pessimism—perhaps that was implied somewhere in the academic language.) That I required a very challenging atmosphere. Strong discipline, standards, challenges (evidently it was felt that The Haverford School did not present these, but I continued there.) A bunch of other stuff which sounded to me like it was being suggested that I be sent to one of those very strict New England prep schools. Not a military school, god forbid, because of low intellectual standards. Well, all and good—but nothing changed. I continued on a mild disaster course ...

In summation, for a future occupation, it was suggested that I be A FARMER! Good God, how was that to come about? From my citified suburban environment I was to become a farmer? Or rancher, but that Philadelphia psychologist did not mention the notion of ranching. That might have been more appealing. Was I to attend an agricultural college and then my father or grandfather would buy a farm or ranch for me to indulge in? Growing what? I think my grandfather had a good laugh over that—a farmer!

But, looking back, it was not such a bad suggestion, impractical aspects aside. I did not take to discipline, I liked the outdoors, I was creative, individualistic, innovative. I might have taken to farming. Or ranching. I don't know about the dawn to dusk aspects of that way of life. "Gentleman farmer" might have been a better suggestion, if only the necessary money were there to purchase a farm in Virginia, or a ranch out West.

I think my mother wasted her money. The hot cross buns were delicious. And I did lock the car door ...

HORNBECK AT SEA

Just after Christmas of 1957 Hornbeck got a job on a merchant vessel. It had been a bizarre, complicated and complex process. To be employed at sea one had to have a merchant seaman's card from the Coast Guard. In order to have that one had to be a member of the seaman's union, the National Maritime Union. To join the union one had to have a letter from a shipping company offering a job (which of course had to be filled only through the union.) Hornbeck's uncle came through. He knew somebody with a shipping company, who knew somebody with the union. It was all arranged. Hornbeck appeared at the union hall, with his Coast Guard seaman's card, somewhat uncomfortably, to be told that there would be a ship for him in a week or so. They would call. He went up to New York to visit a girl he knew there for a couple of days.

When he got back his grandfather told him that the union had called, to call them right away. He was excited. A ship! See the world! He called, only to be told that there had been such a ship but it had sailed. He would have to take the next one, that was all they would do for him. It would be a Cities Service tanker, which did not sound like what he wanted.

He remembered that his mother had tried a few years earlier to do a good deed for a bright young Italian caddy at the golf club who wanted to go to college but had no money. She arranged through somebody to get him on a Sun Oil tanker where he could make real good money for a year. Somewhere in the course of that job he had a breakdown in the heat of the Persian Gulf, tried to kill himself or something, and had to be taken off to a British naval hospital in Bahrain. When he recovered he seemed permanently affected and never did go to college. His family blamed my mother for all that, for "meddling …" So, tankers …

At the end of December on a gray rainy afternoon Hornbeck presented himself as instructed with a small duffel bag to a maritime terminal on the Delaware River near the Philadelphia airport. He had his union papers but no "Z number." He was instructed to tell the purser that it was coming through, but had been held up somehow, that the purser should hold his pay deliverable on demand in cash when he left the ship. Something like that. He was told to keep his "mouth shut" On the tanker he was greeted with disdain, but taken to a small single cabin which he thought a luxury and was very grateful for. He was shown the locker of foul weather gear, and given a tour of the ship, which was indeed very large.

He was assigned the eight to twelve watch—again a stroke of good luck—meaning four hours each watch, starting at eight am and eight pm, leaving four hours, two to six each afternoon for overtime at time and one half, and double on weekends. Union was a good deal. It would all add up to quite a bit of money.

That evening, sitting in the large mess waiting for his watch to begin he was quietly reading a magazine, ignored by a bunch of older seamen who were playing cards and evidently drinking from brown paper bags—in spite of the rule of no liquor on board. Suddenly a scuffle broke out, the table overturned and a man lay on the floor bleeding heavily. Two men restrained a third and the Filipino cook summoned the purser and bosun's mate. Shortly medical personnel came on board, examined the wounded man and took him away. Coast Guard and Philadelphia police took the perpetrator away. The blood was mopped up and nothing was said about the incident. He wondered what he was getting into.

The second excitement of that first evening came as the ship got under way slowly down the river in rain and mist. A few days earlier there had been a collision in the channel and a Greek tanker was still burning slightly. An ominous sign as they slipped by it. Hornbeck was told to ring a large brass bell on the bow for the two hours of his watch there.

The second and third two hours of the four hour night shift were on the bow, alone and high above the sea. It is not a comfortable spot and tales were told of seamen swept away by rogue waves. The seaman on the bow was to ring the brass bell when a ship was spotted out in the. night, something that surely had been noted long before on the bridge. But arcane marine insurance required a seaman on the bow and that was it. One whistled or sang loudly when approaching to relieve the seaman at the bow. The last hour of the watch was on standby in the mess, delivering coffee and sweet rolls to the bridge, or anything else that came up. A large refrigerator in the mess was amply stocked. The three regular meals a day were also filling and quite good. For the morning watch Hornbeck had "sanitary duty," swabbing and cleaning the crew's quarters and the mess. Not pleasant but not really difficult. After lunch on deck chipping and painting, and in inclement weather various maintenance work around the interior of the ship. That routine was established early. There were a fair number of paper back books in the ship's "library," supplied by the Seamen's Church Institute, from which Hornbeck borrowed liberally. The older seamen ignored him. A few told him not to make a life at sea, just a dead end, couldn't establish a decent life on shore. Most of the seamen on that tanker had been on a long time, because of the routine up and down the coast, allowing them time off to see families. It was, for many of them, like a regular, full time job A couple of the younger seamen were friendly. One invited him into his cabin for a look at a collection of pornographic magazines. That made Hornbeck uneasy. Mostly he kept quiet and to himself, and did his work.

The tanker went to the oil ports in the Gulf, loaded and sailed up the East Coast to various refineries and unloaded. Uninspiring places like Bayonne, New Jersey, Baltimore, Norfolk, Virginia. As far north as Portland, Maine and Halifax, Nova Scotia. On the few runs north it was mighty cold during the two hours on the bow, often with snow, freezing rain and dangerous ice. Cold fogs with other ships hidden in them—thank god for the radar! It was pretty routine, and the novelty of it for Hornbeck wore off rather quickly. At first, coasting through the warmer waters, rounding Florida into the Gulf with all the lit up oil platforms, the different ports, was interesting, but became routine very quickly. Once there was a run to Aruba, and Hornbeck was able to get off for an hour or two to wander around the brightly painted little "Dutch" town. By March he calculated that he had made more money than he had ever before in his life, and it was time to leave the tanker. He had grown mightily bored by all of it. So, in early March in port in Lake Charles, Louisiana, he told the purser that he had called home and been told that his father had a heart attack and was in real bad shape He would have to leave the ship and fly back to Pennsylvania.

With a minimum of sympathy the purser placed twenty two one hundred bills in a thick pay envelope, and eighty some dollars and change in a small cloth bag, and handed these to Hornbeck with some papers to sign. Then Hornbeck collected his gear and walked down the gangplank to a taxi that was waiting with some of the other seamen in it. The tanker was berthed out in the swamps amidst a maze of pipes and tanks, so it was a fair ride into town. Hornbeck thought the tough young Cajun taxi driver was something of a pimp as the man steered the vehicle through the bright sandy white soil with tight black leather gloves on the wheel. Evidently the men from the tanker were going to some sort of whorehouse, but first Hornbeck was to be dropped off, in the early evening, downtown.

He ate a light dinner at a small very "Southern" café, and when finished asked where he could wait for the bus to "N'awlins." He was directed to an unpretentious bar a few blocks away where he was told that he was in the right spot, bus came 'bout nine o'clock, an hour distant. He settled on a bar stool and had a Jax beer. A few men played pool, and two blowzy women sat at the end of the bar. There was of course nonstop country music on a juke box. No one paid any attention to Hornbeck. He had a second beer, interested that from time to time the bartender would respond to a knock on a sliding partition at the rear of the bar. This he would raise and serve drinks to black men who were gathered outside in the parking lot to the rear of the building. The man told Hornbeck that it was almost nine, that he best get outside so the bus didn't miss him. As he walked outside he noticed four black men seated at a card table just to the rear of the bar. They were playing cards, laughing and drinking from beer bottles that had been passed out though the sliding partition. There in the warm night those men seemed to be having a better time than the morose patrons inside the bar. The South …

The bus came pretty much on time, and Hornbeck took a seat near the front as the vehicle lumbered off into the unforgiving darkness of canebrake South Louisiana. He dozed with the throbbing and lurching, and once awoke to find the bus parked in a gas station where passengers could get off for a short stretch. He saw a fat white man in a long sleeved shirt and a straw hat sitting in a chair under a light, mopping his face with a bandanna. He was directing a young black man who filled cars and brought money to him for change. At few places the bus had stopped in utter darkness to take on passengers, usually black people who got on, paid their fare and with downcast eyes trudged dutifully to the back of the bus. The South …

Dawn was breaking as the bus passed across the large bridge over the Mississippi. New Orleans seemed gray and shabby. There was a lot of trash in the streets, maybe left over from Mardi Gras or maybe that was the way it always was. Hornbeck got off downtown and found a cheap hotel where he took a room and slept until late afternoon. He had been too tired to look around. When he awoke he put on clean clothes, checked out of the hotel and went to find the downtown airline terminal. There he checked his bag in a locker, thinking for a moment to put the thick pay envelope in his bag—but no, someone might break into the locker and steal his money. Those things happened, and there were a lot of dubious looking characters lurking around the terminal. So, he put the envelope into an inner pocket of his jacket and zipped it shut. The small bag of bills and coins he put in his side pocket. Then he purchased a plane ticket to Philadelphia by way of Atlanta, leaving later that night. This he placed in the zippered pocket with his money. He was ready to hit the streets and see a bit of New Orleans …

He stopped in a men's shop and bought a dark blue seaman's cap, which he thought looked good with the beard he had grown on the ship, and certainly appropriate since a seaman was what he had been for the last several months. Wearing his new cap he walked east with confidence to check out the French Quarter. There was definitely a lot of trash left over from Mardi Gras, and some derelict looking people, too. It was early evening and it looked like drinking had been going on all day. He thought it a pretty degenerate atmosphere, with a definite undercurrent of violence and danger. He resolved to be alert and careful. He had a small meal of red beans and rice in what he took to be "a place of the people." Very authentic. Old New Orleans. Then he set out to stroll around, figuring to take a taxi back to the downtown airline terminal with plenty of time to get out to the airport.

A man standing outside a bar lighting a cigarette looked up and called out to him, "Hey, boy, come on over heah." Wondering what the man wanted Hornbeck made his way warily over. The man said in a folksy manner, "Seen ya on the bus in from Houston, ya got on Lake Charles. Whatcha been doin' in that dump?"

Not wanting to call attention to anything to do with having been on a ship, Hornbeck mumbled in what he hoped sounded like a "southern accent," "Jest visitin' up on some rel'tives." The man nodded.

"Whatcha goin' be doin' here in the Big Easy?"

"Work fer mah uncle, he the shippin' bisniz."

"Goin' put yah on a banana boat, git some of that Latin pussy, huh? Yo uncle got anythin' fer me?"

Hornbeck said he didn't know about that and the man said let me buy you a drink this here bar's no good, better one down the next block, got some nigras play pretty good dixieland come on. And sort of steered Hornbeck toward the bar down the next block with Hornbeck mumbling about not wanting no trouble and the man laughing pulling his jacket open a .45 stuck in the waistband you won't have no trouble when you with me boy I got protection and Hornbeck did not like that very much.

At the new bar, which was crowded with patrons who looked like they had been there all day, the man bought himself a bourbon and Hornbeck a Jax beer and asked again if the uncle had anything for him.

Hornbeck asked, "You got seaman's papers?" And the man laughed and said, "Hell, no, I ain't no seaman. Timekeeper and security, that's me. Shippin' companies alays have need of my talents."

Hornbeck told the man that he would talk to his uncle about it and they agreed to meet at the bar the next evening. Then the man eyed two girls at the end of the bar and suggested chatting them up. Hornbeck said fine but he was going to the men's room first. The man said OK. When Hornbeck came out of the men's room he looked across the crowd and saw the man talking to the two girls who seemed like they were not welcoming his attentions. Hornbeck slid though the crowd and was out the door, into the damp, humid street smelling of rotten garbage and sea air. He walked quickly away from the bar, around the corner and stood looking for a taxi. Enough of the French Quarter. He sensed danger everywhere.

As he was standing there a police car pulled up to him and a cop got out from the passenger side. He looked at Hornbeck, then took him by the arm and told him to get in the back seat of the police car. From the passenger seat the cop asked, "Where you from, boy. Let's see some ID." Hornbeck showed his Coast Guard seaman's card." The cop examined it, saying, "Philly, huh? Seaman. You sail into N'Awlins? You got a place to stay heah? You got any money on yuh?" Hornbeck sensed danger in these questions and mumbled that he had checked out of a hotel and was kinda broke.

The cops looked at each other then the questioning one had sort of shrugged his shoulders and said we gonna have to take you in fer vagrancy you git to spend the night maybe get bumped around a bit then they give some coffee and dump you at the edge of town and don' come back 'till you pockets stuff with cash to party with in the Big Easy. Don' worry no record it'll be a part of yore education you graduate from high school, boy? Hornbeck said that he had a plane ticket and held it up for them to see. That changed the situation, they said, they was then gonna take him the downtown airline terminal and have their man there see that he got on the bus to the airport now where was his bag if he had one? In a locker at the terminal he said and that is where they went took him inside and talked to an older fat cop who looked like he should have been retired and maybe was. Hornbeck got his bag and talked to the older cop who was friendly enough and explained that after Mardi Gras the town was filled with broke drunks and drifters who caused burglaries and muggings so the cops rounded them all up and sent them out of town one way or another. Telling Hornbeck that was what he got caught up in and in a friendly way guiding him toward the bus that was going out to the airport and American Airlines to Atlanta and Philadelphia, back where he had started out.

As the plane took off and leveled out in the night sky toward Atlanta an attractive stewardess stopped by his seat to admire his seaman's cap. He told her he was a seaman, had just paid off a ship. She asked if it was Houston and had he been in that "beard growin'" contest they had just had over there. He said he had not and she smiled and told him "Too bad. You might have won. Beard looks good on you." She was flirting and it pleased him, made him feel mature and a man of the world.

He dozed most of the way from Atlanta to Philadelphia, but awoke with the change in the pitch of the engines as the plane began its descent. He had been dreaming about returning in some distant future to New Orleans, in an important and romantic role. Perhaps as a private detective. Hornbeck imagined that there was a lot of work for a good private detective in New Orleans. He would wear a white suit and a Panama hat ...

As he got off the plane he said to the attractive stewardess: "Hornbeck. My name is Hornbeck." She smiled but looked at him sort of blankly ...

◆   ◆   ◆

Well, that's Hornbeck's story. But, it is remarkably like mine. I sailed on a tanker up and down the East Coast. Rode the bus from Lake Charles to New Orleans. And was picked up for vagrancy in the Big Easy just after Mardi Gras, but got out of that by showing an airline ticket. And flew back to Philadelphia with pay envelope full of one hundred dollar bills. I still have my seaman's card, "validated for life," although I do not now resemble in any way the twenty year old young man so pictured on that document.

So, these stories are intertwined. That is the way of memory.

It fades and it is sometimes hard to tell what was real and what was not. The mind plays tricks on you What you have to do is to gather all of it up, roll it in a ball, wrap a big pancake or tortilla around all of it, then toss the whole thing to the sharks, let them fight over it, roiling in the shimmering, frothy sea of forgetfulness ...

◆   ◆   ◆

JACKED UP

I am a licensed PI in the State of Louisiana—that would be "The Pelican State." Quite often the nature of my work takes me to the city of New Orleans. Trouble seems to drift to and congregate there. "The Big Easy" is just a magnet for the bad guys. It was during Mardi Gras during the 1960s when I was sent there to look for a very bad guy who had been seen among the celebrants. He had been very foolishly released from Angola, and he was going to go back. It was my job to see to that. Why not the police? Because in "The Big Easy" the police are notoriously corrupt and inefficient. I am neither. I am very efficient. I had a job to do and it was going to get done.

So, I am down in the thick of Mardi Gras. Not something I like. Crowds in the streets, shouting, drinking, fighting. The sound of jazz everywhere. I am not there to have fun. A middle-aged black man holds a wine bottle toward me, offering a drink. I shake my head. No way! He looks at me, says, "Mister, you way too grim lookin'. Y'all ain't havin' no fun …" I tell him I am not here for fun. His eyes widen. "Then what you heah for, mister. Ev'rybody heah for fun …" I tell him, sharply, "I am here to jack up a man. There's one man here goin' to get his fun interrupted."

Then, suddenly, in the crowd I see my man, a sallow, stick-thin, middle aged white man. Holding a bottle, dancing to himself. I begin to move. I hear the black man over my shoulder, "Some fool already half jacked up, huh?"

I move quickly, knifing through the crowd. My man neither sees nor senses me coming. And quickly, like a snake striking, he is jacked up. Yeah!

I done my job and got paid. Took my sailboat out on the Gulf. Fresh breezes. Snapper to grill. No jacking up. For a while …

IN THE SEA OF CORTEZ, JULY 1957

On Monday morning I got my Mexican tourist document in San Diego, and took the bus to the border at Tijuana. I would have to walk over and into the town. The Mexican official just waved me through, not paying any attention to the small duffle bag slung over my shoulder. At that time there was not much of a drug trade in Tijuana, but everything and anyone seemed to be for sale. I was constantly bothered with proposals and said no over and over to everyone. I wandered around for about two hours, got something to eat in a small cantina, and then took another bus to Ensenada, about 70 miles down the coast of Baja California. The starter of the bus was in the back of the vehicle, and evidently there was some problem. The driver indicated to me that I would have to hold a button down for him to start the bus. This I did, to the seeming amusement of the Mexican passengers, and the bus started with a great cloud of black diesel exhaust. We rattled away into country along the coast that was quite like that in Southern California, except for the very evident poverty and primitive conditions. The fare for the ride was 10.5 pesos, or about 85 cents U.S.

I took a hotel room in Ensenada near the beach. Quite reasonable. And then looked up the Loftins, an American couple whose name I had been given by a friend, and who ran a sort of tourist agency. I had been told they could arrange passage on a coastal vessel headed south. My friend had done this and said it was a wonderful adventure. That was my plan. The Loftins were quite friendly and said that they would see about a vessel the next day. But, in the meantime would I come to a small party they were having that night, a sort of informal birthday celebration for their daughter. I said I would be honored. The evening was most congenial but ended early. I got a good night's sleep and was up early to meet Mr. Loftin for a tour of "the back country." He was outside the hotel in a sturdy four wheel drive pickup, and as we headed into the mountains I asked about a blackjack that was lying on the dashboard. "Oh," he said, "that ain't all." And pulled a large .45 automatic from under the seat. By way of explanation he mentioned that "sometimes things get a bit funny up in the mountains." Our tour was brief, a couple of old mines, some primitive villages, and then back to town to check at the agency about coastal vessels. Big disappointment. Mrs. Loftin said no vessel for two weeks, maybe more. She suggested that I take an Aeronaves de Mexico plane to La Paz and see there about a vessel across to Mazatlan. That seemed the only plan.

So the next morning I was at a primitive airstrip to board the plane, an old military DC-3. I was not too optimistic about the aircraft—but, what the hell! It was an interesting ride. My fellow passengers were a Mexican who spoke excellent English named Al Green. (Said there were lots of Mexican Greens in Baja.) And another gent, an American "mining engineer" named Don Yxomer (what it sounded like), who said he was "just poking around."

Well, OK ... The country we passed over, at a low altitude, was starkly beautiful desert and mountains, with occasional glimpses of the very azure Sea of Cortez. The runways of the two towns where we stopped, Santa Rosalea and Loretto, were gravel and very rough. Al Green said that he was visiting his parents, his girlfriend and their bunch of kids. There were about twenty people waiting for him to get off the plane at Loretto. I got off too, and was very solemnly introduced all around. Green invited me to stay with him—there was some sort of casita—relax and get to know the people and country. It was a tempting offer, but the next plane was not for a week, and that was too long for me. I probably missed a real interesting experience ...

The airport for La Paz was a considerable distance from the town, in what was beginning to look like distinctly tropical country. A rickety bus took me to La Paz, where I was impressed right off. The town was on a tropical harbor with a malecon, or paseo lined with palm trees. Commercial buildings facing the harbor were painted in bright colors, which added to the tropical feel. As did the dress of many of the inhabitants, mostly in white. I took a room at what the bus driver had said "is best in La Paz." Los Arcos faced the harbor and was $5 U.S. per night with food. Beer was a peso, or about 8 cents.

That evening as I entered the dining room for dinner, I was immediately invited to join a group of individuals who evidently had been partying it up. The host, quite drunk, was an American expatriate who had a house in La Paz and said he owned "a cotton gin." Others in the party were two young American women from Southern California, quite pretty and evidently "party animals." And three slick young Mexican men who spoke quite good English. I assumed they were of wealthy families, and perhaps were "on vacation" or had some sort of business in La Paz. Their main interest was in drinking tequila and the two American women. At some point our host, Jim something or other ("call me Jimbo") suggested we go to a secluded beach for some more partying and a little swimming. But first we had to stop by Jimbo's house, which was right around the corner from the hotel, for a case of Corona and a bottle of tequila, and his car. Jimbo seemed to think I was a "secret agent" of some kind, and kept pestering me to tell him what sort of "mission" I was on. I remained silent. The Mexicans and the American women followed in another car, while I drove Jimbo's car at his direction out of town a short distance, then down a dirt road where we all got out in the moonlight on a lovely, deserted beach. And that is where the trouble started …

Jimbo wanted to swim but kept mentioning sharks. I told him to stay out of the water, have some more tequila. But he kept wading into the water and I was afraid that if I took my eyes off him, when I looked back he'd be gone. Sunk under the water, drowned. What then? One of the young American women was paying "too much" attention to me, or so the macho Mexicans thought. There were mild threats, then stronger ones. The American women thought it amusing. They were drunk and didn't seem to give a shit. I had enough. I told Jimbo to go sit in his car or would leave him there—I had the keys. Then I told the three Mexicans to fuck themselves and started toward Jimbo's car. There were wild curses and I thought I heard one of the American women shout something about me not leaving them there. Fuck 'em. They got themselves into that, they could deal with it. Maybe. It was not my concern …

I helped Jimbo into his house. He was still mumbling drunkenly that I could tell him what my secret mission was. I thought of telling him that it was "to kill the President of Mexico," but thought better of that. Thank goodness.

The next morning, after breakfast, walking on the municipal pier I noticed what was obviously a small coastal freighter—the "Estrella Costera," or "Coastal Star." Very poetic, except that the vessel was rusted and unkempt looking. At the hotel I inquired about it and was told that it would be sailing shortly for Mazatlan, and indeed one could book passage on it. The company office was just a short distant away, so I walked over and presented myself to an attractive señorita.

"Queiro comprare un boleto para Mazatlan."

"Si, señor, una persona?"

"Si, una persona solemente."

My ticket was 100 pesos, or about $8.50 U.S. I did not have a berth, deck passage only, but thought that would be OK for one night. The ship was supposed to be sailing that evening and would reach Mazatlan 24 hours later, in late afternoon.

I wondered how rigid Mexican coastal shipping schedules were. Back at the hotel I was told that it might be wise to purchase some canned food and drinks, "just in case." I did so, and was later very glad I did. I took the duffle on board in late afternoon and after a thorough inspection settled down with some reading. There were hundreds of crates of empty Coca Cola bottles, some machinery and two old trucks lashed to the deck. Who was captain and who was crew I could not tell. Everyone was very friendly and indicated that some sort of meal would be served the next day. As it grew dark the sunset over the humid harbor was very beautiful. I felt that I could be anywhere in the world. There was no evidence of tourism or gringos. Maybe Jimbo was off managing the cotton gin. But I thought rather not. As we pulled away from the dock shortly after sunset the two other passengers, a young Mexican couple, provided superb entertainment—he strumming on a guitar and she singing beautifully some lilting Mexican melody. It was quite enchanting. Later I wedged myself between some large rolls of canvas and fell partially to sleep with the rolling of the ship and sloshing of water as we cut through the Sea of Cortez.

The next day was cloudless and very hot. Some beans and fried pork were put on tin plates in what might be called "the mess." It was most unappetizing, so I threw it over the side and opened a can of my own rice and beans. I was careful to not be observed, as I did not want to insult the cuisine of the vessel! The ship seemed to be moving very slowly and I wondered about the 24 hours to Mazatlan. At one point I climbed up to what appeared to be a sort of "crow's nest." The view was of nothing but the flat and empty sea. One of the crewmen showed me how he attempted to harpoon some of the large turtles that were occasionally sighted. "Muy Delicioso. Much dinero." I got the picture. I dozed the afternoon away in whatever shady spot I could find on the deck. It was evident that we would not reach Mazatlan that evening. I was concerned toward dusk to notice a bank of rather threatening clouds rising to the southeast. "Si, una tempesta." one of the crewmen agreed, smiling. About eight in the evening a rather severe storm hit the Estrella Costera. Mucho rain, pitching and rolling. A very uncomfortable night. At first light I staggered up to what I thought was the captain's cabin or wheelhouse. There the crew was assembled, all five of them, laughing, drinking tequila and playing cards. "Quanto horas a Mazatlan?" I asked. They shrugged and went back to their cards.

Later in the morning the sky began to clear and I was exceedingly glad to notice through the mist the sight of land. Some rocky islands that we steered around, and then Mazatlan with "the second highest lighthouse in the world." Perched on a promontory above the tropical city, from which the rich aroma of vegetation was wafted seaward. It reminded me of a humid greenhouse. The harbor was crowded, and the captain (whom I could now identify by a large nautical hat with mucho gold braid) kept sounding the ship's horn and shouting over a bull horn. The answer from on shore was evidently that there was no berth for the Estrella Costera at that moment. The young Mexican couple (whom I had not seen since the first night) and I were to be taken to shore in a dubious looking rowboat that pulled alongside. One oar lock consisted of some heavy string. My last view of the Estrella Costera included a severed pig's head hanging over the side of the ship with some wire, the remains of what had been hacked up and served in fried chunks.

When we were deposited on land some sort of official asked for my "papers," and seemed satisfied with my Mexican tourista card. He poked and felt at the small duffel, smiled and asked, "Marijuana?" I must have looked extremely startled, because he laughed heartily and clapped me on the back. I am pretty sure it was a huge joke, because otherwise there would have been "La mordida."—or something worse, but I doubt it because I got the impression that in those days in Mexico marijuana was considered a harmless joke. Those formalities over I took a taxi to a hotel the Loftins had recommended, La Perla, a sort of mini-high rise, or at least taller than the other buildings on Mazatlan's waterfront. At the hotel I noticed that the clock read 9:30. I was 13 hours late getting to Mazatlan, but what did it matter? Several times I had to slap my foot down to remain rooted to the floor—"sea legs," from all the movement of the ship during the storm. But not once during that storm had I felt the slightest bit sick. There did not seem to be much activity at the hotel, but the clerk informed me that only the most expensive rooms, high up with an ocean view, were available. I did not care. I just wanted a shower and a bed, and still, the most expensive rooms were a bargain in U.S. dollars. I slept soundly until late afternoon, got dressed and went out for a stroll. Mazatlan was called "the poor man's Rio," and although that is a very considerable stretch I can see the analogy. It was a sort of romantic place, and attracted middle class Mexican (such as existed) for reasonable vacations. The beach was pleasant but the surf was huge and intimidating, and said to be "muy peligro." I had an excellent late dinner for about $2.50 U.S. and a Negra Modelo beer which I found to be very good. Walking along the waterfront in the hot night after dark I felt perfectly safe, but when I got back to the hotel the clerk was quite concerned. No matter. Next day was a 24-hour bus ride to Ciudad Mexico, or perhaps twice that long, the way things went South of the Border.

It did turn out to be 2 days, and was both extremely interesting and very uncomfortable and exasperating. There were moments when we climbed through very green mountains lined with rows of corn and other crops tended to by paisanos in white outfits, large straw hats, machetes and many burros, when I felt very far indeed from my mechanical and modern world. It was all out of another world, another culture, most definitely. Entering towns or villages the driver would blast endlessly on a loud horn, to scatter animals, chickens, dogs—whatever, and put on a large, braided hat as the badge of his important position in the scheme of things. Several times at night while trying to sleep I felt the bus swerve violently and looked up to see the dark forms of what I took to be cows that we had narrowly missed hitting. The most exciting moment in the trip came when in the steep mountains outside Mexico City a truck passed us on the narrow two lane road. Immediately the bus driver took up the challenge of this insult. The bus groaned faster and faster, overtook the truck and passed it on a blind curve. Good God! That was the sort of thing that one was always reading in the U.S.—"Mexican bus plunges over cliff, no survivors!" Fortunately, there was not much traffic in those days, and the bus got back in the proper lane without incident. I must have been sort of laughing to myself at this insanity, because when the driver glanced up at the mirror to see how his gringo passenger was taking this, and he saw me "laughing" he broke into a huge grin and pumped his fist. Yeah! One for the home team!

◆　　◆　　◆

MEMORIES

The moon,
waning October moon,
rising on Pennsylvania farmlands,
and three hours later
over California mountains
and cities—
microwave these thoughts
across the continent in seconds;
it is all the same
in the weird electronics
of the brain.

The old school,
once a church,
now beside a highway,
burial ground
of Welsh and German settlers,
gravestones wrapped in ivy
in the glare
of vapor lamps,
rock wall still disturbed
from the crash of a car
carrying boys and girls
and a case of beer.

A slow autumn rain
stills the woodlands—
insects,
a bullfrog,
distant roadhouse dance band,
wind and an occasional truck.

Reuben
buried in a foreign land;
he sits forever
in a café,
pipe in mouth,
watching,
smiling at the crowds,
detached.

October moon
through the tulip poplars
still full with leaves;
what has changed?
color distorted,
electronically, chemically,
rush of motor cars,
too many people,
doing too much
in too small a place?

In a tavern,
a toast:
"to absent friends."
Some peace within,
perhaps,
withstands this change—
a stick lying in a woods
untouched
until decay
reclaims it to the earth;
the explosion of a tree
in vernal equinox,

the quiet death
of a rabbit.

Roy Hart
beside his stream
in Idaho,
lights his pipe,
sits down to think—
forty years in
the wilderness—
awaits the darkness
and the stars.

In this season
wood smoke hangs
in the hollows—
corn shocks in the fields,
and pumpkins.
A season,
with all seasons.

The world is
in a state of is,
of becoming;
and what has been
cannot be separated
like humus
into seasons.

California mountains,
black and lonely,
and California cities—
a riot of lights moving,

all is more obvious,
in contrast, with speed.

Drifting on the Allagash,
just north of Eagle Lake—
roar of rapids ahead—
Gus Lantaigne
leans back to paddle,
puts paddle to water;
the canoe moves quickly
over the dark water.

In Pennsylvania,
Paul Lewis
feels his cigar hot on his lips,
and the chill of fall across his back;
he moves his chair onto the porch,
and goes in to bed.

◆   ◆   ◆

10 MAY 1961

I sit here absently, basking in the warm afterglow of a good meal well eaten, of wines and rare meats. The brandy glass glistens in its emptiness and the smoke from my cigar forms ever-so-slight a haze around the lamp. Outside a soft spring rain is falling, and I hear the gentle clip-clop of a hansom fading down the street. A train's whistle sounds, speeding out of the city; carrying whom and what where, I wonder. The faint echo of a woman's laughter, warm and light in the night breeze. Quick solitary steps as some unknown person hurries through the wet street, to some end, for some purpose, I presume. And yet, imperceptibly, the night closes around the city, about all of us, crushes us—presses us into boxes so we may spring forth tomorrow. But for some the box never opens; one never knows.

I sit in this quiet moment and ruminate on the people, places and events which give significance to the brief experience which I have come to know as Life. There are light and dark spots, and many shades of gray. Some few names and faces shine through. An inner sign, perhaps, at what can never be recaptured and yet what was never enough. Has it not been said that "dreaming of the past is but regret for things left undone?" There is so much …

My cigar grows short. I extinguish it and reach for my writing materials. Thus it is in this spirit that I address myself to you. Sir, to Doctor Avis, now serving in a faraway land, surrounded by dark adventure and deep mystery. My writing must take the form of various rambling thoughts and meditations. For these cursory excursions of the spirit I must apologize, but, then, they may be not without some interest for you.

I note with interest vague plans to seek further education, in San Francisco perhaps. What better place? The world functions on and with plans, sometimes to great woe, but this is the way things seem to be set up. Plans are sometimes a little difficult to come by. At times, even, they stubbornly resist revealing themselves to certain individuals. I often find myself faced with this predicament. But what of great plans, aspirations, dreams? There must have been a lot of Jews shoved into gas chambers at Auschwitz who had plans and dreams. To what could they attribute their sorry fate? What plan, what scheme? History, or existence, if you prefer, does not always grant one the freedom or the choice for great plans. A decision somewhere, some unforeseen happening, and a chain of events is set in motion, and current dreams and aspirations. One never knows what machinations in this world will affect individual destinies, or when. But Life goes on; spring and summer come and go. People continue to occupy themselves with the trivial details of existence as they see it. Some more, some less, than others. But, nevertheless, on it goes, and on. Occasionally, "Some men sit down in bohemia and despair." And all the while, the great black crow sits on a limb, waiting.

I have been reading lately the *Alexandria Quartet* by Lawrence Durrell. These books (I am on the third one) are masterful writing, poetic, sensual, exotic. And again, as it is with anything evocative of the human spirit and soul (so-called), one wonders what the devil it is all about (Life). Wherefore and why do these people play out their destinies in these manners? In many cases, sensitive people seem to flee the metaphysical and plunge into an embrace of the sensual. Why not? The metaphysical is a blind alley—far less gratifying to the body. There is more poetry, more mystery, tragedy, more art, in sensuality. Enough of this, however; my mind is not now attuned to this subject ... Seek and ye shall find: universally, BUFFOONERY ...

◆   ◆   ◆

HORNBECK'S "MISADVENTURE"

Hornbeck was driving on the rural back roads of the Pennsylvania countryside in a warm June evening. The smell of honeysuckle and wild rose was all around in the humid air. He was driving a small rental car with the windows open, buzzing along at a steady forty miles per hour in the growing darkness with no other cars on the road. Hornbeck was thinking of various places, situations and faces from his past as the big, leafy trees slipped by the beams of his headlights as he rolled along the narrow road. The radio station he was tuned to faded in and out, snatches of old songs that reminded him of other places, other times. The dark road began a gradual descent toward the river, the Delaware River above New Hope. Hornbeck noticed an increase in dampness as he neared the river. A rabbit paused by the road ahead, then darted into the safety of darkness. Hornbeck sipped from a can of beer he had between his thighs. He slowed down, although his speed was safe and he knew the road, though he had not been on it in fifteen years. No change in this country, he thought. Good. Strange how sometimes time seems to stand still. An illusion, though, he thought, because the world in reality was hurtling ahead, somewhat out of control.

Hornbeck thought of former times on those dark country roads, driving with Meredith in the seat next to him, her fiddling with the radio. Of how her hair blew in the wind and her clean, hay smell, so many years before. She did not talk and sometimes he found little to say. She fiddled with the radio to find some sound to fill the void between them. He did not think that necessary. Later there had been times when there had been much to talk about, things they disagreed about, before she had drifted away into a vortex of strangers he had neither liked nor understood. Well, they had had their moments, he guessed. He remembered those, now driving alone over once familiar roads filled with useless memories of lost times and years.

This time Hornbeck was on a journey with a rather definite purpose. "Perhaps foolish, perhaps not." he thought. "I'll find out." The lights of the small river town appeared ahead and below, about a mile distant. Hornbeck stopped the car and gazed for a moment, thinking. He finished his beer and put the can behind the seat. As he descended toward the town he decided to stop by the old Black Bass Tavern, "for old time's sake," wasn't that what they said? He pulled into the dark gravel parking lot across the road from the old riverside tavern and got out. The air was still and humid, the sounds of cicadas unnaturally loud. He noticed that there were a few cars in the lot, most with New York license plates. As would be the car of the people he was to meet later. "Of course," he thought.

Hornbeck entered the old tavern and stood at the long, dark bar. Most of the patrons were in the dining room which faced the river. There were several tables of men. He remembered that the place had been popular with homosexuals from New York.

Why not, he mused, as he ordered a Guinness Stout from the expressionless bartender. He drank the stout slowly, listening to the recorded classical guitar music. No one paid him any attention, and he mused on his errand later that night. Perhaps foolish, he thought again, but necessary. It is what it has come to. He drank the last of the stout, and went out to the dark parking lot. He paused by his car to light a cigarette. listening to the faint strains of the guitar music that drifted from the tavern, blending with the raucous cicadas. Things seemed peaceful. Not a bad world, Hornbeck thought, standing there, not all of it ...

Then, suddenly Hornbeck had to fight back thoughts of rotting jungle, the crack of small arms fire, and shouts in Spanish! He began to sweat. He drew heavily on the cigarette and blew smoke into the night air. He stood and tried to relax. Then he got into the car and started it. The radio came on suddenly loud, and his first thought was that somebody had been in the car, searching it. But then he realized that it was just that the station came in better in the heavy air along the river. He was being paranoid. THE RIVER, he thought, and felt a slight chill on the back of his neck. Across the water the air horn of a Central of New Jersey freight sounded and he could hear the throbbing of the diesel engine. He pulled a pen light from under the seat and studied a piece of paper, a map. It indicated a left turn off the river road one mile north of the first bridge, then one half mile to a farm house and wooden barn set against trees, the only habitation on that road. He remembered his instructions: park by the barn, facing the house, turn off lights and wait for five minutes. Then flash lights twice. That was what he had written on the map. He turned off the penlight and stuck it back under the seat. Then from that space he extracted a small bag which contained a .38 automatic, nickel plated. He checked the safety on the weapon, switched it off and placed the weapon on the seat to his right.

Hornbeck sat for a moment in the small car, thinking, reviewing his instructions, every detail. Then he pulled onto the road and drove north. One mile past the bridge he saw the dirt lane to the left, and drove onto it, driving slowly with just parking lights. He could barely see the road, but he had good night vision. Soon he saw the farm house, a stone two-story building, and the wooden barn against the dark trees. He pulled up next to the barn, facing the house about twenty yards away, and turned off his parking lights. He sat in the dark for what he estimated was five minutes, probably more. The .38 rested in his lap, in readiness. Then he flashed his lights twice, quickly. The beams seemed startlingly bright in the darkness. Sweat was trickling down his ribs …

Later, across the river into New Jersey, driving toward New York on almost deserted route 202 he realized that he was doing almost eighty miles per hour. Fool! he thought, and slowed quickly to the posted speed. Had not been thinking. It had gone well, Hornbeck thought, almost too smoothly. Very quickly, there in the humid darkness. Only the outlines of figures, muffled voices. No one had a name, had a face. He had stopped just over the river into New Jersey to count the money, then put the bag in the trunk. The money was all there, in small bills, used.

He had stopped in a diner for some coffee and talked to a trucker about baseball, about the Mets, a game he had seen on TV. A regular guy. He felt relaxed, and drove on in the night to Newark airport where he got the bag from the trunk and turned the rental car in. It was still before dawn, and he had a wait before his plane back to Colorado.

Later that morning Hornbeck was on a jet headed west over New Jersey and the Delaware River. He was clean shaven, neatly dressed, perhaps some young businessman on his way to Denver. Except he had a briefcase full of cash beneath his seat, more than any "businessman" would be carrying. Oh, there were some who traveled with large amounts of cash. It had all been quite easy. He might do it again, thinking of the dark roads in Pennsylvania. Meredith had loved June nights in Pennsylvania, the smells of honeysuckle and the wild rose. That had been before …

As the plane sailed west Hornbeck dozed, and dreamed of the recent events, over and over. They existed with such clarity. Then he began to dream troubling thoughts. He had visions of his mountain cabin burned, of people coming after him, of running, running, unable to buy anything of peace or value with the money he had. He woke up suddenly. The man next to him had been shaking him, saying, "Hey, buddy, you OK? You been sorta talkin' in your sleep there, sayin' strange things. People were gettin' nervous. Maybe have some water, huh?" The flight attendant brought some water, and sipping it Hornbeck realized that there had been no night before on country roads, no meeting near a farmhouse by the Delaware, no briefcase full of money. He glanced down. There was no bag beneath his seat. Of course not. He remembered now, there had been only endless rounds of drinking with friends in New York, in the bohemian haunts of the Village. Going back with some girl to her roach infested apartment they had to step over a man passed out on her steps. The other stuff, along the river in Pennsylvania—he had somehow made it all up in his subconscious. An attempt to get back some life he had lost forever. He began to laugh, loudly. The man next to him shook his shoulder again, saying, "Hey, buddy, take it easy. We're almost to Denver. Let me get you a drink, maybe calm you down. My name's Hank."

Hank was a friendly guy in his thirties. Over their drinks he said that he lived in Boulder and sold outdoor equipment. Had some big accounts on the East Coast and was glad to be getting back to Colorado. Hornbeck told Hank that he lived in the mountains above Denver, that he had been back East on business but a big deal had fallen through. Hank commiserated, but said as a true optimistic salesman, "There is always another deal …"

◆   ◆   ◆

A PORTION OF MY LIFE

Once again it is fall;
I know from the way
the shadows of branches
extend across the rough
white-washed swelling of the wall;
I can see it in a leaf
trapped by the uneven window glass,
how it resists the sun
and curls inwardly against itself.

Coming into a glade
I felt your shadow
and knew the spaces
between your fingers,
the soap scent of your hair
mingled with woodsmoke.

That was in Marblehead.

And now, looking toward the sea
it is hard to believe
that it is fall.

With the sun warm on my back
I smile, remembering
that this interlude is called
Indian Summer,
and that the rich moon
already beginning its ride
over the rooftops
is the Harvest Moon.

We stopped for tea
at the small cottage,

and I admired the big white pine
between the house and the barn.
While you helped
his wife with the tea,
my friend, the artist,
showed me his latest painting
in the chill of his barn studio.
It was of a ray of sunlight
between trees, catching
some golden leaves and birds in flight.
I thought it very nice,
and told my friend, the artist, so.
He seemed pleased.

Years later,
when I mentioned that visit
you said you didn't think
the artist and his wife were still together,
since they were too gentle
to avoid the things
that come between people.

I remember the way your hair
glistened in the hazy sunlight
that afternoon in the glade
as we held each other knowing
the things that stand between people.

I know that it is fall;
the chill of the afternoon
now that the sun has gone,
and the way a dog barks,
tells me;
coming down the path
from my walk

I am aware of leaves underfoot
and I can almost smell
cinnamon in the air.
I know that this is Marblehead
from the way that shadows fall
against buildings,
and I remember that once
when I turned a corner
I was filled with the thought
that I might find you
standing there,
but it was only a faucet dripping
and my neighbor raking leaves.
I can tell
from the brick of the buildings
and the white frames of the windows,
from the way that branches
scrape in the wind,
that this is New England
and I am experiencing
another fall.

My friend, the artist, is dead;
and his wife gone away
to live in New York.
I have tried to find
his painting of the ray of sun,
the leaves and birds in flight,
thinking I would like to buy it.

My walk consumed the afternoon,
inspecting all the familiar things,
and now I am satisfied that fall
is progressing as it should.

There is no quickening of stride
down the path toward my house;
I am thinking of you,
of our meeting in the glade,
and of the years that lie scattered
all around like the leaves.

My neighbor greets me,
and I appreciate his friendliness.
I shall light a fire
against the chill
and have a glass of beer.
I think a rainstorm may be coming;
there was a hint of one along the beach,
though in the woods everything
was sunny and still.
I remember you always
liked the sea,
liked the rain and the damp mists,
and I remember the time we spent
on the island, with the rain beating
against the window
as darkness crept across the room.

I see that my wife has been out shopping,
and I break eagerly
into a package of oatmeal cookies.
I have tracked a few leaves
into the hall,
and I admire the way they look
stuck to the pine floorboards.
I decide to let them stay the night.

Flames crackle from the log,
and sitting in the glow of warmth

I reflect on the things of the afternoon,
the tiny and subtle changes of fall on the land.
They are good things, and I
am glad to have seen them.
Were I an artist I would paint
some of the things I saw,
but perhaps it is better
to leave them alone.

Later, after dinner,
I shall go for another walk,
and the sky will be bright
with stars through the trees
and the moon will be riding
toward the west, solitary
in the secrets it holds.

Perhaps some wind will have come up,
and it may be catching
in the tops of the pines.
I love the way the long boughs
sway in the moonlight,
and the way the owls
call to one another
across the fields.

I think I remember you sewing,
though I never saw you sew,
but I do recall the way
you looked with your glasses on.
Funny, the way a tree
assumes a shape and
the years peel away.

My wife never questions
my frequent long walks alone.
In the summer we sail a lot together,
drink beer and laugh with our friends.
But when fall comes
I find that I have to walk alone
to watch the changing season and remember.
My wife understands;
I guess she knows.

◆   ◆   ◆

MEMORIES

Summer thunder storms—
at first a humid stillness,
then a rush of wind,
crashing thunder,
and rain.

The explosion of spring
bursts into summer,
its promise fulfilled
in rich growth;
the sun crests the sky,
recedes,
leaving the tide of harvest,
in turn a stillness.

Gus Lantaigne
reaches his village,
stages his canoe
and prepares his traps.

Roy Hart awakes
to the first snowfall.

Paul Lewis walks
in the Pennsylvania woodlands,
feels exhilarated by
the fall color
and swings his stick
through the leaves.

Strange Arabic music
drifts around Reuben,
clouded in smoke
at his table;

the crowds mill,
he strikes a match,
relights his pipe
and smiles.

The woodlands,
     fields,
Indian summer
Indian corn
     Indians
something else
     beyond.

Roy Hart
sleeping beneath the Idaho night—
Gus Lantaigne
smiles at his wife and the Cachette de Noel—
Paul Lewis
finds his winter coat in the closet—
Reuben
dead.

◆   ◆   ◆

GEOGRAPHY OF AMERICA

Do you know the sand and pines of Carolina?
The long ridges of Pennsylvania
Folding and curving to the south,
Marshes of the Jersey shore
And Pine Barrens?
Or the limestone of Missouri,
The flat wheat and corn of Illinois,
Green Mountains of Vermont
And neat white towns?
The coast of Maine,
Rocks, coves, and forests
Right down to uneasy water,
Better than Oregon!
The swift bubbling of the Allagash
As it rushes toward Canada,
Or the sea of dark conifers
Ebbing away from Mount Katahdin,
Where dawn sun first strikes
American soil each day?

Have you seen
The great wrinkles
West of Amarillo,
Where a canyon suddenly
Breaks the land to say:
"The West!"?

Waking on the Rock Island Line
Somewhere in Eastern Colorado,
Prairie gives way to distant mountains,
Pike's Peak and the Front Range.
Mid-September in Medicine Bow

Brings fourteen inches of early snow
And stranded travelers sleeping
On the floor of the Virginia Hotel,
Laramie—eighteen below.
Zero in Montana's Flathead Valley
Means a mild and sunless winter.

The Anthony Lakes of Oregon,
Random-named ranges of Nevada,
Vermillion Cliffs of Arizona at dusk,
Sudden thunder storms breaking
Over Sangre de Cristo,
Sunrise in Steens Mountain
Across all the emptiness of Eastern Oregon,
Green, dark depths of Olympic rainforests.
What have those to do
With the broken lengths of
Shenandoah, Genesee and Tionesta?
Or how Dakota is divided into sections,
Geometric from the air?
Checkered farmlands of Kansas,
Minnesota lakes, remnants
Of ice invasions?

How different from
Placid farms east of the Blue Ridge,
Tidal coves of the Chesapeake,
Strange sand shores of Superior and Huron,
Deserts of Now Mexico,
Ceaseless winds and lost cities of gold,
Palmetto flats of Florida—
John Muir was there once, too,
Before glimpsing the Range of Light
From the crest of Pacheco Pass.

Tidewater and the Piedmont,
Rockies, Appalachians, Coast Range,
Boston Mountains of Arkansas,
Ponca, Shawnee and Osage ...

◆   ◆   ◆

QUESTIONS

only this
I ask you to remember

a number of weeks
(we do not count them)
have flown by now since you went away
and all the questions of our being
lie unanswered
like the scattered sections
of the Sunday Times.

When the many forms of memory and desire
lie down together in strange array
like so many grinning cats before the fire
all our friends and lovers
and their fragile essence
burning will not be found
on the farthest
shores of recollections,

as if tall pine shadows
falling on whitened hillsides
and strange winds of once
blowing fearfully in the night
meant return to me
oh self
when a season meant so much.

Judge Van Duesen's magnificent
coach-and-four rumbled past
on West River Drive
that sunny afternoon
July 1901
stiff collar chafing

my neck I could hardly
turn to catch your smile
the waters running gently
and little did we know
along those banks
of summer 1901
where the river ran.

And strange
that nothing is still
even for a moment
but always flowing onward
in never-ending forms of future
into distant changes of now.

◆   ◆   ◆

AS THE EARTH TURNS …

They had driven west in the warm night, from the hotel where Hornbeck had picked him up in an old, nondescript Ford 4-door sedan. No air conditioning. For a while they drove on a sort of freeway. Very dark along the sides. Big trees. Occasionally office parks, things like that. Warm air flowed into the car, hot and humid like Mississippi, Mr. James thought. He was in the back seat; Hornbeck and Mr. Moore were in the front, talking about old times, it seemed. Mr. James tried to concentrate. He was being taken to see THE BIG BOSS, somewhere out in the country, his hide-out in the woods or something. Mr. James was nervous. He didn't know what to expect. They left the freeway and drove for a while on a regular highway, then entered another freeway. More dark trees, lots of darkness outside. It seemed like a long ride. The radio began to fade, and Hornbeck switched it off. They were out in the country, for sure. Headed to the BOSS'S hide-out. Mr. James knew that much. They turned off the freeway onto a country road. Hornbeck sure seemed to know where he was going, Mr. James thought. Hornbeck must have been to the BOSS'S hide-out plenty of times before. They turned left by a lighted building, "Nick's Airport Tavern." Mr. James could tell it was a roadhouse or something. Off to the left were some strange lights in the darkness, an airport, Mr. James realized, but a small one. The car moved more slowly now, on a narrow country road, into darkness. Agricultural smells drifted into the car. Mr. James was reminded of rural Mississippi. He thought, the BOSS is really out here, in the middle of fucking nowhere. Like he had said. They turned left onto an even smaller road, past two farmhouses, and then into nothing but darkness. The tires were crunching now on what seemed to be a gravel road. Mr. James was sort of uneasy, this meeting with the BOSS and all. But he was with his two "partners," who knew the BOSS. Or so it seemed. They slowed down. Ahead in, or by, the road Mr. James could see a car parked in the darkness, an older American sedan. Mr. James thought he saw a figure standing by the car, a man holding something. What? It looked like a shotgun, but he couldn't tell because the guy stepped back off the road. Hell, it might have been a golf club, but it LOOKED like a shotgun, probably was. The BOSS would have security, out here in the woods, right? Hornbeck slowed down to a full stop by the other car. A very bright flashlight beam shot out of the darkness, played on Hornbeck, over to Mr. Moore, then into the backseat, full on Mr. James. It seemed to stay longer on him, Mr. James thought. He sat rigid, there in the backseat. Then the light switched off. The man said, softly, "Go on in, the BOSS is expecting you, he's waiting." Hornbeck eased the car forward on the gravel road.

Mr. James looked out the rear window, saw a young broad-shouldered guy standing there in the darkness. It was a shotgun! Of course! The BOSS would have sharp young guys for security. Out here in the woods. Probably more of them around. The car moved slowly among dark trees, not a light anywhere. It was sort of spooky, Mr. James thought, the BOSS out here in the middle of nowhere, in all this darkness. They passed by a barn and then crossed over what seemed to be a wooden bridge. The car's lights flashed on a white house, not a cabin but a small white house set back a ways. It looked almost like a school house, Mr. James thought, like one of those country schoolhouses that he remembered. There were dim lights coming from the house, and Mr. James could see a small Mercedes car parked up on the grass next to the house. Sure! The BOSS would have a Mercedes Did he drive himself? Mr. James wondered. Guys following? Hornbeck pulled into a parking area and killed the lights. They all sat for a moment in the dark; it was very quiet and very still. Insect sounds seemed very loud. It was hot and humid. Mr. James didn't move in the backseat, waiting. Mr. Moore opened his door and the interior light went on. He turned to the backseat and said, "Remember, Mr. James, just answer the BOSS, and always call him SIR. Got that?" Mr. James as quiet for a moment, then said, as to himself, "SIR … Ah shorely will, call him SIR." Mr. James thought that maybe he sounded unsure of himself, He cleared his throat and got out of the car with Hornbeck and Mr. Moore. They started toward the house, which was about ten yards away, up a small slope. The door of the house suddenly opened, flooding the area with light, or so it seemed in all the darkness. And then an immense figure appeared in the lighted space of the door, taking up almost all the space, it seemed to Mr. James. A huge man, he thought, it HAD to be the BOSS! He had been told that the BOSS was a big man, but still—he was startled! A deep, rumbling voice addressed them: "Come on up, boys. I been waiting for you all. But you're right on time. Like always, huh, Hornbeck?" He seemed to be chuckling to himself, there against the light, Mr. James thought. He had been told that Hornbeck and the BOSS went way back. The large figure retreated from the lighted doorway as they approached. Hornbeck went in first, followed by Mr. Moore, and then Mr. James, apprehensively. The BOSS was clapping Hornbeck on the back, embracing him in a sort of bear-hug. Then he turned to Mr. Moore and shook hands, somewhat formally Mr. James thought, and said, "Mr. Moore, good to see you again, Sir, here at my humble country place. A bit warmer than the last time, isn't it?" Mr. Moore mumbled something followed by a loud and clear "Sir," rather deferentially, it seemed to Mr. James. And the BOSS turned to Mr. James and said, loudly, "And you must be Mr. James. I've heard good things about you, son," extending a hand that enclosed Mr. James' hand in a powerful grip. "Come on in, I've got some Pennsylvania Dutch snacks for y'all, and whatever you'd like to drink." Mr. James remembered to say, "Thank you, SIR!" He was proud that he remembered that. The BOSS was smiling. Mr. James saw that the BOSS was indeed a huge man, well over six feet, close to 300 pounds, he thought. But not fat. Heavy and powerful, balding, with a thick bull-neck. Penetrating eyes and a loud, deep voice. A man used to giving orders and seeing them obeyed, Mr. James assumed, somewhat uneasily. The BOSS turned toward a table which held all manner of foods and drink, and waved expansively toward it. As Mr. Moore and Hornbeck moved toward the table, Mr. James had a chance to look around the large room he was in, and he was amazed. There were model trains on all the rafters, lots of them. Old leather chairs and a stone fireplace. A real country place. Shutters seemed to be pulled across the windows. Hornbeck and Mr. Moore were loading plates with food, listening to the BOSS tell some sort of story. Mr. James moved over to join them and load up. The food looked heavy and substantial. Snacks indeed? As he moved toward the table he glanced to his left and caught sight of some sort of dark uniform hanging on the door, lots of gold braid and everything. Books and papers were piled everywhere in the room. It looked like the BOSS got a lot of work done here. Or something. The BOSS put a huge hand on Mr. James' shoulder as he was filling a plate, and said, "A beer, Mr. James? Get one out of the fridge over there." It seemed like an order. Mr. James went over and got a can of Ballentyne Ale out of the fridge. The BOSS moved suddenly, rather swiftly, to cut him off in the kitchen area. Mr. James looked up at the huge man, not knowing what to say, waiting. "… Sir," he stammered. The BOSS broke in, saying, "Good Southern boy, you are, I'm told. I like the South. True Americans, you agree, son?" Mr. James quickly said, "Yassuh," just like the good Southern boy he was, thinking of the BOSS as some old-time plantation owner, of himself as "a good nigger," wondering why the BOSS had this effect on him. The BOSS held Mr. James' eyes for awhile, then propelled him toward Hornbeck and Mr. Moore, who were standing by the fireplace eating and drinking, talking quietly, looking relaxed. The BOSS helped himself to a huge plate of the Pennsylvania Dutch food, and a 16 oz. beer from the fridge, and joined the men by the fireplace. "GODDAMN!" he said, very loudly. "Goddamn good y'all could come out and join me. Here in white man's country. I'm gonna flash the lights for my man Preston to join us from the barn, get some victuals, then he can relieve the other fellow in the woods." So there WAS another guy somewhere on the property, watching, Mr. James thought. Protecting the BOSS. He wondered about dogs, were there dogs out there in the dark woods? The BOSS seemed to fill the room, talking quietly with Hornbeck and Mr. Moore, turning occasionally to smile at Mr. James, who ate listening, not saying anything. Hornbeck and Mr. Moore, both big men, seemed small beside the BOSS, who was fiddling with a light switch, evidently to call in Preston from the barn. It WAS impressive, thought Mr. James. The BOSS! He was standing here with the BOSS! The inner circle! At last!

After the food and drinks were consumed, when Hornbeck and Mr. Moore were sitting in the leather chairs, the BOSS motioned to Mr. James to join him over by the kitchen area. He "fixed" a penetrating look on Mr. James, who felt small and weak in the presence of that very big, powerful man. The BOSS said, quietly in his deep voice, "Ah have a job for you, a most important job. And I think you are the man for it. Am I right, son? Are you mah good man for this job?"

Mr. James hesitated before answering, worried about what the "important job" might be, then cleared his throat and said, "Yes Sir!" loudly, "Ah am shorely the man for yer job!" The BOSS smiled, and clapped Mr. James on the back, and said, "Good! Ah knowed it! Let's have some more drinks, rouse Hornbeck and Mr. Moore. Discuss the job."

SOMEWHERE IN INDIANA—CIRCA 1972

It was a typical Saturday afternoon in Groveland, Indiana, hot, dry, and quiet, very quiet. A cluster of bicycles stood in front of the old movie theatre and an occasional car wandered up the faded street in search of a shady parking spot. The town appeared to be deserted except for a group of men who were gathered in the shade of the large cool trees that grew in front of the courthouse. Some stood talking quietly while others sat on the base of a statue to Civil War heroes and stared out into the hot street. There was a bang of a screen door as an old man came out of the drugstore and started toward the courthouse. As he crossed the street he noticed a dog lying in the shade of a parked car and he bent over slowly to pet it. The dog, pleased with this attention, stretched and wagged his tail, causing a wisp of dust to curl up into the hot still air. The man then straightened up and continued across the street to the courthouse. As he approached the group of men in front of the old Victorian building he drew a red checked handkerchief from his rear pocket and mopped his face. "Hello Mr. Hornbeck," someone said.

The old man had been a scholar and a diplomat; he had graduated from Yale and been with the Foreign Service for a number of years until a nervous breakdown had forced him into retirement. When he had first come to Groveland he had remained aloof from the townspeople, spending his time reading and working on historical papers, but in the years which had elapsed since his arrival he had become adapted to his environment and was a well liked and respected member of the community. As he entered into small town life, the marks of his former existence passed one by one from his exterior. His mind was still sharp, though, and he had maintained a cosmopolitan outlook by subscribing to many journals and papers; these kept him well informed about political and literary events along with other significant developments in the world, but lately he had been neglecting them. In outward appearance, however, he looked like he had lived in Groveland all his life.

As he acknowledged the greetings of the group he removed his old straw hat and wiped his forehead with the red handkerchief. His yellowish white hair was moist with perspiration and lay plastered in thin strands across his glistening scalp. He was dressed in faded overalls, a pair of scuffed high shoes, and an old work shirt. The shirt was buttoned at the top and the worn collar fit loosely around the old man's wrinkled neck. There was a white stubble of beard on his chin, with uneven patches indicating unsteady strokes with the razor. The skin on his face was blotched and wrinkled, and there were traces of tobacco juice in the cracks at the corners of his mouth. His face was deeply lined, with dark hollows under his eyes, and his nose, which was red and bulbous, was pitted with many small holes. The features had the appearance of a classical ruin; one could still detect the fine quality and the proportion which existed once, and the impression was one of tired dignity and quiet knowledge.

He sat down wearily on the base of the statue and crossed his legs, exposing a stretch of white hairless skin above his sock. The man sitting next to him said, "Hot today, ain't it Mr. Hornbeck?" "Yes, it sure is," he replied quickly. Someone else commented on the current need for rain. Tom's mind began to drift back through the years, as it had been doing often in the last few weeks, since a letter had come from an old college friend whom he hadn't seen in twenty years. He thought of his nephew, his brother's son, the bright but unpredictable young man who had grown up in a comfortable Philadelphia suburb and had graduated from a good college. Then he had wandered out to California, increasingly out of touch and finally disappearing. He often wondered what had happened to that promising but troubled young man. As the conversation around him groped on slowly, the voices grew dim and faraway, and finally blended with the hum of insects on that hot summer day. He was thinking about the old days, of college and travel abroad, of his years in the Foreign Service, and of the people he had known. Pleasant thoughts, all of them; it had been a good life. The memories returned swiftly, vividly, real—things he hadn't thought of in years and other things he had never stopped thinking about. These thoughts of the past possessed him so strongly that he seemed to be living each moment over again, and he began to smile, faintly at first, then with a broad grin which revealed an uneven row of yellow and cracked teeth.

Later that afternoon, when the bicycles were gone from the movie theatre, the group was still assembled under the trees in front of the courthouse waiting for the cool stillness of evening. They were motionless and silent, and there was a seriousness, perhaps a touch of fear, in their old faces.

◆   ◆   ◆

PART TWO

SPECULATIVE

*(Made up largely, but not entirely,
from notes and writings from the 1960s,
left behind in San Francisco by Hornbeck ...)*

FIRST TIME WEST!

Yes, Ken Ackerman of KCBS and American Airlines' "Music 'till Dawn," I've flown a lot, too; and always found it an enjoyable and interesting experience. But no experience on an airplane will ever equal my first trip west on a train. After a layover in Chicago, an experience in itself for a fifteen-year-old boy, streaking west on the Rock Island Line across the farmlands of western Illinois, dinner in the dining car with the white-jacketed waiters, the ritual of writing one's own order, the swaying of the car. Then, after dinner, sitting in the observation car watching the dusk spread over the incredible flatness of Iowa with the clickety-clack of the rails passing beneath. I had two drinks in the club car, Tom Collins, this at fifteen! And on my way back to my Pullman, some huge Western men in big hats between cars with a bottle, coming from some convention in Chicago. "Hey, boy, where you from? Want a drink?" And into the Pullman, the mysteries of the berths suddenly pulled from the sides of the car and the heavy curtains. In the washroom some conversation with the ancient Negro porter who told some about the wrecks he had been in. Then into my lower berth with the clean white sheets and blankets, all with a certain smell of their own; and that strange net that hung along the window. I always remember some baseball story about a young pitcher, a boy from the farms, who thought it was to rest his arm in and did so. Next morning he had the sorest arm you could imagine and couldn't pitch for a week. At least I was farther ahead than that of the game, and put my watch and wallet in the net. Sleep was fitful, and every time the train stopped I had to raise the shade. There were always men in denim outfits walking beneath the window with strange cans, peering and poking beneath the cars; carts with baggage and boxes being wheeled down the platform in the lights. Then, I raised the shade and outside the moving train was a landscape that was unmistakably western, the dry prairies of eastern Colorado. I raised up in my berth and watched, fascinated as prairie dogs and jack rabbits scattered from the rushing shadow that was the train in the morning light. And later, as the train swung to the south on a curve, in the distance the great range of the Rocky Mountains standing to the west in the sunlight, much as the first white man had seen them. I knew that the tallest was Pike's Peak. I tarried awhile in Colorado Springs, which I found intolerably dull; but that was largely due to my ancient great-aunts. The trip began again in the one car train that headed south from the Springs, through Pueblo, Colorado, where I was amazed by the tall smokestacks of industry (years later I came to know something of Colorado Fuel and Iron), and the barren dryness of the land. In La Junta the train from the east was delayed by floods at the Mississippi regions, and our car was shunted onto a siding outside of town. I walked into the town and saw a movie. The whole experience was an adventure, especially seeing all the Indian-looking people in "western costume" in the theatre. The film was over early, and the town was dark and deserted. I walked back to the darkened Pullman along the tracks, the wind blowing and the stars incredibly bright in the western sky. The next day the connecting train arrived, late in the evening. The Santa Fe Railroad, by way of apologizing for the delay announced that for us (residents of the stranded Pullman) all meals to LA would be "on the house." There was no diner on the train, only "sandwich facilities," so stops were made for formal meals at Fred Harvey Houses—and how I remember those! Leaving La Junta we creaked through Raton Pass in a rainstorm, and I was interested by the rocky, piñoned character of the landscape, and the definite Spanish-Indian aspect of the dwellings and people I glimpsed from the window. It was all new and exciting to me. We stopped at Las Vegas, New Mexico, for a meal, and to me this is THE Las Vegas of the west. The land was dry and barren, the wind blew and the food was mediocre at best. But what did that matter? I remember Albuquerque in the heat of late afternoon, or whatever time—it was hot. We stepped for another meal, and I remember Indians at the platform selling their goods, turquoise and silver. How the time passed I don't quite remember. There was a large mountain somewhere off to the left of the train with a large cross on it, and I remember that this was in commemoration of some massacre or, I think, starvation, in the period of Spanish rule. How I learned this, I don't remember. I think there was some sort of sign by the tracks. There were many soldiers and sailors on the train—it was during the Korean "conflict," and I remember the Indians on the train, with their strange clothes. Possibly the first Spanish word I ever learned was *vaca*, as an Indian father pointed out the window to a herd of grazing cows and said to his small child, "vacas." I remember the vermillion cliffs of Arizona as the train rattled along. We stopped again for a meal with Fred Harvey in Winslow, Arizona—this must have been for dinner because after this I remember the climb into high country, the creaking of the train making its way around curves in the mountains—and I now remember a great curve somewhere earlier when I could see the front of the train, the great locomotives and all the cars; this was somewhere in New Mexico, I think, and is considered a great engineering marvel—or was. At Flagstaff the train stopped for a while in darkness, and I remember standing at the end of the train where a gate was pulled across the path of the last car, and smelling the clean, crisp night air, full with the smell of burning sawdust from the lumber mills of the region; and seeing the stars incredibly bright in the night sky behind the tall pines (Ponderosas) which I hadn't seen before. I must have climbed in my berth after this, because the next thing I remember is raising the shade in Needles, California. The same denimed men were performing their same ablutions, and suddenly the train creaked and got underway, very quickly into an empty land that immediately revealed to me a great desert, unlike anything I had seen in New Mexico and Arizona. Then I guess I dozed off, and the next thing I remember is the slow winding through the east approach to Cajon Pass. At the summit were some scraggly pines, but mostly the country was dry and rocky until the train began to descend toward San Berdoo (pardon the RR lingo I somehow picked up). From San Bernardino we rushed, at a sedate pace, across the flatlands of the lush California citrus country. I remember the stop at Pasadena, and the quaint attractiveness of the station there—it could have been some other stop. And finally into Los Angeles, where my father was waiting, worried because the train was long overdue, though he had been assured by Santa Fe officials that all was in good order. The Los Angeles terminal impressed me while we were waiting for the unraveling that inevitably follows a trans-continental trip—and it still does. I must admit I think that there was some red tape about cashing in meal-chits off the trip, which the Santa Fe had promised to reimburse. Finally my father and I loaded ourselves into his Nash Rambler for the trip down Sunset to Wilshire toward Santa Monica. It was an interesting trip, and is still more interesting that the trip from LAX to Santa Monica. Can it be that somehow this entire way of getting to California gave me more of an understanding of this great continent of ours than flashing across in the sky in just under five hours, satiated with fine food and wines and liquors, lulled into not caring whether or not the great ship sinks from the sky over Grand Canyon by the latest absolutely lousy offering from Hollywood? I think so, and I am eternally grateful that I have had this experience, repeated several times in both directions (and these experiences will have to await another time). And now that I have driven by motorcar some dozen times across the continent, I am more aware of all that lies in between the points that I travel to and from. Today we have jet transportation, and since the basic reason is to get from one place to another, we do it in as little time as the means afford. But remember what loss of understanding we suffer. As Robinson Jeffers said, "The slower you go, the more you've been there."

◆   ◆   ◆

A VERY STRANGE TRIP!

Just before Christmas in the year 1966 Hornbeck got a drive-away car to take him and some others from San Francisco to Los Angeles. The vehicle was a late model station wagon full of fuel, which would have to be replaced before delivery to the agency in LA. The passengers were a strange assortment. There was Tariq Hamid, a hip Pakistani student from San Francisco State College. Hornbeck had run into him in North Beach, where they had talked about modern jazz. Tariq was a big fan of Dizzy Gillespie, was friends with him even. Had instructed Diz in Eastern Mysticism, which Hornbeck thought Tariq made up. He had also one time in San Francisco taken Dr. Avis to smoke dope with Diz and the band. The Doctor said it was really strong stuff, and that he had to keep from bursting out laughing at Tariq's Eastern mysticism bullshit.

Tariq had with him Roxanne, an Oklahoma girl, recently divorced and studying sporadically at San Francisco State. Tariq was her first experiment with "third worldism," a syndrome that would greatly occupy her in coming years. Then there were two hippies from San Francisco State who seemed to be stoned and in their own world.

And finally there was Parkhurst! Who had just turned up in San Francisco after two years in Bergen, Norway, where his colossal "Goddess of Bergen" had failed to be constructed over the harbor of that maritime city. The Norwegians had finally deported him back to the States—a fairly unusual and rare phenomenon.

He was living at "the Alhambra" (sort of a "student crash pad") with Doctor Avis and a bunch of hippies, and driving them all crazy. They thought they were far out, before Parkhurst came on the scene, but "They ain't seen nothin' yet." Hornbeck remembered one of them asking, "Yo, man, does this dude ever sleep?" Hornbeck had known Parkhurst back East before he had departed for Norway, and nothing about the man would surprise him. To say that Parkhurst was "unusual" would be the understatement of all time.

This made six for the trip to LA. There was some trouble getting going, but this was accomplished some time after noon on a Saturday. Hornbeck drove, with Parkhurst in the front seat next to him. Tariq and Roxanne were on the next seat, and in the rear seat were the two hippies, lost in their own world. But as Parkhurst began to ramble about far-out subjects their interest perked up. One hippie asked Hornbeck, "What's the dude on, man. Got any more?" Hornbeck told them that Parkhurst was on nothing, never had been, it was just the way he was. "No way, man," said one of the hippies, thinking that Parkhurst, and perhaps Hornbeck, had a secret stash of way-out dope that they did not want to share. Finally, as they drove down the Peninsula toward Monterey the hippies gave up and consented to share a joint with Tariq, who was chanting mystical chants.

In order to make the trip interesting it was decided to drive along the coast by Big Sur while it was still light, stop at the Big Sur Inn for refreshment, and climb over the Nacimiento Mountains to eventually join U.S. 101 and straight into L.A. Driving along the spectacular coast it bothered Hornbeck that Parkhurst seemed oblivious of the scenery, so lost was he within his own mind and spouting notions like some day being able to "cross the Universe in a few hours." No wonder the hippies thought he was "on something." So, seeking to divert Parkhurst's attention to the scenery outside he said, "Peter, there is some of the most spectacular scenery in the world out there. What do you think of it?" Whereupon Parkhurst rolled down the window and launched himself out, so alarming Tariq and Roxanne that they reached to grab his legs to restrain him. He was shouting about the eternal beauties of the world, about his plan to sail along those coasts in a concrete boat decorated with Viking flags. Finally he was pulled back into the car, and shortly after that episode they approached the Big Sur Inn. Hornbeck noticed the two hippies looking at Parkhurst strangely.

At the Big Sur Inn, a very rustic edifice blending with the redwoods, they all got sandwiches, beer and coffee. There were not many other patrons, especially in those days and at that time of year. Parkhurst did not join them at a big table by the fire, but spent quite a bit of time chatting up the proprietor, an old Dane who had settled in Big Sur before the road was built and who had built the Inn himself. Then Parkhurst circulated, commenting on the architecture, comparing it to Nordic and Norwegian building styles. Going on and on about all sorts of things. Finally Hornbeck got him to the table but he said he wasn't hungry and just talked away. Hornbeck heard one of the hippies mumble, "What fuels this guy, anyway?"

One of the young, hip waiters asked: "I hope you don't mind, but how do all of you know each other?" They were that diverse a group!

More time was spent than had been planned in the pleasant environs of the Big Sur Inn, so it was well past dark when Hornbeck turned off Highway 1 at Lucia onto the dirt road that climbed toward the summit. There was no traffic, and a bright moon, so it was a pleasant and easy drive. At the summit he pulled into a broad open space with a view of the moon shining on the Pacific. Warm winds wafted from the interior east. Everyone got out to relieve him or herself in some manner, and to admire the view.

When everybody was back in the car somebody noticed that Parkhurst was standing some distance away, outlined against the sea by the moonlight. He was urinating and a great cloud of steam was rising around him. He went on and on urinating. One of the hippies said, "Christ, man, look at that. And the dude didn't have no beer, not a drop of water!" It was an unusual scenario, as though Parkhurst were some vast steaming generator pouring out energy. Finally Parkhurst got back in the car, and Hornbeck drove slowly down the eastern slope in the darkness.

When the road flattened out and got somewhat broader in the valley, he picked up speed toward Highway 101. All this was taking much longer than Hornbeck had anticipated. Parkhurst was beside him, but got out to trade places with Tariq who wanted to stretch his damaged (from polo in Pakistan!) leg in the front where there was more room. In the rear of the vehicle Roxanne and the hippies were dozing off—or trying to.

Parkhurst kept rolling down one of the rear windows to let in the cool night air. The hippies kept rolling it back up, annoyed. One of them said, "Geez, the heat comin' off this guy. It's like a furnace, ain't normal." He had been catching on. Finally one of the hippies said to Hornbeck, with some irritation, "Hey, man, you seem to have some kind of control over this dude. Can you get him to shut up. He's driving us crazy back here!" Indeed, perhaps they were experiencing a new dimension of "far out."

Hornbeck told Parkhurst quite sternly that he must be quiet so others could sleep. He was so for about five minutes, then a torrent came flooding out, mention of the human brain being able to store fifty-seven times all the information in the Library of Congress. That when some scientists had speculated that there might be "billions of universes," Parkhurst's reaction had been, "Why so few?" Hornbeck was amused, if the others were not. He knew that Parkhurst was "a world class nut," without parallel. A harmless and delightful one. Definitely unique ...

When they finally reached the highway they needed gas. Hornbeck pulled into a small country station that was open. One of the hippies offered to drive, and being tired Hornbeck said OK and slid into the passenger seat. Now, while the car was being filled with gas Parkhurst appointed himself cleanser of the windshield, which had a fair amount of bugs smashed on it. He got up on the hood of the car and kneeled so he could get a better view of the windshield He cleaned and cleaned, in small circles, meticulously. Finally the hippie driver blew the horn and shouted, "Get the hell off there, it's clean enough!" Parkhurst said nothing, but smiled like Buddha and kept cleaning. The hippie said, "Good fucking Christ!" and started the car. Parkhurst continued cleaning. The hippie pulled the car into the fortunately deserted highway and accelerated to perhaps ten or fifteen miles per hour. Hornbeck was alarmed, but Parkhurst just cleaned away. Finally Hornbeck shouted at the hippie driver, "Don't touch the brake—he'll be thrown off and badly injured. Just let the car coast to a stop by the side of the road, very slowly." And that is what happened. Parkhurst jumped off the hood. The hippie got out and told Hornbeck to drive on to LA, some hours away, saying his nerves were too shot to drive "with this nut in the car."

The rest of the drive was what might be said "anti-climatic," those in the rear sleeping and Parkhurst in the front going on and on about the cosmos and his plan to cross the continent in a hot air balloon. All that kept Hornbeck awake as they coasted into LA on uncrowded freeways on an early Sunday morning. The hippies were dropped off in Hollywood and walked away from the car saying nothing. They had contributed a few dollars for gas, and in exchange had received knowledge that few others have. Not a bad bargain. Tariq and Roxanne were dropped near the UCLA campus, and when Hornbeck asked Parkhurst where he wanted to be taken he had no idea. Finally, he said his brother's office, but of course it would not be open on a Sunday morning. By this time even Hornbeck had grown somewhat weary of Parkhurst, so he gave him some change, dropped him off on the Third Street Mall in Santa Monica, and told him to contact his brother Monday morning. As he drove off slowly on Wilshire Boulevard, Parkhurst ran along side of the car, clutching his bulging briefcase, shouting, "Billions of bubbling thank yous. It was a spacial ride. The cosmos ..." People were staring. Hornbeck accelerated, and watched in the rear view mirror the figure of Parkhurst growing smaller and smaller. He had to laugh. It HAD been an interesting ride ...

Footnote: Parkhurst was taken on by his brother, who ran a successful magazine for the independent trucking industry. The deal was that Parkhurst was to produce a series of drawings for the magazine and would be allowed to sleep in the office. It turned out that these immensely talented drawings were mocking and contemptuous of their subject matter. His brother had to lock him in a storage room at night with a cot and a bucket so he would not be on the phone all night all over the world!

One afternoon (as Parkhurst later related to Hornbeck) as he was returning to the office and cutting through an alley, a black man appeared with a gun. "Give it up, old head!" the man said. Parkhurst had no idea what the man meant, but seeing the gun surmised it was a hold-up. He told the man that he had no wallet, nothing but the bulging briefcase containing his plans to sail across the continent in a hot air balloon. The man looked angry, started waving his gun around. Parkhurst inquired as to the make and caliber of the gun, then suggested to the man that they find a bench nearby and discuss a path in life better than the one the man seemed to be on. And then, Parkhurst said, "The poor chap started sweating, his eyes grew wide and he turned and ran. I just wanted to help him ..."

◆   ◆   ◆

PARKHURST

came plunging down the mountain,
laughing, running,
carrying an immense paper bag
bulging and bursting
with the vastness
of his papers and projects.

In the distance
we heard Parkhurst,
and suddenly,
with one great cry
he sprang into sight,
laughing
and waving his wild arms wide.

Parkhurst called today—
his voice exploded
like a great gong,
and when he laughed
I had to hold the phone away.

Parkhurst
will cross the continent,
west to east, in a balloon.
Parkhurst
will skywrite
in gorgeous flaming colors.
Parkhurst
has had his electricity cut off,
has not eaten in three days.
Parkhurst

is high over San Francisco,
East Bay and Marin, too.

Somewhere in this city
Parkhurst exists—
that could be him
running down that street,
crossing the park—
somewhere,
Parkhurst is loose.

A frantic mechanism,
like some giant ancient clock,
swings on and on and on,
Parkhurst darting like a needle
through the shabby blanket of reality
stretched to cover all of us.

A gigantic, steaming
Parkhurst running through the dark,
leaving trails of bubbling phosphorescence,
his raft of ping-pong balls
towed by ducks.

Parkhurst—
telephoning from trains,
in and out of tunnels—
a momentous decision,
back to balloons!

No word from Parkhurst,
lost somewhere in urban night,
running, running
through an endless maze of plans;
Parkhurst ahead of us,
behind us,

far above us—
someone must find Parkhurst!

◆   ◆   ◆

RANDOM NOTES ON A TRIP, JUNE 1967

While taking "my ease" in the very pleasant park in Bend, Oregon, several small boys came wandering down to the water. One of them said, seeing me, "There's a man that don't have no home," an obvious reference to my dirty jeans and pack. The oldest boy said, "Don't never say that." And they went about their boys' interests, feeding breadcrumbs to the ducks, while "the man that don't have no home" continued his ease, reading *Time* magazine, addressed to his "home" in San Francisco!

Hitchhiking out of Bend at 12:30 that day I heard a car "wind out" of the north of where I was standing, then slow and stop for me. A young kid, about 18, was at the wheel. Gave me a ride to the edge of town, where the truck stop was—which he said would be a better place to get a ride. Asked me if I was a ranch-hand. A man can go in a lot of directions from Bend!

Earlier, when I got a ride north from Healdsburg, this young kid got stranded with me at the same nowhere place in San Rafael with these sort of older hippies; well, when the kid and the driver were in this place getting hamburgers, the girl asked me some about myself; like, where was I from and where was I going, and all that. When I said I was headed for Medford, Oregon, she said, "Not much doing up there." I thought she meant action, excitement, things like that. But when I said that I was just "awandering," she said she thought I was looking for work. Was my outfit and appearance that convincing? I guess it was. I got a ride with them north through the night to Eureka, where I was left to sleep in the car because I heard the hippie girl say, "Leave him in the car—I don't want him in the house." At dawn I got a ride and several adventures with a guy in a pickup headed to Alaska, who eventually parted ways with me in Bend, Oregon …

Must rewrite all of this since I seem to have had in just a few days enough adventures and material for writing for many pages of notes. Never realized how much until I sat down at the machine to put it all down.

Remember this: that if Reuben were still alive and in Israel, he—the great non-soldier—would be fighting the Arabs. Or would he? Don't know.

100 SAUSAGES AND A SEWING MACHINE

I see your long fingers trailing
sparks from the open windows
of the city as it rockets by.
The tires of my bicycle hum
and the children scatter
from their ball-playing.
Could I shout wildly in Chinese
I might tell them to all go home
and fuck their mothers
(on all the dirty mattresses of Chinatown).

You there,
I have seen you before.
Was it not last week,
in this same place?
You were dressed as a priest
and were speaking of the need
for a new morality in the Church.
I remember well, and how is it
now you go without your priestly garb?

I am called by madness to the window
just in time to see a fantastic child
racing up the hill, her long black hair
streaming behind her as she strides
in her outrageously short miniskirt,
her thighs a paradigm of energy and delight.

(Don't know what paradigm means, just like the sound of it.)

◆   ◆   ◆

FRIENDS?

You who did not like me
now say that you do like me.
How is this,
since I am the same person?
Is it because you have now
figured out some explanation
that satisfies the notion
that it is better to like than dislike.

Horserace Rapids, they were called;
I guess that was because
we went so damned fast through them,
or so it seemed,
in those canoes.
I went through on foot,
hauling supplies,
and rolling stones and boulders aside
to float our canoes down the dried-up stream.
I guess it's all a matter of conditions and seasons,
how one goes through life. The point is:
one goes, and it's the journey what makes the difference.
In a later year we paddled over a dam
we'd carried around. I could even
point into the water and say,
"That's where we ate lunch, right down there."

◆   ◆   ◆

("As I See It"; being the observations and thoughts of Hornbeck to the American environment as he observes it)

(THESE OBSERVATIONS OF HORNBECK ARE VERY PERSONAL, AND MUST BE EVALUATED AS SUCH.)

(The whole problem seems to be simply one of too many people, and thus—urbanization.)

… on my journey today (Sunday, 20 August 1967) throughout some of the peripheral regions of the San Francisco Bay Area, I must confess that I saw almost no aspect of the workings of the hand or mind of man that either inspired or pleased me. And such few sights that did bring some feeling of satisfaction seemed to have their origins in some earlier era. My feelings were a reaction to an unrelieved, uniform, and uninspired dullness that represents, at least to my mind, the mass culture of contemporary America and the atmosphere of living that such culture exhibits; granted that most of this, if not nearly all, is undoubtedly rather comfortable and in vague ways probably satisfactory to the persons who exist in the environments that I observed, and thus is so really and commonly American. I saw no slums, not even in the "ghetto" areas of Richmond that struck me, with my awareness of things better, as somewhat of an outrage to human dignity. What I did see was the vast, comfortable, commonness of contemporary America. And with this I have no basic or real complaint when put in mind of the favelas of Rio and the various real slums that are found in all the cities of this world. My complaint is then a relative, and spiritual one—and as such is admittedly rather unreal and misdirected, since the promise of America has always been a material one, the betterment of (man's) material lot in life. And granted that the various unique conditions and untapped resources of America have made available to the peoples of all lands that have come to this blessed continent the material advantages that they have sought, either for themselves or for their children; now that many, though not all, Americans have passed into the second stages of these advantages we are now experiencing various forms of "backlash"—from the "so-called" top, the "Hippies," and from the "bottom," the form of "crime—it does pay not to work" syndrome. But for most Americans who have variously arrived at this second stage of material advantage, and who live pleasantly, for them, and happily with few complaints in ticky-tack dwellings, drive pickups with campers, spend money in the big chain supermarkets and in "cocktail lounges" on weekends, bowl, go hunting, watch TV, and whatever are the accepted "American" pursuits of happiness these days; I say personally, "There is nothing inherently wrong with this type of life—it is the promise that America is all about. But now that you are here I will also say, THERE MUST BE MORE TO LIFE!" But would you agree? I think probably not, and to be perfectly honest and frank—why should you? All that ticky-tack that depressed me this afternoon is not all that bad, when compared with the man I saw sleeping in a wheelbarrow in Mexico City. Now, as for what did please me on this expedition—the moments of rural throwback, the rounded golden-brown hills of California against that incredible blue sky, with few buildings anywhere to introduce the hand of man, but with enough of a subtle understanding of man living in harmony with nature to suggest that there was something good going on. But this was a moment of "rural throwback," temporal as well as geographic. It did not represent "where America is going." America is headed in the direction of the mass culture, the computer, the ways of handling many persons, and, of course, ticky-tack, which is the result of this sense of inevitability, and also comfort in a bland form (or a sense of absence of discomfort). It is not a movement toward any realization of spiritual values or artistic awareness, or even admittance of dissatisfaction. Minds like mine should not be loose on Sunday afternoons; these American people should be allowed to wallow in their comforts until History makes some judgment. My thoughts are abstract, ephemeral, and personal. NOTE FOLLOWS.

Now, if you will excuse me, dear writer of the excellent and amusing book that I have been reading tonight (*The Floating Opera*, by John Barth), but most of us readers are conditioned to entering and leaving books at the breaking point of chapters, which is, after all, on a formal basis, where you writers leave us. What I want to do is to get down in typewritten form the ideas that I have committed to paper with a pencil, and which will, if left as such, languish in some part of my "neglected files"; which is to say, those that will not be read as "important" by anyone if I should not awake on the morrow. So, to the machine and dexterity, if possible.

I seem to recall being told as a schoolboy that the population of the U.S. was 139 million people (and something perhaps more or less in sheep, horses, cows and dogs, et al.). Recently I read that the population of this country is currently estimated to be 199 million people (discounting fluctuations in the aforementioned nonhuman animals). It seems that we have added 60 million people in the intervening period, and I for one could very well do without them. Perhaps this sounds like a snobbish statement. It is not meant to be such. It is not meant to be directed toward any particular class or group. It represents only that I as an individual do not care for crowds and crowding. This recent surge of population has brought, at least for me, much unwelcome change in the ways of life of our country. Granted, change is inevitable, even desirable when it can be recognized as a legitimate form of progress; but too much of the change that I have seen is simply change, careless, unplanned and chaotic change, and I can't see that we, as a nation of diverse human beings, are any better off for all of it, in a spiritual way. Materially, yes; we are a rich and powerful nation. We work less, and enjoy more "goods and fun." But the whole story is yet to be told; the history of the "world community" is not very far toward whatever point may be the destination of the human experience on this planet. These thoughts prompt me to a future examination of "the quality of human life" as it is currently found in contemporary America. (July 1967)

◆   ◆   ◆

Attempting to analyze my personal orientation toward many aspects of the past (as I perceive them), as opposed to a distrust of the present and its projected trends, I am led to consider one important factor that I believe in and strongly identify with—NATURE. Nature is necessarily a thing of the past, while it is also something that we enjoy in the present and will, hopefully, continue to enjoy in the future. That is to say, nature is something of a continuation of the past, the stable world of nature is a balance to the changes that man indulges in, though nature is a state of evolution and change, too. But we perceive and enjoy this identification with past and present today in what is essentially what is unchanged from a recent or distant past; this is the essence of nature in a largely mechanized world. But I enjoy nature, or a nature oriented environment—I suppose because in whatever form I find it, it represents something relatively untarnished by the heavy and accelerating hand of man. Most ideally this is found in a primitive form, as in our wilderness areas; but also found in the guided and manicured fashion found in parks and farmlands, since in these is found a balance and harmony not disruptive to the basic norm that I take to be the foundation for human existence in this planet. ("Art is a harmony parallel to nature"—Cezanne.) But, given the present direction of "art," is this any longer true? Identification with nature does not necessarily represent an escape to the past, but does mean some recognition of a better form of present. (Parenthetically, I wish to add that I am also much interested in cities, their development and problems, since these I consider to be the appropriate arena for mechanization and modern technology, though somewhat grudgingly.)

I predict that as these technological and urban forces that we have let loose in our land continue in acceleration until they have spread over everything and penetrated every aspect of our individual lives, there will be an increasing interest in the concept and memory of "virgin America," particularly the frontier of the American West. And with this interest there will be a great need for competent persons to study, interpret, and recreate the atmosphere and events of that era, as people seek to experience vicariously that which has been irretrievably lost in the American nation.

◆   ◆   ◆

I can see from a projection of the present that California is to become one vast sprawl of people, projects and industrial developments of every sort. And as this process occurs, that element that is the source of our being, the natural, the primitive, the mystical, the LAND, will fade more and more into the vaguely remembered past. The landscape will be an altered and arranged landscape. No longer will men position themselves with regard to natural features. Men will know only vicariously the feelings aroused by standing alone in dark mountains shrouded by night, of vistas of untouched land sweeping away to a distant sky. Man will no longer seek harmony with nature because he will have won his persistent struggle to CONQUER it, and he will no longer have respect for the sand he shoves around in his play. Climate will be changed and controlled for optimum pleasure and benefit; mountains will be flattened, rivers reversed, and cities planted everywhere overflowing with people. With all this activity and population there will be need for more and more controls, proscribing every area of human existence. Man will increasingly fall victim to his own inventions.

All this will come to pass. As surely as the planets continue to revolve in the heavens. It all began when the first white man crossed overland from the east and entered California, and perceived that there was something special, something unique about the vast land that he had wandered into. The first man to enter California from the east was not one that you will read about. He was Arthur Louis Nikolas de Noilly Sands, adventurer and voyager, captured by Indians in the Huron country in the early 1700s, and a most unusual fellow. He lived with the Indians for many years and learned their ways very thoroughly. In time he came to be regarded among them as something of a holy spirit, a saint, or whatever they thought of for a person who brought big medicine that healed wounded warriors and introduced ways of doing things that were better than the old ways. He wandered from tribe to tribe in this role of saint, always westward, and eventually he entered Northern California. He lived among the California Indians for about ten years, traveling up and down the length of the "state," mostly close to the coast. Surprisingly enough, from the time of his capture he kept a record of his experiences, as best as he could with the Indian tools and systems of recording that he could utilize. Some of his thinking was strangely modern:

"I find that so many of the so-called 'problems' or 'troubles' in contemporary society can be traced to the existence of so much available money and affluence that is prevalent. Essentially there is just too much of all this, and too much in irresponsible, i.e. the wrong hands; and this statement made in a rather generalized sense. This statement does not imply any oversight in regard to the problem of those Americans who do not share this 'affluence' in any organized or real social sense; it recognizes that these people in society do in various ways share this 'affluence' in ways that they would not probably enjoy in other, less privileged areas of the world, given the fate of the so-called average man."

"Again, generally speaking, the American people, like spoiled children, get what they want, what they demand, whether or not it is best, or even good, for them. They get what they want and demand because they have the money that the 'givers' want to get their hands on. This situation exists with no regard to any sense of sophistication or discriminating taste or values that might temper the conditions of such exchange. Thus we have an unhealthy relationship, one in which neither party gains any ultimate, any spiritual value. It is one that demeans the giver and the taker, one in which each, in his separate sense of values, is fooled into thinking that he has gained something. The real loser is society; that is, that which involves us all in the longer sense of existence."

"I do not say that people should not be rich, nor do I say that this richness should involve power and the use of power. I say only that, given this richness and the concomitant power that is very real, there should be realized some understanding of values, of what power and money ought to be all about, some sense of ultimate responsibility to the vaster segments of mankind; of how money and power ought to be used to achieve a fuller and better life for the rest of mankind as well as for oneself. The problem thus seems to be one of the relative advantages and positions of the individual versus society."

"This continent is generally a land of children, and seems to be becoming more so, for better or for worse (this will be decided in the future); but for the reality of the land of children—this can be very beautiful and good, or it can be destructive and ultimately bad. We see today much of this child's view of the world, and his actions in it that is not very attractive to mature and reasonable minds. There are many attributes of childhood, of the child's view of life, that are both good and bad. Who is to choose? There are also many negative, unrestrained and destructive aspects. If Nature, or God, had intended us to live on this earth as children, then we would not pass beyond that stage …"

Remember how Lenin wrote—on extra large paper in long-hand, using only two-thirds of the paper, leaving a wide margin for additions and/or corrections? All in all, a rather good method for committing one's thoughts to paper. Advice to myself—try to adopt this method; in a sense, BE A LENINIST …

The power of the PEOPLE—this power is rather undisputed, but it is necessarily vague and formless, like the ranks of the people themselves; it needs channeling and organizing, and then into some irrational felt needs of the people as a collection of individuals; and also into some perceived direction of the so-called intellectuals who envision some idealized state of the people that cannot be real until it is achieved, and then all thoughts of the real past are left very far behind. The unrealized power of the people is the impetus of such movements, when organized and unleashed, but when such power is ungovernable, it serves no good purpose for the achievement of logical and immediate ends. The moral is—those who make revolution never gain any sense of immediate satisfaction; and those who reap the eventual benefits of revolution never experience the realities that make revolution inevitable. What is best is to make "people" comfortable.

THE ACCURSED LAND OF GOLD
(MEANT TO BE CHANTED!)

Acid rock and porno-violent,
blown mind, bad trip, freak out,
high on HOG, DMT, LSD, STP,
shooting speed, dropping acid, blowing grass,
California has destroyed my soul.

Encounter groups, nude therapy,
nomadic cults of death,
sound and light shows,
love-in, be-in, spaced-out,
far-out, wasted,
California has destroyed my soul.

Free university, non-university,
non-student, non-knowledge,
good vibes, bad acid, burned,
out of sight, wow, commune, get it on,
satanic church, guru, right on,
California has destroyed my soul.

Wino, homo, hobo, derelict, drunk,
action bar, uni-sex, free sex, nude-in,
wife swapping, street people, spare change,
mill-in, riot, freaks, punch-outs, love,
mystic, drop out, turn on, heavy, high,
California has destroyed my soul.

San Francisco, Berkeley, Big Sur,
Hollywood, Venice, Haight-Ashbury,
North Beach, Muir Beach, Bongo Beach,
Main Street, Tenderloin, Telegraph Avenue,

Jamestown, Stockton, Volcano, Eureka, Redding,
California has destroyed my soul.

"I get high with the help of my friends,"
"We'll have fun, fun, fun, till her daddy takes the T-Bird away,"
"Beach Blanket Bingo," "Motorcycle Stomp,"
Family Dog, Jefferson Airplane, Grateful Dead,
Hell's Angels, Gypsy Jokers, Satan's Slaves,
California has destroyed my soul.

Suicide, divorce, alcoholic, insane,
free church, magic theatre, Krista House,
cult, tribe, pad, new society, freedom,
beautiful person, got it together, head straight,
where it's at, what's happening, 21st century,
California has destroyed my soul.

Beethoven, Bach, rock, Moog synthesizer,
action painting, action poetry, action,
restless, bars, kill, love, neon fun-jungle,
noise, solitude, shuffling dance, bizarre,
Christmas turkey stuffed with pot,
Easter ham with acid dressing,
California has destroyed my soul.

Piles of gold, plenty money, plenty women,
under thirty, ride the wild surf, sky dive,
nude frisbee, peace march, liberation, disorder,
beer, wine, whiskey, pot, acid, speed,
Golden State, Golden Gate, Golden Hills,
California has destroyed my soul.

◆   ◆   ◆

"WHAT DO YOU WANT TO BE WHEN YOU GROW UP?"

A poem by J.D. Stoat, set to music by "H-Bomb" Harrison

Seriously, now, I ask
What can you think of a young man
Who identifies with a hog,
A young man who can,
When an occasion demands,
"Dress well and talk right"
Who professes a fascination with boiler explosions
and discusses such occurrences in great detail?
What can one think
Of a young man who says
"I have no hope and no plans,"
Whose last address was
The Men's Shelter System?

I just want to drink beer and laugh,
then perhaps go out into the street
and do a strange shuffling dance,
to spin through the crowds
playing a kazoo
toward the "neon fun jungle"
that waits in the night.

I have plans, great plans,
but they have not yet
revealed themselves to me.

I eat pig liver for strength,
and take sassafras root for magic.

There is a boiler I have been watching,
the safety valve is rusted shut,
it's due for an explosion, a big one,

bigger than the United Manufacturing
blast in 1934,
bigger perhaps than the famous
Hemphill Department Store
explosion in 1921.
I regret the loss of life,
but when a big boiler explodes,
well, that's bad.

There are strange sounds in the night,
the crowds are restless,
somewhere a disjointed flute
plays the same tune over and over;
the police captain is drunk,
slumped on his desk while the
telephone rings wildly.

I do my shuffling dance down the street
through a crowd of freaks.
When I grow up I want to be
the world's foremost authority
on boiler explosions.

◆   ◆   ◆

One sometimes writes a poem (so-called)
about the smallest and most trivial incidents.
Setting: man reading alone in his apartment, 20 September 1967, San
Francisco:

Warm (for San Francisco) night,
"Tales of the Vienna Woods" on the radio,
book (*The End of the Road*, by John Barth) open,
I sit reading,
smoking a Marsh-Wheeling seegar
and drinking Rainier Ale,
sometimes thinking
of letters that I have sent,
things that I have said
and how I might recall them all;
mind drifting
from the printed lives before me
to the dream that I inhabit
at no particular moment
WHEN
whirling out of the smoke-filled air
Onto the page in my lap—
at just the spot
where my eyes are resting—
lands a winged insect.
In an instant
I knew that it was
the same insect that earlier
brushed against my face unseen,
on the left side, and quick,
was lost in the hidden
recesses of the room.
In a flash,

without thought,
my fingers crushed the bug;
its twisted form
rolled down the page
and settled in the V
of the book.
I flicked the body off onto the floor
and began again to read.
All this in an instant.
Then, I think,
how fast a life, any life,
can be ended;
from life to death
in a second,
with no prior warning.
Strange.
Earlier tonight
at the liquor store I heard
that tonight a liquor clerk
was shot and killed
down on Powell Street.
A human being and an insect;
how quick from life to death,
and where lies the meaning?
Mourn not the dead,
for they drift on
in whatever awaits.

But what about the living,
running hunted in the night,
twisting sleepless
on a stolen bed,
alone,
soaked in sweat?

◆   ◆   ◆

1:55 A.M., 22 September 1967
San Francisco

Here one must interject a philosophic note. The whole problem that the world seems to face is essentially a religious (so-called) one, be it Vietnam, crime in the streets, relations between the races, or whatever. The problem does not exist for those who embrace and believe in the various established religions; they know what to do, what they must do, and in so doing add to, if not actually create, the problems that beset this world. It is those who wander in the vacuum of insecurity and uncertainty born in modern free thought the intelligent sensitivity of liberalism in conflict with Real Politiks. No more. Let the poem stand. We cannot yet do or say more. *Lacrimae rerum* ...

Social commentary, January 1968; or a rambling report on the events of the weekend of January 13–14, 1968, Berkeley, California.

This is mostly for Tricia and myself, and my typewriter, sometimes the only friend I can really talk to. For Tricia because she asked what I thought of the weekend, and I answered that it had its ups and downs; she asked what were the downs, and I begged the question; I guess because there weren't really either ups or downs. Now for specific commentary.

Roxanne bothered me; it seemed that she is trying to become some kind of nun, or some sexless mind, and in so doing getting away from the vitality and vibrations of life, both good and bad. I thought things went real well up to and through dinner; John seemed to be enjoying himself immensely, though in anticipation of a vague and formless threat of "anything can happen," but with the burden that nothing will happen, and nothing is desired to happen since perhaps all of human activity is empty and meaningless; seeking only some intangible and drink-induced atmosphere of false euphoria. The shift to the Cousins household, and the subsequent smoking of pot was rather a disaster, since it shifted the scene from any form of a group oriented experience to a separation of individuals and previous associations; all this against the backdrop of the alleged impossibility of involving too many diverse elements in any social experience.

To jump around; now back in my apartment, Sunday night, surrounded by the semblance of order, which is, I guess, rather real, I find a sense of peace and perspective that has been lacking all weekend. This peace, so-called, was more or less present during the afternoon, walking in Tilden Park in Berkeley in the light drizzle, seeing the smoke drift up from the lean-to shelter, and knowing of the appreciation of all the nice greens and browns of nature.

CHAOS & COSMOS: ORDER & DISORDER; nature is, I presume, more order than disorder; at least, there seems to be some overriding scheme or explanation for whatever happens or is. Human life is disorder; and like the disorder that John seeks in the Steppenwolf, or the Albatross, this is both amusing and distracting; distracting from the immediacy of one's own situation in life. But disorder, whatever the ramifications, is not good as an end as a means of life; presuming that life has a definable end. And about this I have never been sure.

It was strange seeing Charles, or Charlie, sitting there with his young wife, the mother of his child, neatly suited up in a way that I think was rather not like him at all. It was a view of a man trying to be something that he is not, but done so in the realization that there is no viable way to be what he might be. So it is better for him to try that way; else he would be dead, like Reuben. But, in a way, Charlie seems more dead, since death in life is more of a burden. Perhaps it is better to abandon oneself to CHAOS, since in this there might be some appreciation of what life is, or is not, all about. The vanquished knows far better that the victor the meaning of the victory, and the defeat. The man with the empty stomach knows better the essence of food than the "gourmet" who attempts to satiate himself on rare viands.

Life is, I suppose, a one-to-one ratio; and, of necessity, since we are told that "no man is an island," some form of social contract. But life will always be best lived on a personal and rather private level. Thus, you either live alone and be a real "loner," or you get involved with one other individual in an intense way. But always, "to your own self be true"; which is like saying, BE YOURSELF, BOTH IN AND OUT OF CONTROL! Because only in contrast do we live, do we know anything of order of chaos. For myself, I must have both; I must involve myself in disorder in order (no pun) to again find and appreciate order; and vice versa. In music there is incredible order, and in modern jazz incredible disorder; this is a reflection of the times, and of life. LIFE is to be lived, but we cannot beg the end of life.

◆   ◆   ◆

Wednesday evening, 23 October 1969

Well, I note that Jack Kerouac died yesterday, in, of all places, St. Petersburg, Florida. Forty-seven years old, which may seem surprisingly old to a lot of people, but one must remember that he went all through that Beat Scene and wrote ON THE ROAD when he was about 35—no kid. I think that he was an extremely important American writer, for involved reasons that I won't go into fully, but I think that he perceived and portrayed certain things about this country that were very special and unique to the American Scene. There was a vitality in his books—not all of them—that is pretty important, and so too with his stream of consciousness style that gets to the core of things and people. I was personally very turned on by his work, and he is probably the reason I am in San Francisco; to live, that is, since I had visited here twice before but hadn't understood much about the city. He had no use for hippies or any of that scene, though much about which he wrote had a certain similarity; he viewed the hippie scene as adolescent and anti-intellectual, and he was probably right. Kerouac could really dig the meaning and experience of many forms of American work, brakeman on the SP, logging, Forest Service, etc., without getting all hung up about the greater implications of "the system." He understood all its deficiencies, but chose to concentrate on individual experiences and characters. He celebrated existence, and his awareness came from a real involvement with people and situations, and not from dropping out. And because of what he wrote, and the way that he wrote it, he will be remembered—and I hope by more than persons like me. His death diminishes me, more than the usual.

◆   ◆   ◆

Funny, I don't want to go to bed tonight, haven't wanted to for many days now, but I do look forward to waking up tomorrow and to whatever the day may bring. Perhaps I don't want to go to sleep because I am somehow afraid that I won't wake up, and then of course I would never see you again, but there will come a time inexorably sooner or later when I will realize that I have seen you for the last time; will I realize this at the time of parting, or will the realization come much later? But nonetheless this time will come and you will dwindle into the fuzzy realm of memory wherein at a point I will strain to remember just how you looked and perhaps won't be able to fix any image, and that is when I will get out your picture, but of course I will wonder what you really did look like because the picture is fixed at a certain point and your face was always changing into so many different expressions and moods as you gave a toss of your hair and walked away or were suddenly wide-eyed with a smile that related to a certain thought or words. This is what is so sad about never seeing a person again, that they float away into a limbo of memory that can play so many tricks, like almost thinking that you see someone coming or going down a certain street and being lost in the crowd before you can run up and find out if it really was that person, knowing that it probably wasn't but nonetheless hoping that it might have been, that after so many lost and wasted years you could come face to face once again and recapture that old feeling that once existed, but knowing that this is impossible and that if you did meet that way by chance you would just stand there and say something foolish like, "You look just the same," knowing that that was not true at all, and then eventually wishing that the meeting had never taken place at all because it intruded into an area of memory that had grown very fine and remote and ideal, fond and sad, sustaining in some strange way the reasons of things, those reasons then broken into fragments of realizing that whatever happened in those old and great times was just a simple accident of time, mood and personality, something that just as easily have never happened at all or happened with some different person, and then there would be an entirely different set of memories and you would be to me no more than just a person that one sits next to on a bus, some old woman with no past or present that no one cares about, with a worn shopping bag and a tired expression; or me a bleary-eyed old man mumbling to myself, unshaven and with piss stains all over the front of my pants.

It is the memories that will keep what we have known and shared fresh, alive and wonderful, and any chance meeting in the future will only serve to diminish those memories.

◆   ◆   ◆

I always have the same feeling about Oakland. It is like a sort of dream, but I have never had this dream during the sleeping hours. I have had it while awake. IT seems that I have been dozing, and when I wake up I am on a bus. It is late afternoon, and it is gray and overcast. It has been raining and the streets are wet. The bus is going through a neighborhood of frame houses and small stores, obviously Oakland. For some reason I feel that the year is 1943, eternally 1943. I don't know why, but I remember a picture I saw once in a 1943 magazine of a man on a tightrope in Oakland in 1943, in a 1943 issue of *Newsweek* magazine, and the whole atmosphere seems to fit in with this picture. It is really weird. The bus grinds on through these neighborhoods of frame houses. It seems that I have been on the bus for an eternity. The other passengers are bundled in old over-coats, and I cannot see any of their faces. There is no noise other than the sound of the bus, and there are no people on the streets. Occasionally the neon of a sign flashes by the window; it is usually of a bar. I don't know where I am coming from or where I am going. All I know is that I am on a bus somewhere in Oak-land, and it is 1943. That is all I know. I have the feeling that I will never reach any destination, because perhaps there is no destination to be reached. Oakland is the destination, is my destiny. I am not scared. I am very interested in the passing scenes outside the bus window. I have the feeling that things have not changed for many years, and that the people have taken on the aspects of the frame struc-tures that seem to make up each neighborhood that I ride through. I don't even wonder where the bus is headed. It doesn't seem important. My mood is one of curiosity. And that is all.

I know now what it is that has affected me so. It was my stay in Berkeley, which somehow jolted me from the ambiance of my residence, mentally and physically, in San Francisco. I became aware of something magical, in the hills, in the trees, in the people I saw around Berkeley, and I was aware of all that was passing, unnoticed. My stay in Berkeley made me notice where I was living in time, and where I would be going. That is what happened; it must be so, because a great change came over my thinking as a result of living in Berkeley for those few weeks. I thought of all that I should have done and been in recent years, and it made me sad. I thought that I was right at the borderline, and that something had to be done about it. I didn't know what, and I still don't. Perhaps the thing is to grow up. But what if one cannot grow up? Just cannot. Then one remains a child for all of one's lifetime.

◆   ◆   ◆

REMEMBERING—WHAT?

Three dry leaves
rustle in the wind,
and taking one
I crush it
into crisp flakes
and let them blow away
into the afternoon.

Yes,
that is about the way it was.

Taking the trolley home
I wondered if anyone
was thinking about me,
not that it mattered.
I rather had the feeling
that someone was thinking
about me, but there was
nothing to be done about it.

Later,
when I put some
water on for tea,
I turned suddenly
to look at the window,
a cat was perched
just outside the glass.
But as I reached
to open the window
it jumped and vanished
into the darkness.

I remembered the desert
and how there was nothing

civilized or tamed about it.
At least there were no mistakes.

Sitting by the fire
I watch people
I used to know
do little dances
among the flames.

I am running a secondhand clothing store
in the ghetto, and I know
that most of what they bring
is stolen, but I ask
no questions since
my living and theirs
depends on this arrangement.

◆   ◆   ◆

A TALE

I write this down because I think that it is something that should be written down, and thus recorded; and because I think that it says something about a human personality, about those rather indefinable qualities of heart and soul.

While hiking on Mount Tamalpais, Saturday, 4 November 1969, a gray, overcast day, with the threat of a rainstorm hovering somewhere off the California coast, and with a layer of fog or cloud reaching across the Mountain at about the 2,000 feet level so that Rock Springs and the environs were enveloped in a heavy, dripping mist; the temperature was just about right for brisk walking, and the wind was in the tops of the trees only, a faraway sound like the crashing of surf on a lonely beach; the immediacy of the situation was one of solitude, of walking on god's earth as he created it, with only the intrusion of the expected birds and small animals, and, on the trail, of a nice, sensible-looking man and woman who were on in years but who obviously had, and shared, a valuable sense of life, people who accepted, and reveled in, the beauties and vagaries of nature, who moved toward the end of life with ease and satisfaction of having shared.

And so; on this walk with my companion, after a short expedition we came to a broad, open meadow. I mentioned that I wanted to stray off the trail to point out something interesting. In a slight dip, just west of an outcropping of rock, I brought my companion to a small Redwood tree, enclosed in wire mesh to keep the deer from eating the tender and succulent shoots of the tree. Standing at that spot I made approximately this comment:

"When I first hiked along this trail in October of 1961, I found at this spot about half a dozen small Redwood seedlings arranged in a semicircle, and in the center was a typewritten note under plastic, affixed to a rock, reading: "In loving memory; Jane Marshall, 1943–1961." (The name of the girl, and the exact dates, have been lost to my memory, and I only suggest here.) Through the passing years the note has been lost, and all but one of the small trees have died or been eaten by the deer. Whatever; now, in the fall of 1967 one small tree remains, as a last testament to someone's grief and desire to commemorate a lost love, a love that must have been very strong and which the survivor wanted to remember by the planting of a Redwood grove, something that might last for many hundreds of years, a fitting memory. But, alas, nature has only permitted on lone small tree to survive. I wonder how many people who walk this trail are aware of all this?"

And as I related this story, which is badly recapitulated here, I noticed that my companion turned away with tears in her eyes. When I asked what was wrong, she said, "That is so sad and so beautiful. If I gave you some money would you plant some more Redwood trees?" I had to answer that this was a spot wherein nature did not plan for Redwood trees to grow, since the moisture tended to drain away. I said that I considered it a miracle that one tree had survived, but that I would do all in my power to see that this one tree did live and continue to grow; and if it died I would plant another one, or several more, so that this gesture of romantic love, of a loved one taken in the prime, might continue to exist. This I will dedicate myself to, and will enlist the assistance of those who coexist with me or those who may come after me.

So, when you are hiking on the Mountain, you must remember that there are many tales of human existence, of aspirations and hopes cut short that are always around you. It is indeed a "Magic Mountain," and all the small moments and gestures must be revered, cherished, remembered; for such is the stuff that Life is made out of ... there endeth the tale ... and what beginnith herewith?

21 April 1970

On this rail excursion today was just about the most unlikely collection of human beings that anyone could imagine. There was one very light-skinned Negro couple (one would have to look twice to even discern this), very distinguished and intelligent appearing people; two young Oriental girls, who seemed to be with Caucasian husbands or boyfriends; and the rest of the passengers were made up of a hodgepodge of white middle-class American types of every description (actually beyond description or classification). Let me begin with my "seat-mate," who boarded the train with me at Berkeley. About a youthful 60 years, born in SF, worked for UC in plant research (whatever that might be). Had ridden a bicycle all over the state—but had never heard of the Warner Mountains or the Surprise Valley (good thing, shows how remote and unknown the aforementioned are). Sierra Clubber, etc. Lived through the Depression, said he thought that could never happen again but now thinks that it could. Country in bad shape. Too much irresponsible freedom, too much nihilistic anarchy. Was taking trip for reasons of nostalgia, general interest. Seemed to feel that the automobile was a force out of control with ultimate destructive effect on the human psyche. But we are hooked on it. Health addict; his lunch was of that sort. Other passengers: older people, seeking nostalgia; people with children, seeing some new experience, perhaps to give their children some sense of a past; the usual RR buffs, including some that must be considered nuts, since they were dressed in real RR costumes, looking like engineers; four teenaged girls, "teeny-boppers"—and god knows why they were aboard, or what they expected to get out of the experience. The RR club organizers, much like Sierra Clubbers or boy scouts, overly serious and enthusiastic; one man well into his thirties with what I first took to be his daughter, then had to recognize that the affection being shown was hardly that of a father toward a daughter—and the girl could hardly have been over 14; also teenaged couple who spent the day curled up in a seat with one another; crowd of deaf and dumb people, probably take trips like this regularly; strange solitary individuals, like the man who got off at Martinez on the return; heard him talking to the wise old porter who answered respectfully but not without a certain tiredness that came from years of being a man used to such things. Martinez man said he was born in Martinez, pointed out his mother's house, his uncle's house and his brother's house; tall, stooped figure with a large shopping bag, made his way from the train across the platform with the air of a man who has spent his entire life in a sort of limbo, the man who habitually gets off a train with no expectancy of being met; what is there about trains, and this type of excursion that attracts this sort? God knows that it is hard to talk to other people—and I guess booze compensates for much of this, but does one have to be the sort that gathers in the vestibule talking to the porters in desperation? Seven hundred thirty-five people were aboard that train today, and I tell you it was a weird assortment. Coats and ties, and every other assortment of dress that can be possibly imagined. Beards and moustaches. Only one fellow I would call a real hippie. Several marginal individuals. What about that woman who hailed me and asked if we had met aboard the Queen Mary? I must presume that she meant on that last voyage to Long Beach. She and her husband were of the most ordinary appearance, but probably with the money that accrues to strange people in America to make every weird excursion possible. When I answered that I was not the person she was thinking of, she apologized, not "trying to be nosy" as if such were possible.

SOME THOUGHTS ON RAIL TRAVEL

From the window of a passenger train one sees an America not seen anywhere else, a vanished America of yesteryear.

One sees:

a hobo "jungle," with a few figures going about their meager affairs; footpaths along the tracks by which individuals not in the mainstream of contemporary American life trudge to town and back, the RR being the most direct and safest path;

shirt-sleeved station masters coming blinking into a bright sun to watch the train, hands held in a nonchalant salute as the gleaming cars rush by;

a family standing by their farmhouse, seemingly fused into oneness in their mesmerization as they watch the train roll by;

small boys coming back from a day's fishing, waving to the engineer high in his big cab—he never fails to wave back;

the rancher waiting in his battered pickup at some lonely crossing, straw hat just a faint blur behind the wheel;

grasslands stretching away to a distant horizon, unsullied by road signs, billboards, and all the other junk of the automobile culture;

great herds of cattle fleeing from the noise and movement of the train, like a wave receding, then standing at a safe distance to gaze blankly back;

a man with a knapsack, miles from nowhere, pausing a moment in his million miles to watch sixteen cars hurtle by at a mile per minute;

And everywhere, all across the land, people standing, taking a moment from whatever they were doing to watch the silver cars flash by, listening to the blast of the air horn. They all seem to be thinking, "Yes, there is something awfully important about that train. It's going somewhere."

One sees these things and many more. One relaxes in the plush and solid observation car and watches the rails rush out behind. One sees an older, different America flash by and recede with the rails as they extend into the distance. One has the feeling of having been somewhere, and of going somewhere, but most of all one has the feeling that the journey itself is not without meaning, is not without value.

◆   ◆   ◆

Long after you have left the train the "clickety-clack" and the swaying movement of the train remains with you—I suppose some "modern" psychiatrist would evolve some "learned" theory from all of this ...

◆   ◆   ◆

(The Notes of Hornbeck, retrieved from the briefcase:)

> *"The meaning of the world is as inaccessible to men as the behavior of the chariots of kings to the scorpions they crush."*
>
> —Andre Malraux, *Anti-Memories*

This statement, as I take it, does not imply that there is no meaning of the world; but rather that whatever it may be we shall never know it. Small comfort. But then, is there any particular reason why we should be apprised of the meaning of the world, or should even be presumptuous enough to assume that indeed it has any?

◆   ◆   ◆

Count Herman Keyserling described himself as:

> *"... helpless in the face of life, the passive object of every influence, practically incapable (because of my aptness to see every side of a problem simultaneously) of making a decision, of going through with anything ..."*

We might add here a statement made by Henry Adams of himself in *The Education of Henry Adams*:

> *"Young Adams never quite got to playing the game; he lost himself in the study of it."*

Or Schopenaur:

> *"Life is a sorry affair; one had best spend one's time in speculation on it."*

◆   ◆   ◆

One of the most tragic aspects of the "fin-de-siecle" world of Europe was the knowledge of a growing cloud of mass war. An observer to the 1899 Hague Conference on limitation of armaments made this comment:

> *"Watching Dutch fishermen's children playing in the streets and pairs of smiling girls who strolled by coquettishly, he (the observer) wrote, 'If this*

great assembly does not achieve its purpose, the stupid rivalries of states may one day mow down these young people and lay their corpses by millions on the battlefields.'"

The assembly, which was a charade and tragic farce, did not achieve its purpose, and we well know how "the stupid rivalries of states" ended in August 1914. This observer was not alone. Many saw the way that Europe was headed, and tried to introduce deterrents. But the course of Fate was set. What of our own age?

1:7:68

◆   ◆   ◆

Lying abed, smoking a seegar and reading, alone in a western hotel room, about 10 by 12 feet, with scuffed bureau, double bed, no pictures (bare walls), overhead light; outside, crickets and an occasional car down the main street of the quiet small town; from time to time footsteps in the hallway, a door opening or closing; from the bar downstairs loud voices, guffaws, and western tunes from the jukebox; then the bartender's voice, "Folks, it's about that time." Silence. A car starts and goes off in the night. Crickets. Sleep. Murphys, California.

◆   ◆   ◆

TRIP TO GOLD COUNTRY: Murphys, surprisingly unchanged. A few art galleries, bad sign. Too many people. But still a unique and fine spot. Drive up to snow, very deep for May. Bright blue sky. Road to Sheep Ranch. Sort of scrub country, scraggy pines, red earth. Pioneer Hotel in SR, for sale—$45,000 (too much). Cross-country horse race about to start. Finish at Mountain Ranch, 8 miles away. Time, over rough country, 45 mins. Fine crowd at finish. Just local folks. Lunch by Mok. River. No gold. Stop for iced tea at Sutter Creek Beer Garden; unchanged. Fine. Drive back through wonderfully green and lush valley area, result of much rain. Rich smells.

◆   ◆   ◆

Two fortunes that were found in Chinese fortune cookies awhile back: "It is better that you go into a quiet life temporarily," and "Whatever your desires are, for the present decline them." Could these in any way be predictive? Do they have any bearing on the conditions obtaining in the spring of 1967? How interesting that they have been saved and posted in a prominent spot.

15 May 1967

◆   ◆   ◆

"… coyotes, indeed, were revered as the creators of the universe. The wizards, or medicine men … often chewed the seeds of the jimsonweed to induce delirium … Stephen Powers … found them lacking in breadth and strength of character, with no grasp, vigor or boldness. They were, he said, cunning, shrewd, and selfish and intriguing; in games they were little chagrined by defeat; their hilarity was limp and jelly-like; they never bragged and never exulted. They were great thieves when it was safe to be; they were grossly licentious, marrying as early as the age of 12, and were "endowed with the illimitable power of doing nothing." Residents of the Haight-Ashbury 1967? No! Yokut Indians of California described in 1870.

◆   ◆   ◆

I remember riding west in the summer of 1955 with Tony Healy in his English sports car, in the heat of Indiana we stopped for refreshment in a small-time town. A farmer looked at us sitting in the low-slung car and remarked, "Goddam, your asses must get mighty hot, damn near scrapin' on the road, they is." Another time a similar rustic type, looking down at the knock-off type wheels with the word "undo" inscribed with an arrow, asked, "Say, what year Undo is that you're drivin'?" Good-hearted fun all, I should say. And remind me to tell another time of that interlude we spent in the Ozarks when the fuel pump gave out. It is that sort of thing that gives this country some context, not TV and all the urban bullshit.

◆   ◆   ◆

The 1:00 A.M. news on KCBS brings word of an English biologist who announces he has completed a period of time during which he has been busy "doing nothing." Among other things he has neglected his taxes, and now faces a tax probe. He stated that he has "let the wildflowers grow, allowed the bees to multiply," and so forth. When asked what he had accomplished in his thirty years of research, he replied, "Nothing." I hope we learn more of this man and his long period of "doing nothing." Perhaps what this world needs is more "nothing."

23 May 1967

◆   ◆   ◆

Reuben used to sit out front of the "Boars' Nest" at 1830 Pine Street in San Francisco in the afternoon sun and watch the rush-hour traffic build up on Pine St. "All those machines, Sneeze." Well, the traffic is more each year, and Reuben is in a grave in Israel, and what does it all mean? I remember Reuben, or "the Prophet," as he was called, taking the sun out back of the Boars' Nest in the garden, "the Garden of Allah," as he called it. Sitting there, sometimes talking to himself, he used to say all he needed was about 75 dollars a month and he could spend the rest of his life there, drinking some tea and eating some cheese and fruit, sometimes a bit of meat. In the garden of Allah. Reuben.

◆   ◆   ◆

I have often thought that I would like to live on a farm in Bucks County, Pennsylvania. The countryside there is unsurpassed for a rural charm, much reminiscent of England. There is culture, too, and a sense of a past and heritage. But I have come to see that I can no longer entertain this vision, because that countryside is becoming despoiled with too many people, with housing developments, motorcar traffic, "projects," artsy-craftiness, and so forth. In short, it is becoming ruined, and it would be naive to think that the future might portend any reversal of the present trend. The area lies too close to Philadelphia and New York City. To escape this bullshit that springs from our urban culture one has no choice but to go to a wilderness, and even these areas promise no protection from intrusions of urban America.

◆   ◆   ◆

Regarding Hill 881 in Vietnam, so heavily contested in vicious fighting the last few days between U.S. Marines and North Vietnam "Elite" troops, it seems to me that the world has not progressed very far when men are still storming up slopes, fighting "hand to hand" and killing, to gain possession of a small piece of territory. Granted, the whole idea of war seems outmoded and primitive when viewed in light of our "advanced and enlightened" concept of how man should live. But it seems that our idealism and sensitivity has gotten ahead of the real world. There is a dangerous gap between what our education leads us to think and the world as we actually find it.

2 May 1967

◆   ◆   ◆

Guns is mainly for killin'; and it allays pains me to see kids playin' with guns, sayin' "BANG*BANG, YOU'RE DEAD." Seems to me that guns should be withheld from kids till they're ready to go out and kill something, to eat 'cause they need it. Guns is also fer protection, with the threat of killin' or hurtin' implied. Only use I can see fer guns other than real use is fer practice. They ain't no toys, and shouldn't be used fer play. Times might be when a man's life, or a bunch of lives, depends on a gun and the good use of it. That's serious. But I just don't go fer this play with guns like killin' people is some kinda game. Remember one time I shot a rabbit for no reason other than killin' it, and had to catch up on it and shoot it agin through the eye to kill it. Allays felt bad over this; but wouldn't have no qualms 'bout killin' a man iffen I felt he needed killin'. Not much good in any of it though.

25 April 1967

◆   ◆   ◆

While "book-reviewing," I must praise the superlative historical novels of H.L. Davis. Primarily Pacific NW in locale, the best two. They really give one a feeling for the country and its people. Dialogue is particularly good understanding of the country and its development very well worked out, characters come alive; through all of this one gets a real picture of the forces at work at the turn of the century, history as made by the real people. All the forces of the times in good perspective. And plus the craft that elevates these works to the position of art. Davis' novels are, I think, among the very best of American fiction and history. The man himself was fascinating. Should have a better place in "Amer. letters."

◆   ◆   ◆

On Russian Hill there is a Chinese grocery on a corner. On the downslope below the store there is a small window opening on the street at about knee-level. On certain evenings at about dusk one can perceive a light behind the metal grill-work of that window; and if one passes close by one can hear the music of an accordion. The tunes are the old sentimental ones popular in a past age, but still recognizable. If one looks in the window one can see a cellar room cluttered with all manner of accumulated belongings. And over against the wall sits an elderly man leaning over his instrument, playing, it seems, for no audience other than himself. The passerby feels a sense of empathy, of nostalgia for something he can't place. Such is the experience of a city. You won't find anything like this around the Golden Gateway and the like. Is it possible we lose something of value in these modern projects?

28 April 1967

◆   ◆   ◆

Cannot really think of California as a place where families have tea and cinnamon toast in front of fires, where kids go to dancing class wondering about girls, where people go to grandmother's house for Thanksgiving dinner, or any of the rest of the old-fashioned sentimental stuff. But think of California as land of divorce and affairs, of alcoholism and drugs, suicides and restless unfulfilled lives, of fads and unreal idealism, of perversion and impersonal sex; in short the collapse of the American dream in the Golden Land. Is this the land of the future? Sure California has great natural beauty, and many fine people who live very satisfactory lives. But the greater tone seems to come from the rootlessness and chaos, from the lack of values and stability.

◆　　◆　　◆

SMELLS: The diesel exhaust of (Greyhound) buses always makes me think of one same place—a pass in the mountains east of San Diego, one night in June 1956. My bus, from Yuma to San Diego, had stopped and I got out to walk about. I had been dozing, and I was surprised to find that I was in the mountains; crisp, cool air, large California moon and big pine trees. I was standing absently by the side of the road when a big bus roared by, leaving the fumes of its exhaust diesel in that clean air. Now, for some reason, whenever I smell that exhaust my mind is instantly and involuntarily transported back to that moment; (Proust's "involuntary memory.")

24 April 1967

◆　　◆　　◆

One night last week there was a sudden power failure; I was having dinner when the lights, radio went off. Didn't really surprise me. There was still some light coming in the window and I finished my meal (such as it was). Then I went to the window and gazed out. Quite dark, and I enjoyed the darkness that was in evidence. Realized there is too much light at night, which should be in the old sense a time of darkness. Most enjoyed seeing the candles come on in a few windows around the neighborhood, then more. Finally rooted around this place and turned up a candle; really enough light to do most things by, except read—memories of Lincoln and his books crouching near the fire to get "eddicated." Once man was in bed with the dark and up with the light. And don't see that we are so damn smart today with all our illumination. But I guess we do "live better electrically." Or do we?

25 April 1967

◆   ◆   ◆

That older American, the man making his way West across the continent, wasn't very much concerned with the problems of government or international relations. He was in struggle with more mundane elements, the land, snakes, storms, rivers to cross, mountain passes, and the like; at worst, he had his immediate and fellow man to deal with, be he Indian or scheming white breed. But it was most always a one-to-one ratio. Today it is all changed. Do we still have the right, or the necessity, to conceive of things on a one-to-one ratio? Or must we subordinate ourselves to something we have never really understood, the state? With men at the helm who are alien to what we feel are the immediate realities. What are we to do? We don't know, and therein lies our neurosis.

◆   ◆   ◆

One day follows another; they are much like the other. One life follows another; how much resemblance is there? Is not a life but a day in the advance/story of mankind? Nations follow one another; social theories and needs; are they not all part of this story that we call "life on the planet earth"? This planet that will some day end as a cinder, or a frozen glob of mud, with no minds to comprehend what it all meant? Or will some of our descendants be on some other celestial (or other) body, studying the records of what was once known as the "earth civilization"?

◆   ◆   ◆

Don't tell me that history is "under control." Is the war in Vietnam under control? Is anyone in control of the forces that are operating in Southeast Asia? Or India or Africa, Indonesia, or anywhere else in the world? I certainly don't think so. I think that man does initiate certain programs with the hope of controlling the outcome. But this doesn't seem to be the case, the control that is, in reality. The results are most often very different from what might be desired. Action then becomes reaction. And so it goes. I do see a certain overall movement, but can't see that man can take any credit for it. It is what has happened; it is the "course of things." If man is to control anything, let him control overpopulation. This, I think, is the greatest problem we face. The time to act is perhaps past, but it is not too late to do something more than what is now being done.

21 April 1967

◆   ◆   ◆

When I went outside this morning I was suddenly put in mind of northern Minnesota. There was a quality and feeling in the air, cool and breezy with a slight tinge of a burning smell. The coloring of the sky, and the clouds, added to this feeling I had. Just for a moment I felt that I was somewhere up near the Canadian border, in a small town with the woods rolling away in every direction, with a lake and a sawmill, and an old man burning some trash somewhere up wind.

9 April 1967

◆   ◆   ◆

I have just finished dinner and am about to sit down with my cigar and coffee. The radio is playing, and I am rather comfortable here alone in my apartment. Outside, the Chinese children are playing and some dark clouds are drifting in from the Pacific. We have had a lot of rain lately. Tomorrow is to be a big "peace" parade and rally. I won't participate, for reasons of my own, though I think the war is a mistake and should be ended.

Friday, 14 April.

◆   ◆   ◆

"The wet weather is going to continue in the Bay Area. Well, it's been a hard winter in the Bay Area, and it's still with us ..." So the voice on the radio says. Hard winter, bullshit! A little wet weather, a few hard showers; what the hell is so "hard" about this? California is sure as hell a soft land! Everybody is complaining about the weather. What the hell do they expect out of nature anyway? I get sick and tired of th is bullshit. So it rains. We all do what we have to do anyway; what the hell difference does a little rain make anyway? You might get wet, then you dry out. What the hell! What is life all about anyway, that we are supposed to be so damn comfortable all the time? Shit!

◆   ◆   ◆

I don't think Castro is such a bad guy. He seems to have a sense of humor (at least I hope he has). Anyway, he amuses me. And whatever he's trying to do in Cuba, that's his business, certainly more than it is ours. He may make something out of the country, or he may not. Let history judge him. This country's gotten to damn big, complicated, and out of control anyway; meddling in two-third's of the world.

19 April 1967

◆   ◆   ◆

Looking over some old maps, which show ancient (so-called) railroads, disappeared towns in Nevada and other places one can only conclude that the Past is so-far gone, so unreal and remote, as to be only a rather frightening dream, a half-grasped fancy, remote from anything that exists today, the present. Will we, and the world we inhabit and know, become so unreal and remote? Or has some thread of continuity been established? In Europe the past is not nearly as remote and totally gone as here in America. Is this then a uniquely American phenomenon, this divergence between past and present, because our past was so brief and transitory? Is this why the present seems illusionary and insubstantial? Is the whole American experience a series of transitory jumps from one position and period to another, with no, or little (at best) sense of continuity, like the modern American executive moving so many times before he and his family finally come to rest in some unfamiliar community where the only common denominator is money? What is the reality of it all; where does the truth of the story lie? Tell, tell.

◆   ◆   ◆

One should, of course, make a study of the misusage of the English language and its words. There is a richness of "folk-talk" here that should be appreciated. One of my favorites is the word "confisticated," used by a cop in Pennsylvania to inform me of what had happened to the fireworks I was arrested with. One that I just thought of is, when referring to an unfortunate incident: "That's to be lamenated" (meaning, of course, lamented). "Orientated" is so common in usage as to be not usually thought of as an oddity. A friend once referred to "an obituary of the Ohio River," and I was concerned because I was unaware of the demise of that particularly waterway. A girl I once knew mentioned that someone was "mentally insane," which is interesting since it raises the possibility of other forms of insanity, but what they might be I know not. Well, this is a rich field, and each person is invited to submit his favorite "misusages" for compilation and study; it's part of all this jazz about being human; and finally it is something unique to America, this "folk-talk" is ...

(Some hogs should be crated.)

◆   ◆   ◆

ON THE PRINCIPLE OF "JUSTICE OF WAGES"

It seems to now be the case in this country that a working man be paid a "fair and decent" living wage as a result of the condition of "his being in labor," without regard to his economic usefulness to his employer, or any other consideration. I think that the wealth of the country in general would support this, as do notions of human decency; but do the hard-nosed facts of economics, to say nothing of the even harder-nosed realities of the human personality? IF the latter do not, then perhaps these must be forced aside by some concerted action. If, in order that the itinerant grape-pickers of the San Joaquin Valley be paid more, might we all pay a bit more for such derived products, such as CHEAP WINE, etc.? I think so ...

◆   ◆   ◆

COMMENTS ON THE "CURRENT MACEDONIAN PROBLEM"

"I saw an editorial in the *New York Times* today that I did not think I would see in my lifetime; it concerned a renewed outbreak of the Macedonian Problem. It seems that Bulgaria is celebrating the 90th anniversary of the Treaty of San Stefano, which treaty awarded Macedonia to Bulgaria. But a few months later Disraeli and Bismark reversed all of that, and now Bulgaria is claiming that justice is 90 years overdue at the expense of Jugoslavia. When Franz Josef ruled, Sir, those people were kept well in line. I wonder if they are now happier in the People's Republics? IF the Treaty of San Stefano is still in dispute, then there is no hope for any of us. Can you imagine World War III starting over the Macedonian question? Can you fully grasp the ultimate buffoonery of that? I think so ..."

13:2:68

◆   ◆   ◆

Reading the latest O'Hara novel—*The Lockwood Concern*—I must say that O'Hara certainly knows his people; and he is a damned good, consistent writer. His are not arty, poetic novels, and admittedly they are all much the same—but then so is life. I remember a remark made by my grandfather, a real gentleman if somewhat locked in another era of thought, when I mentioned that I had read and greatly enjoyed some O'Hara novel: "He's a dirty writer." I was surprised and shocked by my grandfather's appraisal, but then he WAS from another era of thinking, whatever that means. But *are* O'Hara's novels "dirty"? Certainly they don't approach anything like *Candy*, and they are certainly a closer approximation to LIFE than the current sensational, over-preoccupied-with-impersonal-sex "literary" works. I think that O'Hara really knows what he is "talking" about; but, then, the greater part of the impact on me is his recreation of the Pennsylvania upper-middle class scene. This notwithstanding, I still say that he knows his people, and writes what he knows with excellence. If, as Hemingway sardonically suggested, somebody had taken up a collection and sent O'Hara to Yale, these books would perhaps never have been written.

◆   ◆   ◆

The UNIVERSE—now believed to be 4 billion light-years "wide"; formerly scientists thought it to be merely 2 billion light-years in width. Parkhurst has told me that, using his new concept of space travel, if one went, say 4 billion (?) times the speed of light—which he said "really isn't such a wildly impossible concept"—then it would be possible to cross the entire universe in one year's time. Now, wouldn't that be nice?
PARKHURST CALLS FROM LOS ANGELES, ENVISIONING THE POSSIBILITY OF TRAVERSING THE UNIVERSE IN ONE YEAR!!!

Now you tell me, being exposed to this type of thinking, how does one retain a sensible perspective on things?

◆   ◆   ◆

If we employ the English language, as we do, to express our feelings and thoughts relative to life, then I feel that we should use this language in the optimum form; that is, according to the highest rules and form that have evolved through the long history of the language. In pronunciation and usage we should strive for the highest degree of accuracy and expression. Inaccuracy and imprecision should be rooted out and discouraged; colloquialisms, while appropriate in common usage, have no place in formal expression, such as the broadcasting and press media. One must bear in mind here one of the objections to Adlai Stevenson as a presidential candidate: he "talked funny." Now, as we well know, Mr. Stevenson was one of the few individuals in public life who employed the English language with remarkable accuracy, precision and wit. But to the public "he talked funny." To me that is sad. To achieve an audience. or election to public office, must one scale down one's talk to the level of the common man? It would seem so; thus, contemporary American life is a game, a seeking of approval by the mob; not any striving toward perfection, toward the highest. And this is sad, that's all. Sad.

7:9:68

◆   ◆   ◆

Up at High Rock Lake, or just off of there in Little High Rock Canyon, in NW Nevada, I picked up off the ground a feather. This seemed to me to be an owl feather, and my feather agreed. It was an owl feather. What this suggests to me is that there lives in that wild environment a big old owl which sleeps all day and comes out at night to swoop down noiselessly on field mice and rabbits, trap such in its sharp talons, and devour such with savage rippings of its sharp beak. How primitive and raw! Yet how vital! Who made this owl, and why does it function thus? Does nature come red in tooth and claw? Is not all of this "reasonable" in terms of the scheme of creation, considering all the rest of the animal world? But what of man? What is he, and how is he meant to live? I remember a girl in Vesuvio one night; her male friend had gone to get food, in this instance this amounted to paying for a few things at a Chinese market; he returned with some smoked fish, which we all devoured at the table. But while he was gone the girl said several times that she just wanted to know "What are we; what is man?" Like Dostoevsky's question in the *Brothers* (Ivan) "I don't want millions, I just want answers to my questions." Brethren, they're there, but it seem they ain't adequate ... Owls, High Rock Lake, coyotes singing in the distance under a half-full moon. That's answer enough for me.

7:9:68

◆   ◆   ◆

Concerning the new automobiles that advertise as part of their equipment, "shoulder harnesses": these, I take it, are for the contingency of breakdown in which case it might be necessary for oneself or one's passengers to draw the vehicle by means of such harness arrangement. How thoughtful! But does it beat pushing.

15:10:68

◆   ◆   ◆

RE: *THE KLONDIKE FEVER*, BY PIERRE BERTON

This is a truly amazing book. Beautifully written, it is a chronicle of madness, futility, and disaster without parallel. Of all the books I have read, I cannot think of one that equals this one as an unending account of horrors, of doomed undertakings, blind naiveté, greed—and so much more that a string of terms becomes repetitive and meaningless; a vast panorama of human frailty played out amidst one of the world's most inhospitable environments. The tale of the Klondike Gold Stampede was truly one of the world's great dramas, albeit one that ended in untold thousands of disasters for every success that has been recorded. To sum up, inadequately, when the many parts of the drama are viewed, the whole thing can only be called INCREDIBLE! Nothing like it will ever again occur. It was a rare combination of time and circumstance, of misinformation and feverish aspirations. GOD, words can hardly deal with a thing like this. Berton has done a magnificent job. This is very likely the most incredible thing I have ever read.

21:2:68

◆   ◆   ◆

I think that I know something of the feelings of "power" that you say you have experienced at various times when addressing a class or giving a speech, impromptu or other. I sensed what a desire people have to be TOLD, to be LED. I realized how men get caught in the grip of political ambitions, of giving speeches, making pronouncements, influencing the minds of others. It is basically a sense of and desire for POWER; and this derives from that sea of faces and minds waiting to be told the WORD. There is something frightening about all of it. Speeches and leadership should be outlawed. Something there is about people that makes them too easily led (and led astray). I think that it is because of something that has to do with all of this that I have never been a follower, or much of a participant. Because to be a participant one must ultimately accede to the philosophies and leadership of others, or seek power and leadership oneself. Either course is inconsistent with my personal ideals, except in times of extreme personal involvement (of an involuntary nature). But can one ever be an island, the master of one's own destiny?

15:2:68

◆   ◆   ◆

I often think that our greatest men are those who have never played on the stage of history and events, except when forced to such roles ... those, who by their reason, detachment and moderation, chose to stand aside; until, events, and their position in relation to such events, commanded action and involvement. When this came, it was not the prejudiced or premeditated action of the already involved, but the measured acts of the strongest of those who were forced to action in difficult times; those who had both the vision and the strength to forge the prevailing policies and actions. Such is the story of human history ...

◆   ◆   ◆

NOTE:

Can a chemical foam fire extinguisher, capable of extinguishing a fire resulting from a ruptured gasoline tank, be carried in an automobile, even if it takes up the whole back seat? If so, it might be a good idea if a certain number of individuals who travel the highways a lot carry such a device. There are too many people burned to death in what might otherwise be relatively minor accidents. This thought is prompted specifically by memories of a news item I saw about a year ago in the Santa Monica *Outlook*; sports car involved in a wreck. Driver, young man, caught in the wreckage. Gasoline tank explodes. People try to get him out. He cries out, "I'm stuck. Please get me out, for God's sake please get me out." People work frantically, until they are driven back by the flames and heat. Cries continue, then cease, while people stand helplessly. This tragedy, and many others, might have been prevented if someone had been carrying the necessary foam firefighting equipment. Perhaps, if this is not feasible for passenger motor cars, large trucks might be so equipped. This matter is certainly worth looking into.

5:7:68

◆   ◆   ◆

RE: *THE KLONDIKE FEVER*, BY PIERRE BERTON

Of the many accounts I have read of travel in the American West, I have always imagined myself as being more or less equal to the hardships. But the conditions described in the Klondike Stampede boggle the imagination. One factor is, I think, the inexperience and naivete of gold-seekers; their total unpreparedness for the conditions that they were to face. But, considering all, the experiences were such as to make me seriously doubt if I would have been able to survive most of them. Influencing this thought are the many instances of despair and self-destruction which are recorded, evidence of individuals having got themselves into situations totally unexpected and for which they were completely unprepared, both physically and psychologically. The sudden impact of reality was too much for many of them, especially those who had gambled EVERYTHING on what was all to realistically revealed to be A HOPELESS VENTURE. The other annals of the west were for the most part undertaken by men who at least had some understanding of what they were getting into and who were psychologically and physically prepared, at least to a reasonable degree. Then, too, the period of initiation was more gradual.

21:2:68

◆   ◆   ◆

A COMPENDIUM OF THOUGHTS INSPIRED BY A VACUUM

"The Men's Shelter System"—a NYC institution; but I can only think of a vast shed of some kind with a crowd of men huddled beneath it, keeping out of the rain, their overcoats steaming.

Just what is meant when it is said that someone has made "a hopeless recovery"?

Favorite short story title: "Disorder and Early Sorrow," by Thomas Mann.

A mild wave of drunkenness breaks over me, inspiring a false sense of euphoria ...

A recurring phrase: "There is something about our friends' misfortunes that doth not displease us"—from La Rochfaucoult's *Maxims*. And oh how true that is, given a certain bent of mind, which many of us share but some do not. When I mentioned this to a friend, she did not agree at all but said that her friends' misfortunes sorrowed her greatly. Obviously there is herein some divergence of thought and attitude. (The original French quote is somewhat different from the English version I have included here. The meaning is the same, however.)

I wish to comment here on "sweet Betsy from Pike": now, when I first met this girl some weeks ago I had rather positive vibrations (the only hippie term that I think is valid and which I find applicable to life). She is another Alison, i.e. a girl whom I consider as a female person, a personality and an individual rather than as a sex object. Naturally, the sex factor is present and important, but the relevance to the last mentioned (sex): when we were talking about our schools. Betsy mentioned that one time she attended a wrestling match at my high school, and while at the gym she happened to glance down through the stairwell and saw a naked young man with an erection, commenting that it was the first time she had ever seen such a phenomenon. Now, this seemed a rather strange and somewhat unnecessary story to tell me, and it struck me as odd. To comment further, I must observe (a) that at that high school gym it is (as I remember they layout) virtually impossible to "gaze" down to the lower level through the stairwell; and (b) in all the years I have spent in and around men's gyms, and elsewhere, I have never observed anyone walking around or publicly displaying an erection. I don't say that such a thing has never occurred, but I consider it highly unlikely. Thus, I must conclude that Betsy did not see such a thing, that in some way the story was a figment of her imagination. And in conclusion, why would she tell me the story? But, she might have seen such a thing, at some time or another, even in some strange way at some other school. Who knows? But, all considered, it seems an odd story.

◆   ◆   ◆

I live beside a railroad track.

Periodically, huge trains thunder by, laden with life's goods and speeding toward a variety of destinations. I cannot help but notice these trains as they pass. The rumbling and the vibration shake the foundation of my small house, and cracks have appeared in the once solid walls. I wonder if someday these walls shall crumble, for the cracks seem to grow with each passing train.

Sometimes at night I stand beside the track, watching for the trains to appear. I can hear their far-off rumble long before the unsteady beam of the engine's headlight flickers in the distance. Once in sight the train approaches rapidly, growing swiftly in size and sound. Often I think of standing between the rails and allowing the monster to rush over me. I struggle with this urge, but never seriously. I used to stand beside the track and watch in awe as the engine and coaches hurtled by, but the swirling cinders and deafening noise forced me to retreat within the walls of my house.

I cannot recall how long I have existed in this fashion. I seem to remember that it was a train which brought me to this spot a long time ago, and perhaps a train will carry me off sometime in the distant future. These thoughts, however, are neither points of origin nor departure; I only live from train to train.

I think that if a train should stop—they never do—I would climb aboard and ride away to some distant land. I feel my house is crumbling and shall not stand much longer, and if I do not move I shall crumble with it. I am not sure I wish to go, and yet I must. The time has come to move, to become part of one of those trains which thunder by.

◆   ◆   ◆

I noticed that people were laughing and staring. And when I turned around I saw that a horse was following me. Right down the street. Followed me everywhere. And when I had finally gotten used to the idea, I turned around and saw that the horse was no longer there. But the whole thing gave me an interesting idea; that to believe in something you must somehow feel that it isn't really possible. And the worst thing was when people began throwing apples. Of course, I ducked and none hit me. But the idea of such a thing. What can one expect next? The only thing is not to let anything surprise you, and if nothing surprises you, then anything is possible. But even in the realm of possibility there are some things which are not permitted. For instance, whispering softly is governed only by the limitations of words. And it is obvious enough that words carry the mere absence of meaning and absolutely no finality. Permission only intrudes into the realm of possibility, while the limitation of existence holds the measure of infinite possibility. Reason shall triumph beyond the limits of existence. Because reason carries the intrusion of permission beyond the tangible limits of the possible world, it would appear that permission is the child of reason. But in reality, if one follows the development of permission by reason as an abstract, it can be seen that the realm of infinite possibility is extended by reason rather than limited by it. By forcing reason, and the ultimate rationality of infinite possibility, beyond the restrictions of permission by experience, the entire scope of rational existence is widened to include even the most irrational of definitive actions. The power of rationality is only supreme beyond the limits of permission and experience. Which brings into the picture the doctrine of rational opposition. This doctrine presupposes that all rational action, governed by a force of ultimate permission, is directly opposed by the forces of irrationality which spring from a concept of permission as limited by experience. But if the concept of rational action is forced beyond the limitations of permission, practical or ultimate, thus removing the foundations of irrationality, reason is then purified in a world of infinite possibility. Irrationality exists only in opposition to reason, not as an ultimate concept in itself. If, by placing reason beyond the limits of permission, which is in reality the product of irrationality, the concept of a world where all is possible rather than permissible, then the irrationality of existence is grounded in the doctrine of rational opposition and is refuted by the removal of the limitations of the concept of permission. Thus reason stands in supreme triumph in a vacuum of infinite possibility in which existence becomes the embodiment of the ultimate rationale of an entirely free universe. The question of ultimate freedom, based on a concept of infinite possibility, presupposes the triumph of rationality over the limitations of practical irrationality as suggested by the doctrine of rational opposition and the notion of ultimate permission. Freedom, as expressed in the finality of Reason, exists only in the absence of irrationality in the sense that the doctrine of rational opposition springs from the concept of permission. Reason replaces permission in that it eliminates the foundations of irrationality by expanding beyond the limitations of practical experience. All existence, therefor, is grounded in a concept of ultimate freedom which springs from the triumph of Reason over the forces of irrationality which exist only in the practical concepts of the limitations of experience. Thus the limitations of experienced existence are expanded into the realm of infinite possibility if they are to be determined by a concept of ultimate freedom as governed by the finality of Reason. Existence is by nature the embodiment of Reason, both as an abstract finality and as a practical limitation. Ultimate freedom is the application of Reason to existence.

◆   ◆   ◆

Last Saturday night I met a girl at a party. She seemed, unaccountably, to be very much attracted to me. It wasn't my fault, though. I mean, it wasn't any credit to me, it was just something that happened. Most often it is difficult to understand why such things happen. It's just easier to go along with them, that's all.

The girl was really nothing special. There was nothing about her that you would notice in a roomful of people. But she was rather appealing in a demure and sympathetic way. And when she talked of man's loneliness in the world, you could sense her difficulty in trying to be detached and indifferent. She seemed quite intelligent, and was pleasant to be with.

I don't remember how I came to talk with her. I think I was tired and sat down on the couch, and there she was, friendly and curious, next to me. Talk came easily, and it was a relief to gain a moment's escape from social pressures. But I had trouble resisting a great temptation to assume a role. I don't mean a vast fraud, but only an urge to accentuate certain feelings or moods which somehow didn't seem entirely true. I guess it is a natural thing to want to slip away from an over personalized image of one's self into some sort of special role which might be alien to ideals, particularly when the role is a success or is appreciated. You always sense when you are a success. A few drinks have a lot to do with it, too.

What happened was more like some kind of predetermined chemical reaction. Something less definite than any scientific formula, but apparently as strong and true. Circumstances, fate, sex, personality—all these things combine to cause social events. And so, with some manipulation and small embarrassment among friends, I took the girl home. That she was much attracted to me was all too obvious; and she could easily sense that my enthusiasm did not quite equal hers. I suppose my relative indifference, although I really did like her, gave her a tragic conception of our relationship. I could see that she didn't want to be hurt. When she said, "Even if you don't like me very much, please call sometime," I promised her that I would. And I promised myself that I would call her soon, partly because I wanted to, but mostly because I was too well aware of how much it meant to her. There was a certain pathos in the resigned acceptance in her mind of the thought that I didn't like her very much. "I guess I'm not very sexy," she signed, as she pressed against me. But she was trying to express herself, to grasp some of the communication which she had said earlier was so impossible for man to achieve. Loneliness, yes, she believed in it. I could tell that she had been hurt and had known loneliness. To understand loneliness one needs experience.

I'll see her again. She is a warm, sincere, gentle, and sensitive person. I hope I can show her something more than kindness. I hope that I don't become indifferent, as some have become toward me, or, most of all, that I don't lead her to believe, as I myself sometimes feel, that ultimately there can be no real communication between people.

◆   ◆   ◆

A central problem is that of theory versus reality; how to bring these two approaches or interpretations together for reasonable action. Also, what is the influence of history on the present and the future, and how does it affect the tensions of the conflict of planning versus fatalism? And if there is a need for a basic optimism in society, can we justify either this need or the optimism from the course of past history? Man seems to be by nature a social or gregarious animal, but there is a tremendous conflict between the individual and the community, a tension resulting from the ambivalence of man. We tend to look upon the capacity for Reason as the source of man's uniqueness—but what is Reason, and why should men live by it if it is so often at variance with our felt natural drives and instincts? And what are the roles of freedom and knowledge in relation to the capacity for Reason?

Man is hopelessly ambivalent—but the vision to see the Truth exists, as does the Truth itself, i.e. REASON, the highest embodiment of free existence.

Man's concern for his condition—Consciousness, a never to be explained phenomena: this seems to be as near a proof of a higher order as man can come. "Cogito, Ergo Sum": a rationale of existence.

There is a possibility that, as society and civilization become outwardly more virtuous and humane, the (innate drives) for evil and violence, cruelty, etc., manifest themselves in many strange and different ways, both in the individual and society.

If we consider the concept that religion is the product of man's Reason, a "reasonable" solution to the problems of existence, then the hypothesis that God is Reason seems logical.

Everybody is out of "adjustment" to some degree, which establishes a norm of sorts. And this means that there really is no "adjustment," and that no one is either in or out of touch with a reality which does not exist; so let's work from this point.

Laughter or a sense of humor shows only an awareness of the absurd.

Let us look at the problem this way: it is easy enough to talk about a life or a world without any meaning; but how would we define an existence with definite meaning? In both instances we are limited by our knowledge, or our lack of it. In order to envision a life without meaning, we must somehow have a concept of what meaning is or might be. It seems that it would be just as easy, and more reasonable, in the light of our experience and knowledge, to ascribe meaning and purpose to existence and work form there; let us build on the mere fact of existence. Certainly, the world may be totally void of any meaning, but that view seems no more likely or logical than the opposite assumption. Let us then reverse our logic and build rather than destroy. It is just as easy and makes more sense.

◆   ◆   ◆

Think
Of all the good people you will never meet;
all the people you've barely known some little while,
whose lives you've brushed against,
whose faces briefly looked on yours,
from whose lips your name passed a few times,
and who faded as you moved on in life;
They form that great beyond,
      that hidden essence,
      that always haunting "what might have been"

What paths did you follow? what turns did you make?
What brought you to this point in life? Where did the choices lie?
The words never spoken, countless hesitations, a gesture too late,
All the contingencies of a lifetime …

A good cigar is like a woman; it is up to each man to provide his own.

A coal miner, working deep within the earth, hears that thud, and knows …
      go easy on the adjectives, old boy.

URDU … lapses into irrationality, in reach of us;
                            we must admit these
primitive urges, and control them; there must be CONTROL! But who—
which group is to do this? How are they chosen, or do they prevail,
emerge due to superior force? Whatever the case, the prospects are
frightening.
      Has man grown weaker or stronger over the centuries?
Who is on the way up, and who on the way down, which races, which nations?
Where do they meet and pass, each to its own oblivion?

What desires, what primitive urges, rule this world?
                        Technology changes, man tags along.
What have we gained? Some thinkers, yes; common man, I wonder.

"People don't want REALITY; REALITY is harsh and cruel. What they want
is ILLUSION—" and the doctor leaned back in his chair and lit a cigar.
"LONELINESS—that is at the root of human existence." And later Doctor

Avis remarked, "I shall never forget that man—that great surgeon, known and respected so widely, sitting in his paneled library in his great suburban house, surrounded by his family and guests, talking about LONELINESS."

    WHO IS Chandler Brossard?   man must admit his failures, and live with themthe trouble is with this primitive desiring ...
This chase goes on and on, and the goal recedes. The question is, will man sink or swim? He has been swimming for many centuries now, and he is tired. The goal is as far as ever ... there is no agreement, in the jungle, over the tables at Oxford. Civilized disagreement, ending in, what? What means to settle this predicament, what end?

                  All over the world—from the distilled products of fine Scottish streams to the palm beer of the Kaffir tribe of South Africa—men are indulging in the same alcoholic pursuit, this liquid which they pour into themselves, which makes them drunken and foolish;
              IN VINO VERITAS

we lose, you lose, they lose ... everybody loses; what is lost?
                    In order to lose, must something have been gained? Win or lose, this game goes on and on.
CRAZY * WIND * GONE * MAD *   galathea kroen   Swiss mountains

◆   ◆   ◆

OK, so the world is getting to be a better and better place to live in. Well, in some ways maybe it is, but these are hard to figure out. Sure we zip around from place to place faster and easier than before, but it seems that getting there is what counts, and knowing where you have been and all that's in between. So we have radio, television, stereo and all those marvels, plus boats, go-carts, motorcycles, night baseball, miniature golf, and god knows what else. So what? Seems like people are more bored today than they have ever been. Dissatisfied too.

Take a small case in point, of how the world is changing. You live in a place not too far from the city. There are plenty of open fields and woods around. You enjoy your environment, the changing seasons, the quiet summer evenings, long walks in the fields and woods. Sometimes drives in the countryside, or to town to do some shopping. You might walk ten minutes to the station and take the train into the city, or you might drive—it's an interesting half hour or so, not much traffic and a variety of routes to choose from. If you are a kid in winter you have a long wait for a car to throw a snowball at, or if you are an adult there is a good chance the car coming up your road is bringing the guests you have invited for dinner. In summer you sit on the lawn watching the fireflies in the dusk and the bats darting in the darkening sky, ruminating in a peaceful silence broken by the occasional slam of a screen door, the rumble of a distant freight train, or an occasional passing car. If it's a still night, and most of them are, when the rustling of the leaves of the great scarlet oaks dies down you drift off to sleep with the faint music from the dance band down at the open patio of the Covered Wagon Inn about a half mile away. It's not an unpleasant or disturbing sound. The big bullfrog croaks in a neighbor's pond; the old widow thinks the frog is a reincarnation of her late husband, or so the neighbors say. It's not a bad life; you're close to the city, yet far, far away. You know the folks in your community and they know you, but not too well. There is a separateness of space and dignity, if you want it that way. You choose your friends from those who appeal to you. There is no leaning across back fences, or seeing who is coming and going, who comes home late or not at all; no thoughts about what types of cars people drive and all that sort of nonsense. This is part of the scene. Idealized perhaps, but real enough to be the way it was. Sure there were annoyances, frustration, problems and unhappiness. Life is never without these; they were mostly personal things, out of your own life and the people in it. Well, things change, and let us explore some of the changes that have come about in the external world of environment.

First, the fields and woods fill up with tract houses, unlike the individual dwellings of the old community. Traffic increases until the narrow roads are filled with a continual stream of cars, and noise. There is no longer any place to park in town, and if you do find one there is a parking meter. Shopping centers come, catering to the tastes and buying habits of the new residents. Traffic lights and vapor street lights are put in. Streets are widened and new roads built. There is a freeway to the city, but it is ugly, dangerous and nerve-wracking to drive on anytime except late at night. Actually, it takes longer to get to the city. Even the train takes longer because there are so many people getting on in the mornings, but this is still the best way to go. But the parking lots are often full; then the railroad makes you pay. Sitting on the lawn at night you hear a roar of traffic, see the night sky reflecting all these purple lights. The neighbor's pond is dried up because a housing development has cut off the source of the stream that flowed into it. The frog is long gone and the widow has willed all her money to her postman. There is no place to walk, since dogs rush out from strange houses and there is a constant danger of being run down by some speeding car. A drive-in theatre goes in, a root beer stand, dozens of gas stations and countless cheap stores and service facilities. Still, traces of a once pleasant community remain. But they are all threatened. Perhaps the new residents find the place a good place to live, compared with other existences; but for those who have lived there for awhile and who have an identification with a past, it is hard to see how the change represents progress or improvement. I would challenge anyone to take such a stand. One can observe these changes and be happy, indifferent, or unhappy. I fail to see how any sensitive person who enjoyed and appreciated life as it was could be happy under the circumstances of these changes. Taxes go up, land becomes difficult to hang onto. Assessments are made for sewers and other "improvements" that were never necessary before. More and more apartment houses come into being. More crowding and congestion, more noise and glaring lights, more impersonal stores and less service, ugly structures going up everywhere. Oh, lots of money changing hands, but little taste and sophistication in evidence. Then a huge Sears store goes in, with acres of floodlit parking lots. Freeways are planned to slice through the countryside. You fight these and are designated as one of a handful of reactionary citizens who seek to impede progress; you never realized that you were such an enemy of society, did you? You could have made a lot of money on all of this, had you been thinking in those terms. But you were thinking in more static terms, enjoying something that money couldn't buy, something that for some reason or another struck you as a pleasant and satisfying environment to live in and raise a family. It seemed to mean something. This new order well it just seems like some temporary way station to oblivion. Better perhaps than many other forms of existence but somehow (?) dissatisfying to you. I guess you are meant to sit in front of a television and let Johnny Carson or Phyllis Diller or some continually interrupted drama amuse you. You mustn't think too much, or remember the way it was. That's fatal. You must tell yourself that the world is getting better and better. Look how well the streets are lighted, how full the supermarket is of goodies. In many ways it is not all that bad, but it is not good; and certainly not as good as it used to be. This is, at least from the point of view of this outburst, a fact. But the world changes very rapidly these days, and one must be in tune with the changes and appreciate them. To not do so induces dissatisfaction; I suppose all old people feel out of tune with the times. But when this occurs when one is in one's early twenties, something is wrong somewhere. And I have enough faith in what I knew good to say that something is at least not good with the changes I have observed. They may be good for others, but I have heard too many other complaints and think that this is universally so. Change comes and I don't think that individuals, with rare exceptions, can do anything about it, or even channel it in satisfactory forms. What does all this add up to? Lament of a malcontent? I don't think so, though there may be elements of this present. It's just the way it is and I guess that one must find whatever good there is in all of it, and try to overlook the rest. But it's hard to overlook a 90 percent factor.

End of lament …
19:9:68

◆   ◆   ◆

21st October, a rainy night somewhere by some future sea ...

Letter to no one in particular,
or to anyone, or even to someone.

Tonight is a rainy, misty night. I rather like it. One remembers other places, other times. One remembers that there have been nights like this since the beginning of time, when men huddled in crude shelters and looked fearfully into the night. There have been rainy nights in small villages, with the stamping of boots and the smell of damp garments around the fire. And with the muffled sound of the sea, rolling across the land poised in its autumnal stillness. And in a flash, as one's hand trails absently across a piece of cloth, a vision lies like a single leaf withered in a roadway, just before a breeze sweeps it away. Life is a series of promises, some of them broken, some of them kept, some of them not real at

Faces stare out from the pages of the album, all of them from moments captured in time. One remembers such moments, and knows that they were real and had meaning. They are things of lifetimes, but they have meaning and reality only so long as someone remembers something about them, can associate them with moments just before and just after. When there is no one to remember this sequence of moments, whether or not the sun shone all that day, who laughed and who cried, or where they all came from and where they have gone, then those faces are nothing more than the faces of strangers staring out at the eyes of the beholder. They are the mysteries that are all of us; they are people about whom nothing is known.

The rain drifts down from the dark skies and gathers in the roadsides. Out in the bay a foghorn blows, and in a moment another answers it. A man listening hears the voices of his past calling, and he wonders. He remembers people he hasn't seen in years, and he wonders where they are now. Perhaps he remembers one person in particular, and the thought of her fills him with a wrenching sadness and sense of unease. How had it all happened, all the whys of it that he could never understand nor answer? He simply remembers that it was good, very good, while it lasted, and that there should have been more to it. But there was no more to it. It had ended as quickly and quietly as it had begun. Something that existed strongly suddenly existed no more, and that was all there was to it. Still, for the brief time that it did exist it was very fine. What more can be said? The foghorn blows again, but the man seems not to hear it. He is drifting somewhere with the mists, remembering ...

The rain has a soothing effect, and seems to bring a quietness that is not ordinarily present in the city at this hour. And in this quietness there seems to be nothing more to be written. As things begin, so shall they end. All things are contained within a circle, yeah ...

◆   ◆   ◆

Here is this dream I had, or what I remember of it, the morning I left LA to return to San Francisco—a journey I was rather uneasy about:

In the dream I was delivering a child, a boy of perhaps three, to a woman friend, unspecified. The child belonged to another woman friend, again unspecified, who was dying somewhere up north, perhaps in Seattle. The idea was that I was taking the child to a "new home" where he would be well cared for and would be happy. I remember driving north along a coast, stopping somewhere and playing frisbee on a beach with the boy—he must have been older than three because we had conversations. I told him that he was going to live with an "Aunt" and that he would be very happy there. The boy seemed skeptical, but trusting and accepting. I remember delivering the boy—a woman standing in a doorway, and a wooded path leading up to it. I had mixed feelings; I was fond of the boy and perhaps wished him mine. Perhaps I was "fond" of the woman, too, and wished the whole scene mine. But for some reasons this was not to be. I remember the boy saying, "We'll play frisbee again, won't we?" And me saying, "Of course we will...." And then me trying to kiss the woman, and her turning from me saying, "No, no ..." and me walking back to my truck feeling somehow rejected, and very, very alone. But also with the feeling of having done something very worthwhile. I could envision my "woman friend up north" lying in a bed, dying, knowing that I had delivered her child to a good home where he would be well cared for and happy. But I had this feeling that I was somehow caught between these two worlds, a part of neither, left out and alone ... Later, I was driving north again, to no specified destination, along the coast and beaches, when I felt something "wrong" in my chest. "Oh shit," I said, knowing immediately that this was something serious. "Oh shit," I said again, and I was able to guide the truck down to some parking area near the beach. It was about sunset, and there was a patch of sand amongst rocks. I staggered down to this patch of sand and collapsed in a sitting position. I was wearing a red and black plaid wool shirt, and I picked up a driftwood stick and tried to write something in the sand. Then I fell back with my head resting on some rocks. The beach was deserted, the coast lonely and uninhabited. In the last part of the dream I could see the waves come in, wash over my legs, and obliterate the message in the sand. I remember thinking: "No one will know … I have been somehow too proud." And I woke up weeping in San Francisco, a gray morning, at 6 A.M.…

◆   ◆   ◆

All the stars in the heavens cannot equal a column of ants crossing a dusty road in Eastern Colorado in the moonlight while the coyotes sing. There are some things that never stop until they get where they are going. If one had not met a certain person and become her lover, then that person would be no more than someone that one sits next to on a bus some afternoon thirty years hence in San Francisco, Seattle, or Boston. A tired old woman carrying a shopping bag, who looks irritably around the crowded bus because no one will give her a seat, until an unshaven old man, who smells of whiskey and has piss stains on the front of his pants, gets up unsteadily and motions for her to sit down. She flops into the seat with a great exhalation of breath, and smiles weakly at the old man. He nods slightly, and then stares at an advertisement for the painless treatment of piles, thinking of those golden days so many years ago when he was a young man and a golden girl waited in front of the drugstore at Hearst and Euclid in Berkeley, and they went off and made love in the hills. He thinks that if he should get off the bus and fall dead on the sidewalk, there would be no one left to remember those days and those moments. They would be lost to all the world, and it would be as if they had never occurred at all. No one to remember the things of things, that is the instability of the past. Once a moment is gone it can never be recaptured; it is gone forever. There is a magic and a oneness of things, and the energies of our systems are continually being diminished. There are only so many moments in which to make love, so many kisses to be given, so many orgasms to be shared. Then the final skull-popping moment of eternal longing, about which there can be nothing done. The blue lips form as if to say a name, but no sound comes. For the winds are already blowing, and the soul is tumbling end over end across a ruined meadow; all the golden faces blur like flights of starlings wheeling through spindly trees at dusk. Like falling down endless flights of stairs into pits of darkness. There is nothing but the night.

Mark Mitchell, drunken poet of Cambridge, walking off down the street, mumbling about Franny being the ideal country girl. Of course, he was in love with her, poor chap. But who wasn't? She WAS the ideal country girl, he was exactly right. I guess that was his poet's instinct. Franny was embarrassed by his rantings, and asked that he be put out of the car. I did so reluctantly, but it was probably the best thing. He was becoming maudlin with the wine, and with the magic of a June night in Cambridge. Poor Mark, he drowned himself in the Charles not long after that night, for his sadness was more than he could bear. I used to see him around Harvard Square, drunk and mumbling to himself, going into Cronin's and reading incoherent bits of poems to the people sitting there, talking about the time he sat up all night with Dylan Thomas. His ghost comes back from time to time, to proclaim the beauties of Franny, the ideal country girl.

◆   ◆   ◆

The rooms are so barren, so stark. They echo with cries of love. And the lovers wander on, across a severe landscape where strange birds rise in shrieking flocks. Their hands grow cold, and they look at one another with eyes pale as ice. The sea beats against rocks, and the lovers sit gazing out across achromatic space. The Doctor recalls his youth in Berlin, and he remembers the dancers whirling by as he watched through a window. He sees himself walking hand in hand with beautiful Inger through the gabled streets of some Hanseatic town., out across the heaths where the wind blew in from the Baltic, somewhere near Peenemunde. Strange that years later he should find himself forced to work there making V-2 rockets. He remembers all that once was, and how the darkness had closed in on everything so suddenly. Where was Inger? he wondered, and the thought of her twisted his heart as he shorted a circuit in the great rocket, to make it fall harmlessly into the North Sea. Perhaps when all this madness was over he might find peace somewhere, with his books and his research. But still, he dreamed of the golden girl who had once walked by his side when the world promised light and laughter, a few tankards of good beer at a country tavern, and the moment of emptying sand from shoes, before blowing out the lamp and snuggling up to the warm, supple body beneath the feather comforters. How the world could change so in a few short years, how the forces of darkness could close in.

One remembers the last light of a June evening, the way it filtered through the trees. Somewhere nearby a girl was playing a guitar and singing. "World without end," that was what they said in the services. Perhaps it was, but the end of a life was always in sight. What about that? One remembers the way the girl played the guitar and sang, how sweet and plaintive her voice as. And the words of Shakespeare came echoing, "All golden girls and lads must, as chimney sweeps, come to dust ..." Why think of such things in the midst of beauty? Because beauty cannot last? Remember Pound, looking out his window in London, watching the wandering buses in the rain.

The Northern Lights flashed, oddly for that time of year, across the stillness of a Maine pond. The coals of the campfire glowed strangely, and everyone talked in hushed tones. There was a feeling of a spirit abroad on the land, a huge dark shape that threw its shadow across the mountains in the moonlight, that stood like a giant bear across the rivers. The Indians had a name for that spirit, Keen-a-way-sha, the spirit of all that is past. There is a place on the Nevada desert where the Indians say that all the spirits live, a canyon where all the spirits call to one another in the night. And he who hears the spirits call thus is soon to join them. The Indians avoid this place assiduously, even though it is rumored that gold and silver are to be found there. And they say that white men who have gone there to search for this treasure have never returned. On cold nights, when the wind blows from the north, the spirits play the games of their youth, and from a distance one can hear their cries and shouts. The gaiety always ends in wails and moans, and the spirits drift back into the rocks with the first rays of dawn. Those who have heard these sounds never forget them, and when they are camped on the desert they are always aware that at any moment a stranger may join the campfire, to sit quietly until the coals die down and the moment for sleep comes. One will dread to sleep, but sleep is inevitable and one feels that somehow the dawn might not come. It is up to the spirits, and men are specks of sand blown by the wind.

Van Gogh's villager is always rounding his corner, and the clouds build in the sky, with all their strange and mad swirls. A moment is always about to be happening, and another moment is already of the past. Doors are opening and closing, and one is both inside and out. A golden girl smiles from her photograph, and her laughter is like rain dripping from the eaves. Her cries of love are like the singing of birds that fill the trees at twilight and are suddenly gone, leaving only the silence of a summer night, where the moon rides the solitary skies, and leaves rustle slightly in the tops of great dark trees.

Down in the valley a single lamp burns in a farmhouse. A man sits at the kitchen table, a bottle of whiskey before him. He hears laughter and a voice out in the wind, and he starts from his chair, as if to go outside to embrace some old, half-forgotten dream in the night. But he sinks back in his chair and pours another tumbler of whiskey. What is taken is taken forever, and that is all there is to it.

◆   ◆   ◆

HORNBECK'S LAMENT
(Hombre Desperado)

Hornbeck stands drunk in the Plaza, thinking
it was just yesterday that in the sharp distance
of Colorado mountains a young man's image rose
in billowing clouds full of vague promise,
and then his alter ego tramping down from
cool pine mountains like some solitary zen master.
It had been good to join the band of rootless wanderers
who swept him westward in crazy circles
like some dust devil dancing across the sands.
Standing there, thinking "I am Hornbeck, that's
something anyway, but to what end?"
Then reeling in some cantina, once more the music,
the girls with laughing names, promises and
moments half-remembered wiped away
on beer-stained sleeves with the lingering
odor of cheap perfume and gasoline.
Now, standing in the Plaza Hornbeck charts his progress:
"Vague. I am thirty now, standing drunk in Santa Fe,
one small book of poems published,
others started never finished."
Watching through the trees stars careening
across the wide dark mountain sky, far-off memories
and vague expectations of formless plans …
"Why am I Hornbeck?" he wonders. "And does it matter?"
Once more the dusty van, torn and tattered maps,
piles of beer cans and strange names of other cultures, talk
of music, girls, great adventures, freedom always freedom,
then the grinding ascent toward the mystical summit of the icy
purifying mountains—Hornbeck plans to leave New Mexico.

By Sangre de Cristo glowing embers Hornbeck shivers
and drops his fish into the frying pan imagining
it slithering through the dust trying to reach the river,
remembering a sloe-eyed devil of a girl who kissed
him warmly in the deserted street of some old worn out
mining town in Colorado where they spent the evening
reeling through a series of depressing bars.
Hornbeck adjusts his hat, seeing that he has lost
his silver hatband at the drunken desert party
the night before all talk of distant stars
and the mystical little people who were here before.
Before Bobo steers the van unsteadily toward California
perhaps by way of Idaho, Montana maybe, Hornbeck for
a moment in some roadside bar while the rootless
band lies stoned somewhere beside the rusting van.
Hornbeck wants to talk, learn something about
culture and various local values but does not
and cannot form an answer to the question,
"Hey, bro, you like the Hispanic people?"
wondering if he does and does it matter?
Hornbeck sees his hair and beard dimly reflected
in the mirror behind the bar and tries to see
some mountain man or bandido perhaps but does not, orders a
shot of tequila and drinks it off neat, feeling distinctly
out of time and place and disavowing the rumpled image
gazing back at him from behind the rows of bottles.
Hornbeck leaves the bar and staggers through the wind
to the dented van feeling more and more
Hornbeck alone in a wilderness …

And now Hornbeck has gone and done a foolish thing—
No! He is not into home canning of fruits and vegetables, far
worse—he has once more allowed himself to feel things
he swore he would only read about or see in films.

Damn! Hornbeck looks around and sees a moment shared,
sees himself respond beneath the inverted bowl of
Colorado sky Hornbeck caught in sweeping winds of regret,
rushing westward remembers much and more until plunging into
soothing Santa Monica surf in desperation thinking
"I should be, I am, a reluctant sensualist
with the poet's flaw of thinking too much." Believing almost
that the waves embraced the muddy water of an old canal
in a fragrant summer night where soft moist lips brushed his,
Hornbeck skims the waves and is in this moment almost real,
Hornbeck of deserts and mountain passes, of green eastern fields,
fleeing westward until clean Southern California beaches
then damp coastal fogs of mysterious Big Sur amongst strangers
and afternoons with the hazy Nepenthe sun struggling
to burn away the fog and push back darkness before the cool
moments in damp redwood groves climbing slowly into shadow
mountains toward Nacimiento Summit and the small campfire still
legal in those days and sleeping bags pulled tightly together,
the fine moments of love beneath the pure California night
sky Hornbeck holding tight, trying to prevent drifting off
into deep sadness thinking "Nothing lasts …" Just a whirling
vortex of cinders …

Hornbeck more than sad momentarily destroyed watching
tail lights going down dark roads and into tunnels
gleaming silver buses gliding out of San Francisco fog
and disappearing into distant postcard worlds
("Reno—the Biggest Little City in the World.")
Hornbeck now a second time in Nacimiento night
alone beside himself with fire and wine wondering
"Why have I come back so far from going on?"
Hornbeck on a monumental San Francisco drunk,
reeling in and out of North Beach bars drinking
mightily with that old "circle of new friends"

thinking that the next week would be the first steps
toward Oregon and the clean forests of the High Cascade,
cool fall nights chopping wood and time enough
to reflect on how it was all lost and why.
Oregon nights are long enough to confront
the reality that there is never any going back
Hornbeck knows this and begins another small book of poems:
"Berkeley moon of my wanderings
why chase these lost nights
like aimless moths around lights,
like mechanical toys whirling
in uncertain circles around
someone's comfortable rug?"

(Around North Beach
someone wondered about Hornbeck,
where he might be?
One guy said he thought
he had gone up to Oregon.
Someone else said he had heard
that Hornbeck had fallen under a
freight train in Northern California, or maybe
that might have been someone else ...)

◆   ◆   ◆

FRONTERA

Time and our lives
slide down the River
pursued and dissipated
into deep barrancas
like vagrant puffs of
pungent seegar smoke
from somewhere in the soft
moth mad and unforgiving
nights of Mexico.

Dreaming of a pale Nordic princess
playing a guitar of ice—a sudden
gunshot echoing across arroyos,
shouting—Hornbeck! El Jefe!

Gringos slumped in the cantina
while the raven-haired girls
chatter like birds in the zocala
the band playing "Valentina"—
"If they shoot me tomorrow
I pray you, come and claim me."
The wavy layers of smoke and the
vague clicking of javalina
hoofs on slick rock across the River
under a strange moon—luna loca
a tangled mound of brush and rock
where there is something moving
a warm wind draining down the cañon
rattling the mesquite.

Death came
in twos
in the night

with tequila vengeance
on its breath.

Our Winchesters
lay by the River ...

◆   ◆   ◆

PART THREE

ASSOCIATIVE

(1976. Cripple Creek, Colorado. Altitude 9500'. Population 458)

I have just come from a session at the local barber shop, old Wayne Hunter proprietor. Mr. Hunter is a bona fide redneck of the old style, and in the winter some of his old timer cronies gather in the shop to gossip and banter. These fellows are really good old boys of a type that is dying out around the West. Sitting in the barber chair I felt a sudden surge of sympathy for them. What they have been through in this mining town, in this harsh Colorado mountain country—the forces that have formed them and given them the character they have. Life casts one in a certain mold and then places one in a time and place to play out a role. That is the way with the old fellows in Wayne Hunter's shop. Things have changed around them; the town has died, and is now sort of reborn, at least in the summer, as a tourist destination with visitors both unknowable and distasteful to these guys. The so-called outside world is increasingly something that they can no longer understand or relate to. They rarely or never go down to Colorado Springs. In their twilight years their talk is almost all of the past. And why not? That is what they have known, have suffered through. Their lives.

The haircut takes a long time. There is no hurry on these bleak winter days. The barber pauses to join the conversation, relights his pipe, spits in the sink, pauses in some story he is telling to get his thoughts back on the right track. The old fellows don't mind the long pauses. They are used to them. Things should take time. It is a way of getting through the winter days, the long nights. I planned the haircut as something different to do on this day, something to sort of fill up the afternoon. Rather than puttering around the Museum, tinkering with odd repair or maintenance jobs, or staring down Bennett Avenue from my office, watching the cars come up the street, turn in the parking lot and go back down the street. That is all some people have to do, especially the teenagers. They see no one—the cold streets are empty. Nothing different. Just back and forth, mindlessly I imagine. It is a strange world up here. Especially for me as I view it with detachment, knowing I can, will, get out, go places. Not like those caught in the villages and small towns of the world. Using up the resource of Time, which cannot be replenished, their journeys through time unremarkable, passages leaving nothing. Parkhurst said, "Time goes, you say. Alas, not. We go, time stays …"

◆   ◆   ◆

LETTERS TO THE EDITOR

What follows here is a collection of letters written to the Editor of the Santa Fe NEW MEXICAN over a period from 1992 to 2006. As a matter of record, the paper has printed every letter submitted. As will be seen, the letters cover a variety of subjects, and a diverse range of opinion. Some of these letters have gotten the writer of them rather disliked by members of Santa Fe's vocal community of "barking dog liberals." You must sing the party song or you are castigated to the other side, the side of inferior, dark and insensitive forces. This narrow-mindedness is engendered by a deep rooted superiority complex—i.e. "The world would be a far better place if more people thought like ME!" Well, it is hoped that careful reading of these letters and analysis of them will reveal a creative and sensitive awareness, not a narrow-minded, rigid, "right-wing attitude." But—you be the judge ...

Life, land

As a life-long conservationist, I am very concerned about the current barrage of shrill voices raised against grazing on the public range, and ranching in general.

Sure, there are problems and abuses that need to be corrected, but this protest seems to be something more than just concern for the range. I spent a lot of this summer on public range lands and I saw no environmentalists wringing their hands over grazing, only hard-working ranchers, men and women who deeply care about their way of life and the land.

These protesting, privileged urban intellectuals just plain don't like traditional Western culture; they feel superior to ordinary folks who derive their living from the land, and they seem to have no understanding of the real West, its people, traditions and character. Their agenda is to turn the West into a wimpy recreationalist theme park. Well, there is no character in that sort of thing, and a society without character is *nothing!* These pointy-headed anti-grazers wouldn't survive out on the range—they couldn't stand up in a good windstorm.

◆   ◆   ◆

Qué viva ...

I am told that there are some newcomers in Santa Fe who express anger and bitterness at the outcome of the recent election and feel uneasy with talk of "*la gente.*"

Well, such people obviously don't understand Santa Fe and should leave for places like Scottsdale, Aspen and Santa Barbara where they would no doubt feel more comfortable. If you come to Santa Fe you make adjustments—not the other way around.

◆   ◆   ◆

Too late!

These well-intentioned gestures to "take back the Plaza" are an illusion. Let's face it—the Plaza is gone.

Downtown Santa Fe can no longer claim to be a community, meaning that which is of and for local residents. It is simply bazaar for unimaginative and shamelessly materialistic tourists and exhibitionists. It comes mighty close to being a freak show.

It's too late to throw off these particular shackles of "the new slavery of tourism," but there should be a lesson in this: that tourism, and particularly excessive tourism, is not compatible with a strong, healthy, stable and egalitarian community.

Industrial tourism is turning much of the West into a recreational theme park, with an attendant loss of character. The message is going out: "Hang up your saws and saddles, boys, and send for espresso machines. "Your role is to serve the urban tourist...."

We are becoming just a bunch of people hanging-out, living off each other. This bubble will burst! Perhaps only the Mormons and the Amish will survive.

◆   ◆   ◆

Superior attitudes

A recent mocking letter about grazing and other aspects of the West compels comment from this member of five environmental organizations.

The "superior" patronizing and ignorant tone of this letter is typical of the attitudes of certain people, often of Eastern and privileged background, who have sequestered themselves in Santa Fe and have no real understanding or appreciation of this State, its people and their Western heritage. They obviously have neither liking nor respect for ranchers or other traditional Westerners who make a living from the land. These *perfumados* would have us gazing at crystals, chanting mantras, eating weeds or engaging in endless recreation. Innocent as these activities may be, they produce neither character nor sustenance.

Without trying to excuse those things that are wrong—past and present in the West, one must remember that it has been hard work and sacrifice by others that allows these privileged types to loll about Santa Fe with their superior attitudes.

◆　　◆　　◆

City's purpose

I have just completed a trip to the refreshingly uncrowded and honest ranching country of Northern Nevada and Eastern Oregon, where the communities are real places and the people go about their daily business with purpose and pride. They do not have to dance like monkeys for tourists in order to survive.

Upon returning to Santa Fe, I am once again dismayed to see how overcrowded with tourists this town is, and how completely the downtown area is given over to tourism. It would seem that Santa Fe has lost control of its destiny.

The purpose of Santa Fe is, I believe, to enhance the quality of life of those who live here, especially those. who have lived here for a long time and whose roots are here. It is not to provide a horde of tourists with "experiences," or to provide rich outsiders with a place to build immodest homes that they occupy occasionally. I think that more than a few people in Santa Fe have lost sight of the simple truth Santa Fe exists first and foremost for Santa Feans! Let us not forget that.

◆　　◆　　◆

Don't sell religion

There are very sad implications in the current case of Jemez Pueblo men having slaughtered eagles for feathers used in "popular American Indian-style crafts" which were sold to "trading posts. collectors, tourists ..."

While not at all excusing those who murdered eagles for profit, I must trace the ultimate blame for this sad episode to those who have created such a lucrative market for the types of goods alluded to—i.e. the mania of "collecting."

I have always been uncomfortable with the commercial exchange of religious or ceremonial objects of any culture.

Such things are not, in my opinion, to be sold to strangers, who then trade them for profit.

The murdered eagles in this case are, the victims of this materialistic (Anglo) disease of having to acquire and own everything, especially of cultures (they) consider to be quaint or "primitive."

Having this past summer watched five or more Golden Eagles perched on Nevada rim rock, searching for "breakfast," I remember that we can never own what is not truly ours.

◆   ◆   ◆

Charging for chips

It is often small things that indicate where we are and where we are headed. From the beginning of time it has been the traditional hospitality of native New Mexican restaurants to offer free chips and salsa to patrons.

Evidently, no longer in downtown Santa Fe.

Recently at a very popular (and profitable) downtown "New Mexican" restaurant, I was asked if I wanted chips and salsa. "Of course," I said. I was dismayed to find later that I had been charged $3 for these.

Not long ago I stopped for lunch in Lordsburg at the humblest of Mexican restaurants.

As soon as we were seated, the free chips and salsa were on the Formica table; when the bowl of chips was empty it was quickly refilled, with a smile.

Lordsburg is a poor place, but they have not there descended to the level of charging for chips and salsa.

◆   ◆   ◆

Kids no fun on Plaza

For the past several years, I have studied these kids who gather on the Plaza, and my impressions are not encouraging.

These young Anglos who hang out there in raggedy clothes stare vacantly, smoke, converse disjointedly, or play that little game from California, hacky-sack.

Skateboarding is a recent phenomenon, rather disruptive to the peace of the Plaza.

They are not having fun, as your editorial suggests. These are not happy faces.

My impression is that for the most part these are the indolent offspring of weak, rich, liberal parents who don't seem to care how their children spend their time or what they look like.

Yes, they are free to congregate there, but let's not kid ourselves—this is not a healthy scene.

◆   ◆   ◆

Jewels or junk?

It is very puzzling and dismaying to me that the Historic Design Review Board and other city agencies have allowed a junkyard to be placed on a prominent downtown lot—junk consisting of dubious architectural fragments and other items gathered up in India and the Middle East to be sold to "rich Americans"—material that has absolutely nothing to do with Santa Fe, its history, culture or heritage.

In my mind this is just one more nail in the coffin of the integrity of the "Santa Fe That Was." The only saving grace is that this eyesore can disappear as quickly as it arrived.

◆   ◆   ◆

Not so enlightened

Over a month ago, I noticed on a building near the rail yard that houses a business catering to persons who consider themselves "spiritual" and "enlightened," prominent graffiti reading, "Kill Bush!" As of Feb. 15, it was still there, indicating to me approval of this message by the business and its patrons.

Taken literally, that graffiti would mean, "Assassinate Bush." One presumes that among spiritual and enlightened people, it is a canon of ethics that any exhortation to kill someone is decidedly not spiritual, not enlightened, but immoral.

Would the Dalai Lama approve of such? I think not. It is understandable to oppose Bush—I certainly do. But tasteless reference to violence is not constructive and simply indicates that there are some people in Santa Fe whose thinking is severely compromised.

◆   ◆   ◆

Let eagles live

A recent legal case involving a Native American who, following instructions from Tribal Elders, killed a Bald Eagle to acquire feathers for a religious ceremony is full of disturbing implications.

But it boils down to this: It is time for the Great Spirit to cause a revelation that no longer should any eagle have to die, or be kept captive to have its feathers pulled out, for any ceremony, or for any other reason. The eagle deserves to live and fly free. Worship him as he soars in the great blue sky!

◆   ◆   ◆

Cuba no libre

I am not a "fuzzy-minded idealist" admirer of Cuba and Castro, but I have recently entertained the notion of visiting Cuba to see what it and the people are like. Now I learn that those Americans who have done so, through Canada or Mexico, are being legally harassed with threats of fines and/or incarceration, with the intention of preventing any further travel to Cuba by Americans. How repressive and narrow-minded.

I have always felt that this country should deal with Cuba, regardless of communism and its ills, with an open and progressive attitude—i.e., trade and exchange of people and ideas.

Is this new repression the influence of anti-Castro conservative Cubans in Florida whose votes the Republicans seek? Or is it simple reactionary narrow-mindedness?

Whatever—it simply pushes this centrist individual further from the current Washington regime and its ideologies—all of which I have opposed from the outset.

◆　　◆　　◆

To the Editor—there are currently increasing and very disturbing rumors, suggestions even (Krauthammer in Sunday 28 August *New Mexican*)—that the United States plans and should execute military action against Iran to destroy the nuclear capacity of that nation. That would simply be the stupidest thing (we) could do—as opposed to continued international diplomatic pressure. It would be a disaster beyond imagining, like Iraq born of ignorance and arrogance. It would enflame the Middle East and the entire Muslim world. It would guarantee future terrorist attacks within the United States. It would bankrupt this country and severely damage the country socially, and further erode what little respect we have left in the international community. I call upon the people of the United States, if they have the will and the purpose, to unite to prevent another military disaster from dragging this country down.

◆　　◆　　◆

Who needs ski reports anyway?
Dear *High Country News*:

I very much enjoy your excellent paper, even if quite a few of the articles sadden me as they chronicle the transition of an honest working man's West into a characterless, la-de-da, recreational theme-park West. But "The New West's servant economy" truly shocks and depresses me (HCN, 4/17/95).

That these ski resorts, catering, one presumes, to the 1 percent who control 40 percent of all the wealth of this country, should scour the country for the cheapest possible labor, and treat them like dirt, is an abomination. The greed, arrogance, materialism and insensitivity of these useless places are beyond any justification. The West would be a better place, and we a better people, if these worthless and decadent ski resorts disappeared without a trace.

◆   ◆   ◆

Heed warning

I would hope that all Santa Feans would give the utmost consideration to a recent very thoughtful essay in *The New Mexican* on growth and population as pertains to Santa Fe, by Lindsey Grant, and to a book he co-authored, *How Many Americans*, bravely published by The Sierra Club, also on the subject of uncontrolled population growth and its vastly negative social and environmental consequences. But I fear that Mr. Grant's warnings and suggestions will go unheeded—I suspect that Mr. Grant has long experience of "whistling in the wind."

Not long ago I walked with a man in Tonapah, Nev., who had fled the crowding, pollution, traffic, social problems, etc. of California. He said sadly of his native state, "Those folks over there have plumb thrown away a paradise ..." How tragic it would be to hear people say that about Santa Fe, or the United States even.

The time to take the strongest action is *now!* The quality of life that has made Santa Fe unique and enjoyable is already very much compromised. Further growth, if not limited, will destroy what is left, and future generations will say, "They threw away a paradise—how did they let that happen?"

◆   ◆   ◆

Back to basics

I think that the time is at hand for some of our more notable local restaurants to turn back toward things more normal in their menus.

Some of these establishments have traveled so far from food as sustenance into a realm of food as "experience and presentation" that we are threatening ourselves with terminal decadence.

Having recently "suffered" through a variety of these presentations, with distress to both stomach and billfold, I find myself remembering fondly what used to be called "a square meal," served up in working men's cafés (which, fortunately, do still exist locally).

Food does not have to be dull and tasteless. But neither does it have to be overly complex, dainty and unintelligible, and apparently devoid of the concept of sustenance. Come on, Santa Fe, return to Earth before it is too late!

◆   ◆   ◆

People are problem

With regard to the recent rather biased anti-ranching article *Cowboy Socialism*, even if everything stated therein is 100 percent true, the greatest threat to the American West is people—too many of them and their expanding recreation/them-park mentality.

The U.S. population is rising far too fast, and if not severely restrained this growth will render more and more of our landscape a soul-less sprawl of malls, housing tracts, jammed highways, and as we already see, extreme social inequity. We shall be a society of rootless people focused only on the here-and-now, entertainment and materialism.

◆   ◆   ◆

I have gotten a lot of negative feedback from my letter to the paper about the kids who hang out in the Plaza. I guess the tone of it offends some people, as well as what they perceive to be a lack of understanding of "kids." Now, I did lay it on a bit thick in the letter, and perhaps I have misjudged those kids, or some of them. Meredith says I don't know what I am talking about, but I am around that Plaza almost every day, and she is rarely there. I have sat there eating my lunch, listening to "conversation," observing. There is a definite link to the kids who hang out at the bus station in Mill Valley, downtown Berkeley, or outside the donut shop in Watertown, CT. It is a widespread phenomenon. It is said that those kids hang out there because "there is nothing to do in Santa Fe." Not so! Kids are hanging out like that in San Francisco, where there is plenty "to do." Here in Santa Fe I could provide you with a list of about fifty things there are to do for teenagers. Granted, much on my list might be for "squares" or "nerds," but nonetheless things to do. What about a job? Laying up some funds for the future? Athletics? Computers? Hobbies? Homework? Helping out around the house? Working on cars or motorcycles? Exploring the surrounding countryside (which I used to do on my bike when I was that age). And so forth. The point is, the kids are hanging out in the Plaza because THAT IS WHAT THEY WANT TO DO. OK? Now, is it healthy for them to be smoking like that? No! Does Meredith's next door neighbor want her twelve year old daughter hanging out there every afternoon, smoking away, with a bolt through her tongue, saying "shit" and "motherfucker" every other word, etc? Certainly not! As for these kids being "the indolent off-spring of weak, rich, liberal parents"—the behavior does strike me as "indolent"; as to parentage, I am relying on things I have been told, and my own suppositions from the kids' appearance and my own intuition. I may be wrong. The other day on the Plaza, however, I observed something that must have some bearing on my suppositions. A bunch of the Plaza kids were getting into a white BMW sedan, driven by another kid, who while waiting rolled down his window and tossed a rather large crumpled paper into the street. Also, the fourteen year old kid who smashed his mother's Nissan PATHFINDER into the Palace of the Governors last year, having taken the car while his mother was away, is another example. A recent article about a young Plaza habitué is revealing, I think, and when I attempted to discuss it with Meredith she brushed the subject aside. The portrait of this young man is not one of a happy, well-adjusted young man, obviously. Something has gone wrong far before this point. Might there be parallels with unsettled Marin County young people? Of particular interest is the philosophy imparted to this young man by the "alternative educational program" his mother involved him with after he dropped out of high school, the notion "that you don't have to let anyone tell you what to do." I believe that this is central to the notion of anarchy, which seems to be very popular with young people today. I see the symbol spray painted, gouged in concrete, etc., everywhere; when Ted's family was here last January the subject came up and Matthew knew all about it. It seems to be circulating among the young, very popular. Because "no one can tell anyone what to do." How appealing. Just do your own thing. Of course that appeals to young people. But it is neither logical nor healthy. I wonder how and where this got started, and who or what is promoting it? I think there are some "social philosophers" today whose agenda is attacking, and destroying, the middle class and so-called bourgeois values as being repressive and harmful to the "true expression of the human potential." That is, diversity (in every manner), freedom from harmful restraint to "explore your own potential," freedom from dehumanizing demands by petty tyrants who seek only to keep a leash on people—"no one can tell anyone what to do."

And so on. I read recently something by some progressive teacher complaining that dress codes, for both students and faculty, were only "about power," and that what is important is "nurturing the human spirit to love and appreciate all people." You get the picture. So, I submit this in defense of my analysis of the young people who are hanging out in the Plaza. It would be healthy if they were engaged in more productive activity, that they were not drawn toward slovenly appearance and antisocial attitudes. One last thing—a few days before Christmas I was passing through the Plaza and paused to study one young man seated there. He had very short hair, combat boots, and a sullen almost hostile expression. A Christmas carol came over the speakers, "Hark, the Herald Angels Sing." He looked up, and said to no one, "Ah, listen to that SHIT!" and spit onto the concrete. I watched him for a while. He stared at the concrete and spit several times, actually quite regularly, occasionally raising his head to stare sullenly. I thought, this CANNOT be a happy, well-adjusted young man, I bet that attitude carries into all aspects of his life. I cannot guarantee that. It is just intuition. So, my conclusion, that at least some if not many of the kids who gather there are caught in a downward spiral that is not healthy, for them or for society. Some may be good kids who just like to hang out, as Meredith says—before going home to work on their homework, help out around the house, clean their rooms, and dine cheerfully with their parents and siblings, all at the table together! Hah!

I don't know if I make a case for my letter or not. I might, if I had not laid it on so heavily, sounding like a cranky, old, conservative fart who neither likes nor understands young people. And that is how the tone did sound to a lot of people. Poor choice of words and phraseology on my part. But—those kids at the bus sta-

tion in Mill Valley, is that a healthy scene? That is the sort of scene that I am talking about, it is a similar syndrome in the Plaza that I am calling unhealthy. It is
not the end of the world. I would have to know infinitely more about those kids,
individually, what sorts of students they are, how they get along at home, what
economic level they come from, what cultural background, what plans they have,
what they think of society, the country, the world. All that sort of thing. I might
be surprised, and find that I have completely misjudged the situation. I would be
pleased if that were so, because then I would have a better feeling about our society. Not too long ago I read a book, *South of Paradise, High School in the Last Part
of the Twentieth Century*, by a reporter for *The St. Petersburg Times* (Florida), who
spent a year hanging around a middle class, suburban high school, not posing as a
student but circulating openly as a young, hip reporter. His account was worse
than I thought it would be. I was appalled and truly concerned if this was typical
of the middle class public schools in America. You would have to read the book
to know what I am talking about. So, when Meredith says, vis-a-vis my letter,
that I don't know what I am talking about, that is not entirely true. She had
never heard of the popularity of anarchy, was not aware of the symbol everywhere. So, where are we? Where is truth? Who is the Victim, who the Slayer?
Speak!

◆   ◆   ◆

I would like to share with you the following examples of some of Edward Abbey's thinking, as expressed in the book *Confessions of a Barbarian*:

"Santa Fe—A dirty phony little town crawling with queers, promoters, creeps, thugs, vandals and parasites." (p. 146)

"And Taos? Where the fairies and the Buddhists live, and the rich, ugly useless old women." (p. 147)

"The Enemy? We all know where the Enemy is. The Enemy speaks to us all the time—from the radio, on the television, on billboards, in the newspapers and the slick magazines, in the halls of Congress, at the state capitol, in city hall." (p.258)

"Most people should not be allowed to have children. Look around you. Look at them!" (p. 279)

"Susie (daughter) is not happy at Verde Valley School. Homesick, lonely. I should never have sent her to that detention camp for unwanted teenagers of wealthy families. How could I have been so dumb as not to realize what a prep school really is? A lesson for me. The rich, really, are NOT good people. They are selfish, spoiled, greedy, cliquish, clannish, mean-spirited. That's how they came to be rich." (p.282)

"Just read Matheissen's *Snow Leopard*. Good writing, but—there's something ludicrous and pathetic in the spectacle of those rich Americans going all the way to Nepal, trekking through the Himalayas, followed by a string of porters bearing the white man's burden, spending thousands of dollars, in order to—"find themselves"! Good Christ! Why didn't he just stay home and hike the Catskills? Travel Long Island on a skateboard? The colossal egotism of these soul searchers. What makes them think their useless pitiful souls are so god-awful important?" (p. 283)

"(John Nichols) 'sentimentalized' (or romanticized) the Meskins of New Mexico, whom I described as a people now devoted mainly to drugs, crime, spray paint, ward heeling politics, cars and the monthly welfare check." (p. 285)

"Did Jesse James ever say 'Have a nice day' to his clientele as he was leaving? I doubt it." (p. 300)

"These hysterical liberals who keep telling me they love the Mexican culture so much. Then why are they living in the USA? And what IS this much-loved Mexican culture anyway? Tacos, tequila and ranchero music, sure—but what else? Culture means a way of life, the way people do things. Mexican culture includes not only the hot food and the pretty flag, but over-population, poverty and misery, filth and squalor, injustice and oppression, class and caste, corruption and cruelty, brutal police, a Nazi-like military, a fear and hatred of the natural world … One could go on and on." (p. 306)

A "crank"? Like me? Perhaps …

◆   ◆   ◆

AWAKE, AWAKE, PUT ON THY STRENGTH, O ZION! PUT ON THY BEAUTIFUL GARMENTS, O JERUSALEM! I GIVE MY BACK TO THE SMITERS AND MY CHEEKS TO THEM THAT PLUCKED OFF MY HAIR! WHO IS IT THAT SHALL CONDEMN ME? LO, THEY SHALL ALL WEX OLD AS A GARMENT. THE MOTH SHALL EAT THEM UP! ETERNITY IN GOD'S EYE IS A MOTE. AND WHAT GREAT ARCHER BENDS THE BOW THAT MAKES THE DIVI-DIVI TREE—WHO PLACED THE ANACONDA ON THIS EARTH TO TEMPT? BLESS YOU IN SUBMISSION, FOR THE DEVIL HE BE RED. HOW HAVE I WRONGED THEE, MY PEOPLE, TO LET YOU BREATHE THIS FIERCE YACOUB?

COME AND SIT IN THE DUST,
O VIRGIN DAUGHTER OF BABYLON!

If you find the above rather odd, well, so do I. In truth all words of theological origin are a great and vast bafflement unto me. Whatever mysteries they may contain are completely beyond my humble ability to grasp. They seem to be just fragments in the great mosaic of the universe, which some learned scientists now proclaim to have originated from something no larger than a grape! Why not from something the size of a pea, I wonder? Or a speck of dust? Theology is to me as Henry Adams said of philosophy, "The pondering of insoluble problems in unintelligible terminology ..." Be all of this as it may, as the English poet Ralph Hodgson. said some years back, "I don't try to reconcile anything—it's a damned strange world ..."

We are lurching toward the year 2000, and I imagine that at that time we will witness all sorts of buffoonery. Whether the new millennium will prove beneficial I cannot say. I am reminded of a man who not too long ago wrote a letter to the Philadelphia INQUIRER in which he said that he had lived in Bucks County (PA) all his life and had seen thousands of changes, not one for the better. He was speaking environmentally, and it is not hard to understand what he meant. My father used to say that during his lifetime we had added 150 million people to this country and he did not find them that interesting. I don't find them interesting at all—I find them a damned nuisance! We need to stabilize the population of this country or all will suffer a severely degraded quality of life. There may be truth in Ralph Waldo Emerson's comment, "Things are in the saddle and ride mankind ...," but by golly it's time to start bucking!

Here in Santa Fe there is the usual coming and going. The natives are restless, and the rich, smug Anglos pursue their pattern as before—but, unlike the boarhound and the boar, NOT reconciled among the stars! No, these people need a little sensitivity session with Pedro and Carlos, stoked up on Budweiser, to set their small pointed heads straight. Do I have an attitude? Very well then, I have an attitude—from attitudes great things spring, great things both good and bad. Let us then, as we slouch toward the new millennium, build temples in the shining firmament and stretch our thoughts toward things good and fine in this world full of contradictions and attitudes.

My books are on the internet—amazing. Those who are so equipped are invited to visit the Amazon site, and if they have not yet purchased the books perhaps they will be persuaded to do so. To those of you who did buy books I am deeply grateful. I hope you enjoy the books and will share them with others. And to those who declined to send for the books, out of either indifference or stinginess, I can only say that I am quite disappointed.

Since I have inherited the house at 129 Aberdeen Terrace in St. David's, Pennsylvania, I plan to keep it and will spend more time there. And very little or none in California! I have no longer either the interest or energy to deal with the depleted, tarnished or no longer extant (for me) attractions of the Golden State. We have more than enough weirdos in Santa Fe who emanate from regions west of here, and I find myself quite comfortable in the unspectacular and normal environs of Philadelphia and its pleasant suburbs. Of course, everything these days is being subjected to an accelerated pace of development and media-induced fixation on entertainments of all sorts. The fact that I do not own a television leaves me plenty of extra time to play pinball machines, wherein I am told if one can attain the level where one experiences one-ness with the machine a vast enlightenment will result. Consequently, I am importing several hundred used pinball machines to be set up in and about the Plaza in Santa Fe, along with a couple of truckloads of used appliances which I think will enhance the sidewalks of downtown Santa "Fake"—I mistyped downtown as "fowtown," which is typical of the many small mistakes made on this machine which will eventually produce a new and challenging vocabulary of entirely new words. I am at work on a dictionary of such words, to which I will assign my own meanings.

People may eventually learn not to ask "what do you do," to which years ago a friend would answer, "Sir, my career? My career is a hanging on …" My father was always intrigued by an old boy at the Murphys (CA) Hotel who when asked how he was doing always answered, "I'm hangin' on …" On a recent cross-country trip I took two lane blacktops across Kansas (yes, Toto) where one night I fetched up in Medicine Lodge, the birth place of Carrie Nation, who tore up a bar in Cripple Creek one time and vastly increased the saloon keeper's business as everyone wanted to show defiance by rushing to that particular saloon for a drink, or several. Anyway, I diverge, as usual. Medicine Lodge would drive me to drink! But I think none is to be had in the decaying community. Whilst I was having breakfast in a humble locally owned establishment, a troop of farmers entered. Noticing one of their brethren somewhat slumped over a nearby table one of them called out cheerily, "How y'all doin', Homer?" The slumped-over man looked up, rather gloomily, I thought, and said, "I'm here." Period! I got on my way quickly and scooted right out of Kansas, seeking more cheerful environs. I cannot say that I found them until I reached the countryside of central Pennsylvania. Much of the Heartland is given to both brooding and a severely compromised environment. The North Country of Michigan, particularly the region of Charlevoix, seemed attractive to me, but there appeared to be a bit too many men in camo outfits, even if it was bow season.

Activities in December here in Santa Fe included the Christmas Eve "stroll of the luminarias," a formerly simple and humble Hispanic pageant that has been taken over by the Anglos and made into an extravaganza, ever more so each year. Also a meandering trip down into the "bootheel" country of New Mexico, where a jaguar was seen earlier this year. If I did not encounter Jaguar, perhaps I will absorb some of his strength and magic from being in the territory he graced on his visit from Mexico. The Mexicans are quick to shoot a fine animal like that for the value of the skin, when they are not shooting each other for publishing journalistic articles that they deem to be unflattering to them and their narcotraffi-cante empires. A drug lord was seen strutting in Tijuana flaunting a coat made of five or six ocelot pelts, because he knew that the gringos are trying to protect that animal in their "pitiful effort to save nature or something." That sort of thing enrages me and causes me to have unkind thoughts about much of what manifests itself below that border. If nothing else, we must dedicate ourselves to the ecological salvation of this fine earth. You all know the drill—get to work, NOW!

I am starting another book, completely different from the others—I feel I have said all I have to say about the West. The new book will be about the East, manifestations thereof, my experiences therein, family background, and of course environmental observation and commentary. A tentative title is "INNA EAS," which as you may guess is a rather crude variation of "in the East." Whether the subtlety of that comes across I cannot tell, and it may be that the tentative title will be jettisoned for something more resounding and dignified. We never know until we know—and sometimes not even then.

I am reminded of a rather interesting piece of graffiti that I saw on a railway underpass on my recent trip to Pennsylvania. It read, "We will never be equal until we are equal ..." I find the subtlety of that quite intriguing, challenging even.

For my recent birthday dinner I chose "Wild Boar" at the La Fonda dining room. Curious, I asked of the young lad who was our waiter (who, mercifully, had not told us his name) what manner of wild boar this might be. He did not know but said that he would find out. He returned saying that it was raised commercially near Denver. Interesting, but not the answer to my question. He returned a second time to inform me that the chef said that it was a wild pig that was a very popular item eaten in Mexico. Ah—javelina, or peccary, but definitely NOT wild boar, or European Wild Boar as the species is known, or Sanglier in France. At this point the waiter was looking nervous, as was Meredith, so I dropped the subject and turned my attentions to the meat on my plate, which was served in slightly charred pieces with a variety of picante sauces, most notable being a mole-chipotle combination which was mighty good, as they say down in Texas—or used to before all that fancy high tech business came in and brought a passel of spindly damned Yankees with it. Still, lots of pretty women in Texas, and as every derned good ole boy knows, "Texas women is Texas gold!"

In closing, and as a nod to the materialism of the Holiday Season, I want to share with you with you a line from an old Country & Western song: "She got the gold mine—and I GOT THE SHAFT!"

A snowstorm is blowing across New Mexico—the land is still and sere under the gray, lowering skies. There is the usual smell of piñon smoke in the air, and the rumble of low-riders echoes in Española canyons, while pale, spindly Anglos raise toasts of hot mulled cider in their snug eastside Santa Fe houses, the volumes of Spinoza and Proust laid aside, madrigals playing softly from expensive stereo systems—decent people, who are trying to save nature or something ...

◆   ◆   ◆

There are two news articles that have received publicity here in Santa Fe recently, and comment: one in particular about the Hispanic men who were ejected from a tavern in Washington State for speaking Spanish—"Speak English here, or adios, amigo!"—since there is a predominant Spanish culture here, or there used to be.... The new governor of New Mexico, who wants to "execute 13 year olds!" is in many ways a real jerk, and much of his rhetoric is made up of thinly veiled anti-Hispanic sentiment. Fifty-seven percent of New Mexicans drive without insurance, and perhaps an almost as high number drive without driver's licences or registered automobiles. Too expensive, they can't afford it, they need to "get to work," are the excuses. What about drunk driving? It is not at all unusual to read about people arrested for DWI, with seven or eight, or more, previous offences. Just this morning I read in the paper that the head of the DWI program in Española was arrested for DWI and marijuana possession! One man had twenty-five DWIs in a ten-year period.

I feel sorry for the Mexicans. Their country is in dreadful shape, they are starving and desperate. But nonetheless, most people in this country do not want to be overrun with them. And, we should learn to be less dependant on cheap labor. Why cannot this "poor young man" (Anglo) who was featured on the front page of *The New Mexican* stop hanging around down there on the Plaza, get off his ass and get to work. He can do some of this stuff the Mexicans do, that we seem to be so dependant on. So, what it boils down to is—enough is enough, no mas! I have a whole file on why very few more people, legal or not, should be let into this country. Read Ed Abbey on this!

The second article was about the American woman who got involved with a revolutionary group in Peru and was convicted of treason there and sentenced to a life term in prison. Now, as far as concerns that "poor young woman" now sentenced to that awful prison in Peru—well, she is a middle-class radical from New York who for some neurotic reason over-identified with South and Central American guerillas (probably wanted to get it on with Ché, or some similar figure. This is not an uncommon syndrome around Berkeley and places like that). So, she either naively or unwisely became involved with a guerilla group in Peru, where such subversive activity is taken VERY seriously, with the result that she got herself in a shit-load of trouble. At least she got to shout her "slogans of the people"! Now, I imagine that this will be quietly dealt with after a bit; she will be transferred to a U.S. prison, and after a while quietly let out, with the warning that she behave herself. Which she may or may not do, depending on how scared she is. People in this country are sort of coddled in the judicial system, compared to other places in this old world. I am reminded of a prison in Morocco, described as a place "that no one ever emerged from, dead or alive!"

A friend of mine from Colorado was here recently, a graduate of West Point who served two tours in Vietnam as a captain in the Green Berets. Well, in the intervening years something seems to have happened, many things, and now the captain is drawn by higher powers to live in Taos and "save the Earth," and I presume the people on it as well. Meredith, who had met him before in an earlier, more normal manifestation, was rather put off by him. "Awfully serious, disturbingly so ...," was how she put it. The captain, while here, said something about being so outraged at some injustice wreaked upon the Indians somewhere along the line, that he felt that he wanted to "go out and fight white men!" Where and under what circumstances, I did not learn. Well, this is what too much sensitivity leads to, I am afraid, and it is a perfect example of liberalizing yourself out of existence. I look around at the people here in Santa Fe, the refined Anglos, and can see that they are good, well-meaning people—BUT THEY WOULD NOT SURVIVE IN A RIOT!

None of this means that people should be ever treated unfairly. Of course not. There are just certain realities that have to be confronted, and somehow dealt with in trying to make our society better. I read recently about Asians agitating for more Asian immigration! But—thoughtful Asians have come out in opposition to this, in favor of severe limitations on immigration. They understand the many problems where they came from, over-population, etc. Ever been to Brazil, or read much about it? I just finished a long and very interesting book about the place, by a man who professes a long term "love affair" with the country. When I finished the book I could not throw off a very distinct feeling of unease about the whole place, colorful and fascinating as it may be. When the Brazilians say to Americans, "We are your future …," I don't find this at all reassuring; in fact, it profoundly disturbs me.

I suppose what I have written here does not sound "particularly liberal," and I don't intend it to be. I am trying to be honest and fair-minded, without pretending or ignoring anything. Tolerance is what I believe in, not pretending. Not liking something is not abnormal. Pretending to like something when ones does not is abnormal. Self preservation is not necessarily politically correct. And liberalizing one's society out of existence is dumb!

◆   ◆   ◆

I should be walking downtown but ominous clouds have come up and I shall have to wait for them to dissipate—which they usually do with only a few drops of rain. The drought continues …

I just stepped outside and what I predicted is indeed taking place. The clouds are drifting over the mountains, the temperature has dropped ten degrees or so, and there is no indication of any impending rain.

On a more contemporary note—last week Meredith and I attended at the wonderfully refurbished 1920s era "Moorish" theatre The Lensic, a performance by Savon Glover, the world's greatest tap dancer (from NYC) and a jazz quintet. Quite a presentation. Mr. Glover is indeed a virtuoso of his chosen art. Meredith says he has been written up many times in the NYT. I suppose that I have overlooked such articles since my interest in tap dancing is somewhat minimal. But Mr. Glover has taken it over the top. Sold out house, all Anglo of course, sort of "Berkeleyesque" audience. Standing ovation! I began to wonder if perhaps the enthusiasm was perhaps a bit excessive. I wondered if black audiences would be so wildly enthusiastic about Mr. Glover. Because there is something in the tap dancing and the presentation, that has distinct origins in the "old soft shoe shuffle" of the minstrel show, of the darkies entertaining the plantation owners and guests. Blacks might feel a bit too close to all that.

I remember one time long ago when Mr. Blackburn was living on School Alley on Telegraph Hill and had a bit of money. He gave a rather elegant "garden party" in the secluded and luxuriant environs of School Alley (I would hope it is just the same.) Various items were presented on silver trays, drinks were dispensed at a bar, and a black man was playing jazz and show tunes on a piano that had been trundled in to the yard. As the afternoon wore on it seems that the piano player had indulged in quite a few drinks. He got up to entertain "the folks" with various displays of rhythmically slapping his hands against his sides and thighs, of making popping sounds against his cheeks, and so forth. The guests were a bit dumbfounded. When this entertainment ended with the man dancing about with a broom balanced on his nose, slapping his sides and thighs in a sort of soft shoe shuffle—well, Mr. Blackburn's sensitive liberal guests were downright embarrassed. I thought it all highly amusing, but then I was not so enlightened as the rest of the guests, who were from the art and academic worlds. I was a mere frequenter of pubs in North Beach at that time, and sometime graduate student at San Francisco State.

Back from an excursion downtown. Just as I predicted, the clouds dissipated and the evening beckoned clear and calm. A visit to the library to return a book, and then a stroll about. Downtown is in the evenings quiet and much thinned out of people—the tourists are back in their holes. A few couples, Anglo of course, of the better dressed type meander toward restaurants for dinner. There is in the air various cooking smells from these restaurants, of differing nationalities. Last night I stopped in the reopening of the venerable Palace Restaurant, and was given a tour by the young very yuppie manager, including the patio where we were immersed in rich cooking smells. "Ahh," I commented. "Smells good. Yours or the French place next door?" "A bit of both," he said, tiring, I think, of me. I perused a menu and promised that Meredith and I would stop in soon. The long time Italian owner had sold it last winter to a chap from NYC who ran several restaurants there, including the trendy La Goulue on the Upper East Side (Meredith and I stopped in there once for a light Sunday supper—I had Steak

Tartar.) Well, these New York types don't seem to know how to relate to Santa Fe, for within six months he closed and sold the Palace, to some young locals who know what they are doing and how to get the locals in—the only way to get through the winter.

Next day. Spent the evening reading *The Working Poor* by David Shipler, Interesting companion piece to *Nickeled and Dimed* by Barbara Ehrenreich. The extent of poverty in this society is really shocking, and discouraging. We should have an egalitarian society, not one with the greatest gap between rich and poor of any western nation. But, having permitted the country to be flooded with cheap labor from (the Third World) we "suffer what men must." Not a subject that I wish to dwell on. I get enough criticism from Mr. Roberts in Berkeley, who was recently visiting here and was made uneasy with me pointing out the inequities in Santa Fe—the completely segregated societies the Anglos and Hispanics occupy. He prefers the vision of Hispanics rising in the scheme of things, their children going off to Ivy League schools. Well, that does happen, once in a very great while. He would be gratified to learn that just yesterday a "living wage" legislation passed by the Santa Fe City Council was upheld by the District Court. Immediately $8.50 an hour must be paid by those businesses within the city which have 25 employees or more. One wonders how those working at firms with less than 25 employees will feel if their wages do not also rise. The cost of living in Santa Fe is at least 20 percent higher than the national average, and of course the vast service/tourist workforce is very poorly paid. So perhaps this new living wage law will prove beneficial. Maybe.

An extremely rich cultural menu looms this summer for Santa Fe. Rather impressive. Ongoing is THE RUSSIAN SUMMER, treasures from the household of Nicholas and Alexandra. I have not yet seen the exhibit but will do so shortly. There has been considerable negative commentary from individuals who seem quite knowledgeable about things Russian, particularly from the Tsarist era. Over the public head, I should say, and quite likely not relevant. The next controversy seems to be *Fahrenheit 9/11*, which thoughtful commentary recognizes as "over the top propaganda" designed "to get Bush outta there!" Well, if that is accomplished I will be most pleased. But one does have to wonder at the inaccuracies and distortions that evidently Mr. Moore employs for his purposes.

My friend Michael Moore, "Old Man Moore" of Victor, Colorado, passed away quite suddenly a few weeks ago. He had been in poor health, but a long decline was expected rather than a sudden exit. I was thinking of making a short trip to Colorado before I go East, but without Mr. Moore to visit quite a bit of the impetus for going has been diminished. I do enjoy Colorado Springs and

Manitou Springs. Actually feel much more "at home" there than I do here. One at times feels uneasy and oppressed in this "adobe Disneyland."

◆   ◆   ◆

7.6.04
Santa Fe, NM

The following haiku were submitted for the Buckaroo Ball ticket contest.

1. The Texas Zephyr,
   Whistling through dim prairie dusk.
   Someday, Darla—us.

2. Saddle leather creaks.
   All day dusty cattle pass.
   Thoughts of a cold beer.

3. Desert New Year's Eve.
   Our neighbors twelve miles away.
   We hardly know them.

4. Out by the ranch gate
   The old truck sits, out of gas.
   Ranch hands laugh—who cares?

5. All day stacking hay.
   The old dusty barn a tomb
   Of some rancher's life.

6. Mr. Moore reflects,
   Western face a thousand stories,
   In ranch house mirror.

7. Sudden mountain wind
   Brings unwanted smell of smoke.
   The old fear of fire.

8. From ranch house porch
   Mr. Moore stares—all that land,
   Not his—bank took it!

9. Barbed wire cuts and smoke.
   Grass fire, bouncing truck, cold beer.
   Hear distant thunder?

10. Giant clouds rising
    At edge of prairie distance.
    Time to wander on.

11. Sudden desert storm.
    The old familiar sage smell.
    Thoughts of absent friends.

12. Soft Texas twilight.
    Darla swinging on the porch.
    Distant train whistle.

13. A lonely windmill
    Spinning in the prairie wind.
    Place called High Lonesome.

14. The old ranch house creaks
    In hot desert wind rising
    In the lonely dark.

15. At Gold Valley Ranch
    Bud and Tom had no last names—
    Just desert drifters.

16. This night wind lonely.
    I could ride Northwest, or North.
    Looking for my home.

17. My name is Ben Gay.
    An old cowpoke, ride Old Dan.
    My hat is your fan.

18. The Great Western Night.
    Dim light glows from line camp shack.
    Old man drunk in there.

19. I sense distant jazz
    Outside the ranch house like cats
    Clawing to get in.

20. High desert sage smell.
     The old sadness comes with dusk
     In The Great Basin.

Did not win—stupid little (non-haiku*) ditty won.

*Haiku = 5 lines, 7, then 5 … as you probably know.

◆   ◆   ◆

I offered the following two episodes to the Coors Brewing Company for possible advertisements representing the extremes of diversity. I never heard from them. I think that their level of sophistication was not quite up to appreciating what I had suggested:

1. It is a brutally hot day somewhere in the South. A race riot is going on, and from the struggling black and white crowds great clouds of dust are rising. There are cries of anger, pain, racial insult. Axe handles rise and fall. It is quite a scene.

And from this struggle emerges a giant white man, bearded, in denim overalls. He is sweating mightily. and carries an axe handle in his left hand. With his right reaches to a back pocket to extract a red bandanna. "Whew, hoss!" he exclaims to a fellow combatant in a camo outfit standing next to a large cooler. "Beatin' on them coons' haids all morning makes a man mighty dry!" The camo man smiles, reaches in the cooler, gets out a bottle and holds it out, saying, "How 'bout a Coors Light, bubba? Just the thing after a race riot …"

2. Some distance away a giant, muscular black man in a track suit with gold chains is wiping his glistening head with a towel handed to him by another bald-headed black man. The first man says, "Hey, hey, mah man. Kickin' those honk-ies' asses on a hot day makes a man mighty dry. How 'bout a Coors Light?" The second man reaches into a tub of ice, saying, "Comin' right up, brotha. Coors Light. Just the thing to ease racial tension." Both men laugh.

3. At the end of the afternoon all the actors, white and black, and the film makers, are sitting around a picnic table. They are drinking Coors Light, laughing and slapping one another on the back. The mood is very convivial.

4. Voice over: "Coors Light, satisfying and refreshing. Just the thing to relieve racial tensions …"

◆   ◆   ◆

(HORNBECK?) DOWN AND OUT IN BOBODIALASSO

Definitely no place to be! Not at all! Down and out in Bobodialasso, second city of the former Upper Volta, now Burkino Faso, with its forty miles of paved road. Where I was stranded, down to a few lousy centimes. Well, not quite—but that situation was not far off. Where the locals danced nightly in the town square to the backfiring of a two-cycle engine. And where no one at all gave a shit about my Historical Atlas of Oklahoma ...

The situation was not encouraging. It engendered more than just a vague feeling of unease. I had failed in the countries of West Africa to secure exclusive rights for the distribution and sale of Pluto Water. I had not sold a drop of the damn stuff. No one was interested! The trade ministers with whom I had met were all big beer drinkers, and to a man they had indicated that there was absolutely no need in their countries for the white man's weak and insipid Pluto Water. They had acted insulted! More than once the notion occurred to me that if I had left the keys to a Mercedes on their desks a sudden and vast need for Pluto Water might have miraculously arisen. Then again, perhaps the simple truth of the matter was that in all of Africa no one gave a shit about Pluto Water! Whatever—I had reached a dead end. My African partner had for some weeks been "unavailable"—I was told that he was in France, "on important business." Our joint bank account had mysteriously been cleaned out.

The heat in my room at the Hotel Terminous in Bobodialasso was stifling and oppressive. Everything in the room was coated with a film of dust blown in from the desert. I was soaked with sweat and felt feverish and unwell. I picked up my Historical Atlas of Oklahoma, hoping that the old familiar names would ease my troubled mind, but the small print blurred before my eyes. I felt lost and alone. In desperation I decided to venture out to the local café/bar and spend some of my dwindling funds on some cold pombe, the local palm beer, forgetting that the pombe was usually served lukewarm. Perhaps, I thought, some event or idea would materialize that would suggest a way out of Bobodialasso.

The café was dimly lit and stuffy, smelling of beer, tobacco and unwashed bodies. Ceiling fans revolved slowly in the smoky air. Many of the fan's paddles had rusted or rotted away, leaving spindly rods rotating uselessly, occasionally dropping blobs of grease on the tables or patrons. No one seemed to care. This café was the only place where one was likely to run into Europeans, such as there were who washed up in Bobodialasso, usually as bad off as I, or worse. I noticed Klaus sitting at a table with many empty pombe bottles, an over-flowing ashtray, and the sticky remains of many crushed insects. I had spoken to Klaus a few times before, but did not care for him. Klaus beckoned for me to join him, and with a sense of foreboding I picked up my pombe bottle from the bar and walked over.

Klaus was a sallow German who had evidently been in Bobodialasso, and Burkino Faso, for some time, pursuing vague enterprises. Whatever these were, they must have been profitable because he always seemed to have plenty of money, which he displayed arrogantly in large, sweat-stained wads. The locals didn't seem to like him, but at the same time they appeared to be respectful and somewhat fearful of him. Klaus had told me that he was an anthropologist, but his manner was not at all academic. Rather, he gave the impression of a mercenary, or smuggler. I had caught glimpses of tattoos on his arms that appeared somewhat Nazi-looking. Only glimpses, because he usually wore a long-sleeved cotton jacket over a dirty T-shirt.

When I sat down at the table Klaus reached over and pulled my head close to his. He was sweating profusely, reeked of alcohol, and his eyes glittered like those of a rat. His manner was overly friendly, conspiratorial. In his guttural and heavily accented English he whispered to me what I took to be homosexual obscenities. I drew back from him, shaking my head. I took a long swig of my pombe and stared at him. He stared back with a mocking grin. Then he grabbed my arm and said, "OK, OK. I got something else for you. One hundred dollars, for you. I got something all set up. In this village, not far from here, two sisters. Young girls, nice ..." He paused, clutching my arm. He seemed feverish, drunk. I took another swig of my pombe and watched him, preparing to get up and leave, not wanting to hear whatever it might be that he was proposing. But his grasp on my arm was tight and demanding. I did not want an "incident." He continued, "Young girls, ja, nice. The local chief, he say he want to get rid of these girls, they have bad magic. We can screw them all afternoon, and when night comes we decapitate them, for the chief. He boil their skulls down for us, as trophies. I videotape the whole thing. There are people in Europe pay big money for such tape." I was shocked! I stood up and looked at Klaus in amazement. How could he even consider such things? All I wanted to do was sell Pluto Water, and here this crazy fool was trying to drag me into witchcraft, or worse! I stood up and shouted at him, "You're insane, man, that's evil! You've been dreaming too much of Buchenwald and Auschwitz ..." Klaus suddenly lurched to his feet and faced me across the table, I could sense silence in the café as all eyes were on this altercation between the two white men. I felt extremely uneasy. Klaus's eyes were wild and he was waving a large knife in front of me, which he had pulled from beneath his jacket. He shouted, "Fuck you, American shithead! You are weak! You are nothing! America is all through! I am strong! I can tell these people to EAT

YOU!" Crazed ravings! But dangerous—the knife! I had anticipated something like this and was ready. Quickly I smashed my heavy bottle on the top of his head. The bottle did not break. Klause collapsed back into his chair, the knife clattering to the floor. I smashed him on the head again. This time the bottle shattered, and Klaus's head fell forward into the overflowing ashtray. There was a heavy silence in the dark café. Then an enthusiastic burst of applause. Someone at a nearby table shouted, "OK! OK! America number one! NUMBER ONE!" I raised my fist in what I hoped was a display of power. "Pluto Water gives GREAT STRENGTH!" I shouted, "NUMBER ONE!" Then I strode toward the door and burst out into the evening light. The last sunlight was almost blinding. I stood there in the steaming heat for a moment, as if in a dream. What had I done? Insane!, I thought. I really have to get out of Bobodialasso now. Maybe Klause could have me arrested—God knew what contacts and power he might have. Then, from within the café came a strange rhythmic pounding and stamping. I turned toward the hotel and began to walk hurriedly. The pounding and stamping grew louder and more frenzied, joined by some sort of chant. I had the feeling that something was happening to Klaus, something bad, that his power—whatever it was—had been broken. That he was going to be dealt with—sternly. Perhaps terminally.

Back in my room I sunk into the chair by the window that looked out into the palm trees and the mud architecture of Bobodialasso, and into the shimmering desert beyond. My heart was racing, and my mind was filled with all sorts of wild thoughts: Oh, where is my Golden Coat? Where are the Sons of Eternity? I have seen the Fish King and the thousand sequined mermaids that are his dancing girls. Crazy stuff like that! I drank half a warm pombe quickly, then opened the Historical Atlas of Oklahoma. Soothing, familiar names jumped out at me, places where I longed to be: Chewey, Scraper (named after the famous Captain Scraper who came into the Territory after the Civil War), and Titanic (indeed named after the Great Ship—two years after it went down!). How I wished to be in the Everlasting Hills of Oklahoma and not in this end-of-the-world shithole of Bobodialasso! I imagined that at any moment the door of the room might be kicked down, and drunken policemen would burst in, under the command of Klaus. There would be vague and serious charges. Shit! I had heard of these things happening. I had heard there was an American in the prison in Ouagadougou, the capitol. Someone had said that his situation "was not encouraging." I worried that I was in very deep shit indeed. Then I remembered the shouting and stamping from within the café, and wondered if this might be somehow in my favor? I thought that it might be, but it was all so bizarre that I could hardly think straight. I clutched the Atlas, drank the rest of the pombe and opened another warm bottle. Outside the window the palm fronds stirred in a sudden hot, dry wind from the desert. I felt very alone and far indeed from Oklahoma. I should have stayed on my daddy's ranch, riding my pony over the plains, watching storm clouds blow up out of Texas and hoping that the OU football team would beat hell out of Texas that fall. I should have married Darla, had kids and gone to church. All that, things I thought I wanted to escape. I never should have come to Africa trying to sell Pluto Water, it was crazy! I had been talked into it by a Doctor Avis in Lisbon, some sort of business man who said it would make me enough money to retire on. I had invested my savings with him and his African partner, who had now cleaned out our joint bank account. Oh, what a fool I had been! And now I might be done for. What to do? I drank more beer, and must have dozed off in the hot winds from the desert, because I awoke with a start as the door to the room did indeed burst open. But there were no drunken policemen, no wild-eyed Klaus. There was only a single figure swaying in the dim light at the door, in a jilaba, clutching a pombe bottle and a reed bag with many clanking bottles. It was my neighbor at the Hotel Terminous—Darnell!

Darnell was a black mathematician from Berkeley who had come to Africa in search of his roots. He had wandered about the continent seeking "oneness with my people" with a certain good-hearted naiveté, and had finally fetched up in Bobodialasso where he had run out of energy, enthusiasm for "the brothers," and, most important, money. Throughout his travels Darnell had found that the Africans didn't seem to care much for his skin color, but viewed him with suspicion as a stranger. They were always hitting him up for drinks and money, and in his eagerness to oblige he had been reduced to the same state I found myself in—down and out in Bobodialasso. Darnell had lost his enthusiasm for dancing nightly in the town square with the brothers and sisters to the backfiring of a two-cycle engine. He had introduced himself locally as "Rasheed El Makin Rabazz." This had produced vast hilarity amongst the brothers, and Darnell AKA Rasheed had been puzzled and annoyed. One brother had told him, "Shit! You just a rich nigger from America. Buy me a Mercedes!" Another brother had said, "Fuck Africa, man! You stay here, you die of AIDS! Give me your passport and plane ticket, man. I be Rasheed or Darnell, whatever, go to America, yeah—Hollywood!" Darnell and I had had some good talks and a few laughs over all of this, but now he had grown tired of it all, trying to be a brother amongst people who were always trying to rip him off. He had become mightily tired of all of Africa, and he shared with me a deepening concern about how we would ever get out of Bobodialasso. He had come to realize that the racist and imperialist USA was in fact the place to be. He was very homesick for Berkeley, and was growing increasingly concerned that he might never get back there.

I motioned for Darnell to come into the room, and reached for my tape player and punched on the Bob Seeger tape. The song that played was "Those Hollywood Hills." Darnell took the bottles of pombe from his reed basket and arranged them along the window sill. Then he took a giant swig from the bottle he was holding and grinned at me. He appeared drunk, but not out of control. Before I could tell him about the recent events concerning Klaus, he said to me, "How come you sitting here listening to that shit, some white boy trying to sound like a brother? Man, you must be homesick. You got to get with the local shit, you know, the backfiring of the two cycle engine, the rhythmic clacking of the mirababa beetle." I told Darnell that just then what I wanted to hear most was Bob Seeger and "Those Hollywood Hills," James Taylor and "Baby, don't you leave LA, they got nothing down in St. Tropez," shit like that. "You're just as homesick as I am, Darnell, you just won't admit it," I told him. "You know and I know there sure as shit ain't nothing at all going down in Bobodialasso." Then I told him all about the stuff with Klaus, the incident in the bar, the stomping and shouting, my fears of arrest, all of it. Darnell looked worried, and held out one of the pombe bottles, "It's cold—well, cool, man. Drink up, and we'll talk about how we going to find a way out of this shit hole. You might be in some big trouble, you pound that Nazi upside the noggin like that. I hear he got big connections in what they call government here. Shit! Maybe your friend Lesley send her Lear Jet for us, that Commander in full uniform—impress the shit out of these bush niggers. Carry us away to Paradise—not some bullshit Muslim paradise, REAL PARADISE—LA! That's paradise, man—that town a motherfucker!" Darnell was raving like a crazy man. I had never heard him talk like that. He seemed to be slipping out of control. The heat, the pombe, the complete desperation of our situation! He raved on, "But shit! There's no place to land a plane in Bobodialasso, we're fucked! We got to steal a Land Rover from the Army—but there's never any gas in those vehicles. Oh man, oh man—what the fuck we gonna do?" Darnell rocked back and forth in the dim room.

We sat collapsed in the stark room of the Hotel Terminous and discussed our options, as if any of them were real. There was no sense trying to go north through Chad, because there was some sort of vague war going on there. We had heard that General Gigouni Oudadaiyee and his army of rural dissidents, backed by a company of French Foreign Legionnaires, was mounting a heroic offensive for the relief of Oum Chaluba, key to the Bodelé Depression. All caravan routes north were interdicted. There was no chance at all of getting through the vast and formidable Bodelé Depression. And to the south things were equally bleak. The subjects of the Lomida of Rey Bouba were in revolt. The Lomida was reported to have retreated into the cool gloom of his forty acre mud palace in disarray. It was said that strangers entering his lands were beheaded. And there was no sense either in trying to go east into Gambia, a place described in my guidebook as "the soil of the country is sandy and poor—except for the swamps." Darnell suggested that we try to get to Djibouti, on the Horn of Africa. "Why?" I asked in amazement, "That's the hottest place on earth, there's a vast revolution going on there, everyone's starving or killing each other." I could just make out the form of Darnell in the light from the window. He had slumped down along the wall in the shadow of the far side of the room. I did not make his posture to be that of a man full of plans and energy. "I don't know, man," he said somewhat weakly, "I just like the sound of it. You know, young man with a Horn. I know it's bad there, the worst. Maybe if we went there we'd look back on Bobodialasso fondly." He wasn't making sense. I had heard this sort of logic before in Africa, and it seemed to be the sort of thinking that moved one in wrong directions. "Strange logic, Darnell," I told him. "I think we should just concentrate on getting out of here, to Ouagadougou. Somebody in the capitol of this fucking country ought to be able to help get home. Is there a US Embassy? They'd help." Darnell got up to get another pombe from the window sill. "We ain't going nowhere if your Nazi pal Klaus gets the Man on your ass. I got to help you, 'cause black man and white man, it doesn't matter, the man in the street doesn't give a shit if we're bein' busted by the Man. We got to get out of the motherfuckin' country, get to Nigeria, that place that old white senator from the South called, on his trip here, 'The grand and glorious nation of Niggeria.' Ain't that a motherfucker?" "You're right, Darnell!" I told him, "That's the place. They got direct flights to New York from there. Now how we gonna get there?" I asked. Darnell stood drinking beer, his back to me, staring out into the palm fronds and the mud architecture. I could barely hear him say, "I don't know, I just don't know."

We sat in silence in the sweltering heat of the room in the Hotel Terminous. Outside the sun had sunk over the palms and the mud architecture of Bobodialasso. The god-almighty reality of our situation had sunk in, for both of us, though I was the one in possible trouble with the law, not Darnell. He seemed to feel that it affected him as much, though, and we were in this thing equally. A heavy, ominous darkness began to sink into the streets outside the hotel—there were no streetlights at all, and at night most of the buildings were shuttered—against "werewolves and evil spirits," we had been told. Not far off we heard some bursts of automatic gunfire, some shouting and the sound of breaking glass. The Bob Seeger tape had run out, and Darnell was passed out in a chair in the dark room. There was no more gunfire, only silence, then the call to evening prayer rasped from tinny speakers around the town. I lit the single dim lightbulb that hung from the ceiling—half the time it never went on, and I had to creep around the room with a flashlight that was rapidly fading since there were no batteries for it to be bought anywhere. In the weak light I could see that some huge beetles had invaded the room and were crawling aimlessly about. I was feverish from the heat and from the pombe, and I thought I heard the crisp sound of a jet airship whistling through the night sky. Hey! I thought—it's Lesley's Learjet circling overhead, her father the Commander in full uniform, steely-eyed and alert over the blinking controls, looking for a place to land. Then I remembered that there was no place at all to land an airship in Bobodialasso. I could imagine the Commander saying, "Fuck it! There's no place at all to put down, and fuel's getting low. I'm heading to Gabon. President Bongo's chartered this aircraft for a ride to Nice. Tell Lesley her friends down there are on their own …" And I imagined the gleaming Learjet banking and flashing away to the south in the magnetic African night sky, the silvery whine growing ever more dim in the soft heat.

A vast and ominous silence had settled over Bobodialasso. The wind had died away, and the town seemed swallowed up into The Great African Night. The eternal night and vast darkness that had covered everything for half the day since the beginning of time, a fearful darkness from which people shrank and sought shelter and safety. A time of great beasts hunting. A time of evil spirits. A time of FEAR! To thrust back this fearsome darkness people had taken to the drinking of pombe, to mad, stamping dances, to dancing even to the backfiring of the two-cycle engines—all things to keep the mind occupied and to keep the ominous darkness of the Great African Night at bay, to keep from thinking of the terrible things that happened in the night.

Suddenly there was a commotion on the street outside the Hotel Terminous. There were men shouting. I went to the window and looked out. In the dim light cast from the hotel windows I could see what appeared to be a crowd of drunken men dancing in the street. They had long sticks and seemed to be poking at something. I leaned out and looked closer. It was Klaus, or the body of Klaus, and the men were poking at the body with long sharpened sticks, shouting and dancing about. The body was clad only in underwear and seemed obscenely white in the glow from the hotel's light, which was fading as the shutters on the lower story were being slammed shut by the manager—standard procedure when there were disturbances outside. I grabbed Darnell, shook him awake and dragged him to the window. He stared down into the street for a moment, then drew back and looked at me, shaken. "Holy shit!" he said. "They got Klaus out there. And the dude is through. They gonna carve up that motherfucker, have his head on a stake come morning. How come they done that? They must hate his ass! This go down over what you done in that bar? Holy shit!" I was as shaken as Darnell. I didn't know what it meant, or why it happened. "I don't know, man," I said. "I know Klaus wasn't liked, but those people were afraid of him somehow. Maybe when I put him down they felt his magic, or whatever, his strength, was broken, and they just went for him. I told you about that stamping and shouting I heard when I left the bar." Darnell just stared at me, shaking his head. "Whatever it is, it ain't good," he said. "These things have a way of getting out of hand. Whole town could blow up, us with it. WE GOTTA BUST OUTTA THIS PLACE!"

The disorder, the shouting, continued in the street. I leaned out to get a better view. I could see the men waving their sharpened sticks. The body of Klaus seemed to have been dragged away. Several of the faces turned up to stare at me. Then they recognized me and shouted things like, "Hitler dead! America number one! The white giant killed the Nazi! Pluto Water!" I felt as though I was in a dream, it was all so bizarre. Had I really killed Klaus? I didn't think so. I thought he had been knocked out, and those fellows in their frenzy finished the job. But if they thought that I—"the white giant"—had killed the Nazi—probably good for their morale. My head reeled. For some reason I thought of: "Flying into Los Angeleez, bringing in a couple of keys …," and of a gentle winter rain washing over Santa Monica, palm fronds rustling outside room 309 that I had occupied there at the Embassy Hotel Apartments ("Old World Charm"), no crowds of drunken men there shouting in the street, poking dead bodies with sharpened sticks, not yet anyway. I thought of the girls on roller skates there, wired for sound, gliding along the beachfront under a bright, clean and blazing sun. Visions of PARADISE! Suddenly Darnell grabbed my arm. He had a large metal bar in his hand, and was grinning. Evidently while I had been transfixed in my revery he had darted back to his room and retrieved the metal bar, which looked very business-like. "Keep this motherfucker under my mattress," he said, "Found it in back of the hotel. Figured I might have some use for it some day. And that day is here, my man. Come on! I know that shithead third-rate Nazi has all kinds of stuff hidden in his room, money, guns. I seen him driving a big Land Rover onetime, kept it locked in the shed behind the hotel, hidden. The manager told me about it—some advantage to being a brother, huh? Let's toss his room, man, find the Rover key, oh yes, my man, our time is at hand—this be one BUST

OUT SCENE IN OLD BOBODIALASSO!" We ran down the hall toward Klaus's room. The manager was there, key in the door. Evidently he had the same idea. Darnell clocked the man good, and we broke open the door. In a few minutes of mass destruction with Darnell's big pry bar we had guns, money, a bunch of other stuff—and a set of keys that we knew were good for only one thing—Land Rover!

The big Land Rover hummed westward across the desert, the thick tires biting into the desert sand. Darnell shouted, "We got the money to bribe our way over the border to Nigeria—damn, I keep thinking of it as Niggeria! Then we sell this Rover, and we get our tickets to New York, on to LA! We on our way now! 'Baby, don't you leave LA, they got nothing down in St. Tropez!,' Oh, thank you Klaus, and thank YOU, man, for knocking that Nazi upside the head!" I smiled at Darnell, who was driving with firm determination. I was thumbing through a leather pouch that we had taken from Klaus's room. Money—yes, there was plenty of money there, big sweat-stained wads of it jammed into the pouch. There had been a bunch of other shit, pictures and notebooks that I had thrown out. I didn't even want to think about what that evil dude had been into. It was over, and we were on our way OUT! Toward home! Bye, bye, Bobodialasso, bye bye, Burkino Faso! Yeah! I might try to write a song about this!

The border was no problem. The guards were mighty happy with some of the sweat-stained wads we offered to facilitate our passage "into the great and glorious country of Niggeria!" as Darnell confessed he was highly tempted to say to the border guards. I told him, "I think that they might not have understood the brother's attempt at humor. I think they'll dig it more in LA. Hey, hey, my man ..." We flew out of Lagos first class. Had been taken to the airport and whisked aboard the plane bypassing all formalities, which consisted usually of bribes to be allowed to leaved the country. All this had been arranged in a big limousine by an obviously influential man in a uniform—something Darnell had arranged, something about "an important brother." I was tempted to bring up the subject of Pluto Water, but decided not to push my luck. On the way to New York we had some drinks with a Chinese gentleman, a Mr. Wa, who said that he had "world-wide interests", and who, like us, was continuing to LA from New York. Darnell seemed to get on well with Mr. Wa, talking about computers and all sorts of stuff. He told him that I had the exclusive rights for Pluto Water all throughout Africa, and that I was thinking now of Asia, smiling as he enlarged upon all of this. Mr. Wa nodded gravely, saying, "Pluto Water, ah yes, I know Pluto Water. Very good. Number One! Recuperative powers, maybe good for Chinese people. Please have my card, both of you. Perhaps we do business. We talk in LA. I will be at Beverly Hills Hotel. And you?" Darnell looked at me, smiling. "The Embassy, in Santa Monica," I told Mr. Wa, "The air is good there, sea breeze, Recuperative, Like Pluto Water." Mr. Wa smiled and nodded. "Ah," he said …

Indeed, I ensconced myself in room 309 at the Embassy Hotel Apartments in Santa Monica and began to write down the story of my adventure in Africa. In another room Darnell spent much of his time hunched over a computer running programs for Mr. Wa. There were all sorts of projections for distribution and sales of Pluto Water all over the Far East, China, India, Southeast Asia—all of it. Pretty big! Mr. Wa, it seemed, had "important connections." Darnell had taken to calling him "The Man." He had not, so far, called him "a brother." We dined several times with Mr. Wa at The Beverly Hills Hotel. It was, of course, very good. But, sitting in that dining room I could not get out of my mind the image of the crowd of drunken men outside the room at the Hotel Terminous in Bobo-dialasso, shouting and poking at the white body of Klaus with sharpened sticks. I did not tell Mr. Wa about any of this—he would not have understood. Then, on the other hand, perhaps he would have. There was a lot about Mr. Wa that we did not know …

Of course Lesley's Learjet and the Commander were never sent to Bobodi-alasso; she never knew I was in any trouble there, or anywhere else in Africa. My postcards, if they ever reached her, had been chatty and upbeat. I never made any mention of the vague feelings of unease that dogged me as I attempted to sell Pluto Water. The Learjet has now been sent on an errand of mercy. It is on its way to Neosho, Missouri, to pick up John and Brinley and bring them to PARA-DISE. There is a big reunion planned, in PARADISE! Everyone will be there. Except Klaus. Klaus won't be there …

(The following image came to me one night in a dream. I think it was trans-mitted through extra-sensory perception:

The bleached and polished skull of Klaus is sitting on a stake in a village in scrub-land giving over to desert not far from Bobodialasso, where it had been delivered to the Chief in a polished ebony box. The skull glistens in firelight which holds back the heavy darkness of the Great African Night, while two young girls, sisters, dance around it. The Chief sits in an old French dentist's chair drinking pombe, occasionally pushing the ground with his foot to spin slowly around, watching the skull glistening in the flickering light and the shadows of the dancing sisters. He is listening to a Bob Seeger tape, "Those Hollywood Hills", on a tape player that had been delivered along with assorted other stuff in a reed bag. He stares at the sisters dancing in the fire-light, then says, "You girls get on in to bed now, hear! You done danced long enough 'round that third rate Nazi shithead's skull on a stake, done tried to bribe me to do you girls, now his fucking head there where it belong. What sort of fool he take me for?" The girls scamper in to bed in one of the thatched huts, and the Chief continues to sit contemplating the skull, drinking his pombe in the hot darkness, thinking about the two men, a white man and a black man—Americans—who had made off with all the Nazi's stash. Good for them! he thinks. What a bust-out scene in Bobodialasso! "Go to sleep, girls," he shouts to the girls in the hut. "You safe now!"

The Chief continues to sit in his dentist's chair, spinning slowly in the dying firelight. Maybe someday I get to America, he thinks, to LA! Yeah, those Hollywood Hills. He grins and drinks some pombe, then fires off an entire clip from a MAC machine pistol into the utterly dark and unforgiving African night sky. The two girls stir in the hut. The bleached and polished skull of the third-rate Hitler German shithead grows dim in the dying firelight. The Chief muses in the great dark silence. It had been an amusing bust-out scene in Bobodialasso. My people. This is where I belong—as Chief. No, it might not be good in LA, I might end up just another nigger in a doorway—I better stay here. And he loads another clip into the MAC machine pistol and fires it into the sky. Drinks palm beer and laughs, in the great darkness ...)

The Reunion was a disappointment. People were restless and disconnected. Too much, I guess, had pushed us in different directions. I went back to Santa Monica and walked the streets, thinking. I decided to let Darnell have my share of the franchise and profits for the distribution and sale of Pluto Water in Asia. He and Mr. Wa seemed to get on well. I wondered if he had called him "brother" yet, or "my man"? Somehow I didn't think so. Mr. Wa was too formal. He seemed used to power, to deference. I could imagine him, in former times, in an armored train somewhere in China, in command ...

One night I called Darla in Oklahoma. I told her that I was coming home, and that I had lost the Historical Atlas of Oklahoma she ad given me, somewhere in Africa where no one gave a shit about it—or if they did, it was because they were using the pages for toilet paper. She laughed, and said that she was sure it had served a purpose. Then she grew serious. When was I coming? she asked. There had been lots of rain, and the plains were green and the grass was tall. She couldn't send the Learjet for me because her daddy had lost it in a wager on a quarter horse last fall at Ruidoso Downs in New Mexico. I said that I would gladly pay my own way to fly to Tulsa, where I would buy a pickup truck and drive west to the ranch at Lone Wolf to take her out to dinner. One thing, though, I told her, some day, before we are too old, we have to take a trip to Africa, to a place called Bobodialasso. I want, I told her, to dance with you there in the town square, to the back-firing of a two cycle engine ...

I hung up, called a cab for LAX, then went down to wait for it outside the Embassy. Palm fronds were stirring in the wind off the ocean. I thought of Africa, then of Oklahoma ... Home!

PART FOUR

CONSTRUCTIVE

GENERAL SUTTER

Some time ago on a fine fall day I drove to the small Germanic town of Lititz, Pennsylvania, and had a rather bland lunch at the General Sutter Inn—across the street from a restored mid-nineteenth century brick building that had been the home of General Sutter and now is the Farmers & Mechanics Bank of Lancaster County. Idly stirring my chicken noodle soup I asked the young, plump Germanic waitress if she knew anything about General Sutter. "Not much," she replied, "just that he had something to do with the California Gold Rush." "When was that?" I asked. She thought for a moment, then said, "Oh, that was a long time ago." And wandered off. I suppose in her mind Lititz is better known for the local chocolate factory that produces "Wilbur Buds," rival to Hershey's "Chocolate Kisses." Or the Moravian Seminary and the girl's school, Linden Hall. The Inn had a few pamphlets about General Sutter and the Gold Rush, but they were pretty sketchy. Not too many tourists show up, and those who do come probably come to tour the Wilbur Chocolate factory. Or to shop for some local Amish crafts. They do not know much if anything about General Sutter.

On his vast land grant, issued by the Mexican Government in the territory of California, Sutter had hoped to discover coal to fuel industries he was planning. But, at the site of a sawmill he built on the American River his man Marshall discovered something else—gold! It was to be the ruin of Sutter. Eventually he lost everything, and in 1865, when the Civil War had ended, he gathered up what was left of his broken family, and announced that they were "leaving forever the accursed land of gold." Strong words, but equal to the bitterness General Sutter felt at the way he had been treated, how the gold seekers had grabbed, stolen, burned to the ground all he had. So he headed east and settled with his family in the prosperous Pennsylvania Germanic settlement of Lititz. From there he went yearly to New York to attend banquets of former Gold Rush pioneers, many of whom had grown wealthy and prominent. At the banquets there were always lusty shouts: "Three cheers for General Sutter!" There were some who remembered his kindness and generosity to those in need, such as the remnants of the Donner Party in 1846. But not so in Washington, D.C. where he also traveled yearly, to petition Congress for the pension that had been promised, that he felt was owed. Each year he was told it would be approved, but it never was. It was in that city that General Sutter died in 1880, having been promised one last time that his much deserved recompense would be approved. It was not, and the blow was too great for the old General.

Being thoroughly familiar with the story of General Sutter, I had a more definitive purpose than most for my visit to Lititz. Not only did I want to dine at the Inn, visit the brick structure across the street where the General and his wife had resided, but I wanted to visit General Sutter's grave in the quiet Moravian cemetery behind the Seminary complex. So, on the fine fall day, after the bland lunch and a visit to the bank, where nothing about General Sutter is displayed, I walked the few pleasant blocks to the Moravian Seminary. There, behind the buildings is the cemetery. Because, I suppose, that the General and his wife were not Moravian, their graves are off by themselves in a quiet, far corner of the cemetery, rather by themselves. The stone markers are simple, and bear no reference to any gold rush. I stood there for quite a few minutes, moved by what I knew of the General, how one of the greatest events in human history had overtaken him and destroyed him, how the man had sought coal not gold, how he knew that gold would destroy him—and it did. How Isaac Graham and the rough, uncouth Yankee mountain men who had stumbled into California in the years before the Gold Discovery had impressed the General as precursors of ones who would "take everything"—and did!

I walked slowly back to the Inn and the automobile, full of thoughts of the life and career of General Sutter. At least his name lives on in The General Sutter Inn, even if not many know or understand the significance of the man. I do, and that is what matters to me ...

He built a good sawmill ...

◆   ◆   ◆

When I was in Maine recently there was an article in the local paper about locals breaking into the large houses of "the summer people." I was reminded of a time when this was not so, would be unthinkable. Or at least so in my mind.

In June of 1963, on a thickly fogged cool day, Ted and I drove out to the peninsula in Penobscot Bay where sits the old maritime town of Castigne, a place of large summer homes and a few all year residents. We walked in the seemingly deserted town, and a way up the beach which devolved into fir trees. There were no summer people yet, and the big shingled houses loomed up in the fog, silent and empty. We walked in the damp woods and along the rocky shore. Suddenly, we came to a large house that was seemingly abandoned and partially in ruins. Everything was overgrown and falling down. Definitely abandoned, which was odd. Since it was wide open, and there were no signs or anything else indicating that we should not explore, we climbed over the rotting porch and entered what must have formerly been a large living room. There, leaning against the wall was a quite large and very beautiful old gilt framed mirror. It seemed in good shape, and we wondered why anyone would have left such a lovely item, one that would be of considerable value we thought. But, there it was, and none of our business. We left that damp and abandoned house, made our way back to the car and left Castigne.

On the foggy and little traveled road back to "the mainland" we were passing through a wide area of hayfields bracketed by a dark, ragged forest. Just then the old Chevrolet quit and I coasted to the side of the road. I knew the problem—it had happened a few times before, and was easily and quickly fixed. A loose wire on the engine. I popped the hood and began to tighten the wire with some pliers from my tool kit, reattaching it to its proper terminal. Ted stood idly by in the fog, keeping watch, as it were.

With my head under the hood, I was aware of an old pickup truck pulling up, someone getting out and saying to Ted in a very pronounced Maine accent, "You fellers need help?" I looked up and saw a lanky young man holding a tool box. I told him that it was a very small problem that I was familiar with, that it was fixed and the car would run fine. But thanks for stopping and offering to help, out here on this lonely road in the fog. He looked from me to Ted, determining us perhaps as "from away," but maybe not, because of the old car and our "rustic" appearances. Then he said he always stopped for broke down cars, was a mechanic, could get near anything going.

As he was saying this he glanced down at the front bumper of the Chevy and noticed the California license place. Staring at that, he said, thoughtfully, "California, eh? Henry Bell's out theh." Very laconically, as if California was Greenville up on Moosehead Lake, and we were from Greenville and might likely run into Henry Bell "theh." He wished us well, climbed into his truck and was off.

Later, that evening sitting around the cabin on Toddy Pond, listening to the loons, Ted cracked open two beers, handed me one, and said, "California, eh? Henry Bell's out there?"

Ever after in the Golden State, I kept an eye and ear open for Henry Bell. But never did hear tell of him. Maybe he went back to Maine. Back "theh."

◆　　　◆　　　◆

these Maine woods are still,
save for the wind
in the pines
and the lake waters
restless against rocks
we stand gazing north
with miles of emptiness
before us until
the coming and going
of cities the vague
struggles against
collapsing economic systems
are lost behind us.

these maine woods do not collapse.
                    ***
the brightness of your thighs
speckled with sand (speckled?)
boot-tracks in the snow
across the plains of Poland
rusted tangled heaps
of metal, blackened,
smoldering, and
frozen, twisted bodies—
what for?
I wonder.
Helmuth, Seigfried,
dead,
Ruth and Kathe,
dead,
thousands of others,
names unknown,
dead
What for?

The brightness of your thighs,
frozen, white,
traced with blood.   (blood blud bld)
(BLOOD: THE FLUID THAT CIRCULATES IN THE
PRINCIPAL VASCULAR SYSTEM OF MAN AND OTHER
VERTEBRATES, IN MAN CONSISTING OF PLASMA IN
WHICH THE CELLS AND PLATELETS ARE SUSPENDED.)

◆   ◆   ◆

Three dead men riding North.

I see
Them gaunt and lonely
Against a dull sky
And hear
The rattling hoofbeats
On timber bridges
As they
Cross swift, dark rivers
On their journey North.

They pause on a rise,
And in the quietness
Of the empty land
Their slow breathing comes
Like wind in dry grass;
With eyes pale as ice
They gaze across trees
To the distant South.

Then, as by a call,
They turn North once more,
Grim because they must.
Through tall trees they ride
In silence, hunched from
Sudden winds coming
Cold from the black woods.

Three dead men riding North.

◆   ◆   ◆

6.2.04, Santa Fe, NM

Dr. Avis called yesterday morning to inform me that from his internet search he learned that "Brinley MacLaren died June 12, 2002, in Tucson, Arizona." We had suspected that Brinley might be dead, but hearing it was something of a shock. Since I had so long put him out of my life because he had become an annoying and intrusive figure, I wondered what his life and last days in Tucson might have been like. A few years ago he came uninvited to visit Lesley, driving an old Porsche saying that he had "come into a bit of money." But he so got on her nerves and annoyed her that she told him to leave and not bother her again. None of us ever heard from him again. But I sort of felt bad about everything, and thought if we could locate him I might try to make some small amends. Hence the Doctor's internet search. Last night I ran across this bit of fiction that I wrote about Brinley a few years ago. I decided to retype it, to serve as a strange memorial to poor Brinley. For whom, I do not know …

We see Brinley in some God-forsaken, broken down, dusty when it is not muddy, Brazilian town way out somewhere lost in the Matto Grosso. He is in a sort of shabby bar-café, drunk in the white heat and steaming humidity of such a place, his white tropical suit stained and torn, a crushed Panama hat on his head at a crazy angle. Yes, he is fulminating in this primitive bar, many empty bottles on a rough table smeared with crushed insects—drunk and crazed, raving incomprehensibly to the other patrons who snicker and laugh amongst themselves. The untidy bartender hovers, obsequiously—"Another cerveza, Señor?" anxious for the money that this crazed gringo spends in his humble establishment. "Of course, of course!" shouts Brinley, "Many cervezas, for my good friends here!" He pulls out a large sweat-stained wad of cruzeiros. Some of the patrons nod and exchange glances in the gloomy recesses of the bar.

We are standing there, in the doorway of this stinking establishment, John Galey and I, sweating in that awful heat and humidity, staring at the scene of Brinley before us, wild and disheveled, at the end of the Civilized World, this awful town called Remata de Males, or Culmination of Evils. Yes, somehow it has come to this. We have come to rescue Brinley, but something has happened and now we are reduced to his level, trapped, unable to escape this wretched place. We are in the hands of Brinley, drunk and crazed, in some forgotten nowhere town in the vast swamp of the Matto Grosso. Yes, our fate is in his hands!

Brinley has forged some kind of a pact with the Devil, and with a drunken, corrupt Chief of Police in a stained and torn uniform who fawns over him and says things like, "I have nice young girls, Señor. Boys, too! Whatever you wan'. For your frens, too. Is much pleasure in Matto Grosso, no? We are much pleased, Señor Brinley, to be having your great attentions!" Brinley looks up at us with a foolish smile and bloodshot eyes rolling, laughs maniacally, then snorts and coughs endlessly. Finally he shouts, "You have come to rescue me? Ha! Rescue yourselves! We are doomed! This is the end of the earth, the end of everything. This is the END! END OF THE HISTORY OF US ALL!" He laughs wildly and snorts again.

Somewhere in the town we hear automatic gunfire, then a loud explosion—a car bomb? The lights go out. There is some shuffling in the café, the sounds of breaking glass. In the darkness the Chief of Police says, concerned, "Señor Brinley, you did not spill your drink? It is nothing, just the bomb of a car. Everything is under control." The lights come back on. Brinley is slumped at his table, his drink spilled and the glass rolling back and forth on the bed of crushed insects. He suddenly rears up and shouts, "Gold coins, you must put your fortunes in small gold coins, or else you will be ruined!" A fresh drink arrives at his table. The Chief of Police smiles broadly and says, "El Señor Brinley is very wise, he has advised me well. Gold coins, if I could only get some, they no rot. He is my great fren." Brinley beams drunkenly, takes a great swig of his drink, some of it spilling onto his stained suit. He laughs his crazed laugh and shouts, "There is no way out of here. This is the END! His Excellency Chief Alonzo is my very great fren!" He laughs again like a crazy man. The Chief of Police laughs like a crazy man. The patrons, the bartender, they all laugh like crazy men. The Chief of Police claps Brinley on the back, looks up at John and me in the doorway and says, "This the Matto Grosso. This where big things happen!" He looks around the room, then at us, and claps Brinley on the back again. He grins widely. "We all great frens," he shouts, "here in MATTO GROSSO!"

The lights go out again. We can hear Brinley laughing and coughing in the darkness. Suddenly there is a HUGE EXPLOSION! We find ourselves, John and I, lifted in a searing bright heat, our university degrees forgotten and useless. The blackened head of the Chief of Police rolls out into the dusty street, or is it muddy? Brinley and his stained white suit seem to be plastered in fragments against the walls of the bar. Then there is darkness. Our ears are ringing, so we can not tell if we hear Brinley laughing or not. It seems that we do. Coughing, snorting, then crazed, maniacal laughter, fading away.

And suddenly we find ourselves sitting in John's leafy back yard at 321 South Wood in Neosho, Missouri. It is beastly hot, and cicadas are buzzing. A moment before Brinley has been telling us for about the thousandth time about the need to put one's fortune in small gold coins, else face ruination! Night is coming on. We can hear the air horns of the Kansas City Southern freight trains as they whistle through Neosho not far from John's house. We are about to go to dinner at THE CORRAL OF GOLD, but we are puzzled, John and I—Brinley's chair is suddenly vacant where he had been sitting just moments before. We had felt a sort of searing white heat! Then I am alone. John is gone, too. He had been gone for some time, I remember. I sit alone, in the heat wondering where they have gone, those two old friends …

THE NORTH COUNTRY

It was late September when I set out from Santa Fe for Pennsylvania in the Ford Ranger. I planned to go by way of Northern Minnesota, the Upper Michigan Peninsula and so forth. A rather roundabout route, but one I wanted to accomplish. I was somewhat depressed and thought that perhaps being on the road would improve my mood. It did and did not ...

Heading north I stopped by Victor, Colorado, in the early afternoon to visit with Mr. Moore and to see if we might have a light supper in one of the Cripple Creek casinos before I headed "down the hill." I found him at the Victor Museum, gazing as usual out at deserted Victor Avenue. We chatted and he was amenable to closing up early—there were no visitors—for supper. He suggested that I run across the street and ask George to join us. George was a bearded, worldly sixty-seven-year-old fellow who had shown up in Victor and liked to hang around the museum and talk to Mr. Moore. He had done a good charcoal sketch of my father. I thought him a pretty good fellow. By Mr. Moore's directions, I found George in the squalid darkness of a boarded up building across the street. There was junk piled all around, dirty mattresses, the stench of two dogs, old food, body odor. I was shocked. George could barely rise from a pile of dirty blankets where he was huddled, clearly drunk. I beat a retreat and told Mr. Moore that George "would not be joining us." It was unsettling. Is that how things end up? What it comes to?

I opted to stay, as did my father when he first visited Colorado Springs in 1972, at J's Motel on North Cascade. It was run by a genial Hungarian, Josef, a refugee of the 1950s uprising, with whom my father got along well. I had always found J's reasonable and convenient. But this time there was something off about the place. Old cars, not those of tourists. Dubious characters, white men with long hair and beards, coming and going, or lounging about. Mr. Moore confirmed my feelings immediately later when waiting for me in the parking lot: "Welfare motel." It was quiet though, except for a loud crash at one thirty one morning. Josef said, apologetically, "Probably man in number sixteen, drunk. It's awful." Is that how Josef had to make it through the winter? How sad. No more J's for me.

It is a fairly recent phenomenon—people "sans place," living far from their places of origin, far from family or solid friends. Lonely, impersonal motel or hotel rooms. There is too much of the white underclass in Colorado Springs. Distressing.

I wanted to see what had happened to "the old crowd" in Manitou Springs. First, I had a haircut at Will's across from the Spa building. Still cheap at six dollars. Will is a sort of Mexican, very "Anglocized," been in Manitou many years. A fixture. He remembers Paul Burke, and me. Asked if didn't I have something to do with Cripple Creek. I told him I did once but no longer. Not a very distinguished haircut but a good local experience.

While taking some photographs on Manitou Avenue I was hailed by Mike Casey, whom I had induced to purchase my house up on Delaware Way. He now rents it out, being married and living in larger quarters. Told me he is on the volunteer fire department, and might run for city council. An Irish guy from Chicago, the sort of fellow my father would have said of, "a man you can depend on." We need Mike Caseys, to hold the line against decay.

As for other members of the "old crowd," the saddest end came to Andy, who was killed and stuffed into one of the pump houses in front of the Spa Building. The crime was never solved. Eileen is a success story, having separated from Big Eddie and married Wally Pollock, a hard working carpenter who has his head on straight. They have a nice house at the head of Manitou Canyon near the incline. Eileen told me that she had taken Little Eddie out of school and taught him at home, and that he is now in Denver working as a telephone salesman making $2500 a month and living in a luxury apartment. No drugs or alcohol, but Eileen says he still has a fixation on his over-age hippie failure father, who has yet to get it together. Probably an expression of resentment toward Wally, Eileen said. Still, a success story for that malnourished little boy who I found at 25 Ruxton (the apartments I managed for Ted Roberts) playing with a turkey carcass and a milk carton. Bruce Fanning I was told married a dull woman, but is still "a sleeze," promoting projects and going deeper in debt. And Eileen's good friend Kate—whom she thought was a lesbian—is married to an abusive man, highly dysfunctional.

I had coffee downtown with Leland Feitz, former Cripple Creek District Museum Board member and Director after me. He seemed in good shape for a guy in his seventies who has had "health problems." He spoke of hiking in the mountains above Manitou Springs. Leland had been very fond of my father, and they always had breakfast when my father was in Colorado Springs. We spoke of the Museum, how it is getting run down and not patronized now that gambling has taken over Cripple Creek. He wanted to see our old historical photographic exhibit put back up. But frankly, he said, he didn't think anyone cared all that much any more. My eroding links with my early days at the museum ...

One night while Mr. Moore and I were having dinner at the Ritz Grill in downtown Colorado Springs we heard a loud, and we thought unmistakable, voice addressing a couple in a nearby booth. Mike said, "David Justice?" I said, looking at the man standing there, that I thought so. When he had gone I asked the couple if that had been David Justice. They said that it had. I went over to the other side of the room where he had gone. He was with a group of people, voice loud and seemed drunk or crazed—or both. Later Mike and I went over to join him. There was one fellow there from the old crowd, a blond guy who grinned blankly. David Justice remembered us, vaguely, from his monthly parties in his Victorian house filled with antiques, always the first Friday of the month. I remember one of the women telling of having to put him to bed numerous times drunk and weeping. I also remembered the two lovely Hispanic sisters who used to attend his parties, and inquired. One dead, he said, car accident. He invited us to his upcoming big Halloween party. Mr. Moore said later that he might attend …

Photographer Harry Gray, who did such wonderful work for us up at Cripple Creek, seemed to have disappeared from the telephone book. That is always an ominous sign. I drove by his house and did not recognize the vehicles in the drive. They did not seem the sorts that Harry would have owned. So, is he "gone," or moved from Colorado Springs? He seemed too much of a fixture to move. I liked Harry, and his wife and shy daughter who accompanied him to Cripple Creek. I remember our good times and talks, and wonder …

When I had the MG I found a very competent mechanic in Colorado Springs to work on the finicky vehicle, who said he had been trained at the MG factory in England. Armando Palumbo, and his man Dwayne kept the MG tuned for the high altitudes. Armando's nervous wife manned the desk of the Conoco Station where the work was done. I stopped by to fill up, and there seemed to be all new people there. I wonder if I should stop back and inquire about Armando, or just let it go?

When Mr. Moore came down to join me for dinner at the Ritz Grill he brought a large carton of crime novels, "for my trip." When he left, after dinner and our visit with David Justice, I think he might have run into dubious weather up Ute Pass. I heard on the radio of heavy snow in the mountains above 7000 feet. I remember numerous times leaving Colorado Springs in perfectly decent weather and running into snow toward Woodland Park, deteriorating conditions up to Divide, and really dangerous ones on the eighteen miles from there up to Cripple Creek. I hoped that Mike did not run into anything like that in his old Subaru with its weak heater. Hearing near midnight that it was snowing heavily between Colorado Springs and Denver, I decided to wait around an extra day before heading into Eastern Colorado and then up through central Nebraska and points north. The next day was gray and drizzly, with signs of clearing, so I just visited the library, had lunch with my cousin Roland and his wife Lyndall at Giuseppe's Depot, took a long walk around Manitou, and spent a quiet evening reading.

In a lonely, impersonal motel room one has a real sense of having left things behind, of having moved into an unknowable world. I thought of the string of such rooms ahead of me on my trip, not with great pleasure. Something to be endured, spread across the Great American Night. Midnight news indicated that storm front was passing to the east. I hoped Mr. Moore got back safely, to his stuffed trailer with his two dear little dogs (albeit smelly!) I remembered my first experience in bad snow getting back to Cripple Creek in October 1972, my first year. I had been in Denver, and going up Ute Pass it began to snow, more and more heavily. It was touch and go getting to Cripple Creek. I was glad to stop in the Cottage Inn, not that the atmosphere was particularly agreeable, it was safe, a refuge, indication that I had made it. Then back to my cold cabin, to listen to the wind, wondering what I was doing there. Well, that was a long time ago, and I survived. There are a few who did not. Thinking about driving up through central Nebraska, a lonely spot on my map, I put aside a book of disturbing short stories by Ron Hansen, set in that milieu.

Looking around that spare, impersonal motel room I thought of the little treasures that we collect in a life time, to give our existences meaning, definition. I thought of the collection of such things that had been donated to the Sonoma County Museum when I was Director there. They had been the property of a single, retired woman school teacher who had recently died (in a room?) We called this exhibit "all the little treasures of a lifetime." Some found that touching. I thought of my father when I brought him back to his apartment briefly from the hospital, before taking him to the nursing home, of how his eyes had wandered over his things, all so neatly lined up. "My dear, dear things," he had said, tears welling up, "I never thought I would see my dear things again." It was touching. I thought of Meredith's dear, death things lined up on her bureau. Even my things. And then the "de-accessioning" of these objects, when no one really understands their meaning or value. They are just his or her "things." And things become as if they had never been.

It was gray, cold and overcast on the plains of Eastern Colorado. A bit depressing out there, particularly in that kind of weather. Almost no traffic. Turning north into Nebraska I seemed to leave civilization behind. Mile after mile of deserted two-lane blacktop, here and there a sandy road leading away to a lonely ranch. Good grass, though. Occasional pickups with men in western hats who waved. Most of Nebraska's towns are spread along the Platte River, where the railroad runs. I thought of driving through Northern Arizona one winter night and listening to a small Nebraska radio station giving an account of Holdredge playing Gothenburg in basketball. It seemed the most important thing in all that dark night, there in far-off western Nebraska. It probably was. I imagined the fans, who I could imagine cheering in the stands, the perky (I hoped they were perky) cheerleaders, the pale players of those towns I would never visit. Very American …

Wright Morris writes lyrically about his home state of Nebraska, his early, difficult youth there. He speaks of the trolley conductor in Omaha "reversing" the seats at the end of the run. I remember the same thing in Strafford, terminus of the Philadelphia & Western trolley line (the "pig and whistle"), the old (to a small boy at least) white haired Irish conductor in his dark blue uniform doing the same thing. Walking the length of the trolley car, grasping a seat in right and left hands and reversing them. Bang! Bang! Bang! That done, passengers were allowed to enter the car. Some things we never forget. It is that type of thinking that keeps a man company driving alone on a raw gray day through central Nebraska.

Into South Dakota I met up with an interstate, and drove east to Pierre, the state capitol, to take a motel room for the night. It had been a long day of great distance and loneliness. Pierre is a small city for a state capitol. I chose a motel advertising "breakfast" near downtown so I could have a walk around. It was still cold and raw, and most of the downtown was closed for the day. Rather lifeless. A west wind brought the smells of manure and fertilizer. The Missouri River seemed big! I had to get in the truck and drive a bit to find a restaurant, a chain place. Back at the motel an old man hailed me in the hallway, proclaiming "I'm drunk!" As if that were some sort of spiritual revelation. In my room I perused the telephone directory, as is my custom. Two Christian bookstores, no other. Two or so Hispanic names. A couple of physicians who were probably Indian. All the other names in the directory were European. So much for diversity in Pierre, South Dakota. I was surprised to find modern jazz on FM public radio. It was, I suppose, restful after the long day in the lonely Nebraska prairie and sand hills.

Reading Wright Morris, I was amused by how he would not engage in school yard games in Omaha, not wanting to get his only set of clothes dirty. I remember Phil Nalibotsky, a "tough Jew" and good athlete at school once slipping in the winter and getting mud on his trousers. A chauffeur arrived shortly with a clean pair for Phil, who was popular in athletics but did not socialize with the rest of us. His parents sat apart at football games and wrestling matches. Aloof, by choice. Wright Morris speaks of the "colored boys" in his school class pictures—"only eyes and white shirts visible." I remember that from Radnor High School pictures. Unfortunate …

Reading and listening to the most welcome modern jazz in that motel room my mind wandered all over the place, much prompted by Wight Morris' tales of his youth. I wondered how many people in Pierre were listening to the modern jazz? What were lives like there? Not like San Francisco, for sure. Or Colorado Springs even. Wright Morris wrote of a long ago girlfriend in Chicago, one that slipped away, "She was far and away the best friend this boy ever had …" He wondered what had ever happened to Dorothy. Lawrence Durrell wrote that "In the story of love the so-called 'right one' comes either too soon or too late." I think of my childhood girlfriends, sweet little girls one and all, or so I supposed.

Next day the sort of breakfast that motels put on, a collection of people who look like they have state or church business. Polite nods, the local paper, coffee and Danish. Then on north, under lowering clouds, scattered rain showers, endless wheatfields and not much else. Farm or ranch houses few and far between. I can see where the North Country can sometimes "get to a man." Coming south on the highway were the caravans of wheat harvesters. First pickups driven by women pulling trailers, then flat bed trucks driven by men, and finally the immense harvesters. All very business-like. Not much other traffic. Some ducks flying south under the lowering skies. Still thinking about my childhood girlfriends. Josie Reeves, Didi Walker, Missy Missimer, my "tom girl" friend Louise Rice. And, of course, Louise Woelper, she of the "love affair" (Her twin brother was so jealous!) We chalked declarations of our undying love on the rough wood walls of the loft above my grandparents' garage. (Years later I thought to photograph this for whatever eternal preservation.) Bare company for that lonely drive north through the wheat fields into North Dakota—my 48th state! Stopped for lunch at a downtown local restaurant in Jamestown, a place I had the feeling that had seen better days and where there were not many young people left. Substantial turn of the century (20th) buildings. The patrons at the restaurant were pasty, over-weight and not healthy looking. The food was hearty but bland. All part of a package. Let the buffalo have the great plains back!

I crossed into Minnesota at Fargo, ND, a place of seeming substance, at least relatively. Then turned north on a rain slick two lane road and entered what I took to be "north woods country" at a place called Detroit Lakes. The land reminded me of Sweden, flat, rocky, small lakes, the pointed fir trees under lowering skies. Very Nordic. I fetched up for the night at a Super 8 motel in Bemidji, which had a nice downtown but strip malls out of town like everywhere else. At the convenience store were some young Indians buying beer, looking very much like L.A. gang members, their "role models" I guess, but not very productive ones. In the motel room, still traveling with Wright Morris, I was pleased but not surprised to be able to listen to, on Minnesota public radio, a program of Emanuel Axe playing with the Minnesota Symphony. I don't think the Indian gang members had that tuned in! The people I saw in Bemidji—there is a college there—seemed better looking than those in North and South Dakota, more Nordic looking, fitter. My Uncle Charlie from Peru could not get over the "fat women" in this country. And he was not talking about the black women.

Wright Morris wrote about as a kid eating game birds on his uncle's farm in Texas, perplexed by the birdshot in them. I remember the same—the pheasants my grandfather shot that had bird shot in them when served at dinner. I remember my grandfather's canvas shooting jacket, with the plastic compartment on the back to hold his license. And his fine shotgun, which "disappeared" from the house at Strafford. I think my cousins took it—though they steadfastly denied doing so—got scared and hid it in the woods or something. That was about the time my fine canoe paddle went missing from the garage. Morris' memoir, WILL'S BOY, is quite wonderful and touching, I think poignant might be the word. Why did he never try to find Dorothy in Chicago. The loss of a lifetime. I remember Morris when he taught at San Francisco State.

I am hoping that the weather will clear tomorrow, but in the North Country that might be wishful thinking indeed. In a way this lowering gray syndrome is what I expected. Like certain aspects of Northern Maine, that country from Jackman to the Canadian border. We passed through that in this kind of weather. Same vision of ragged fir trees, bogs and narrow logging roads. Route two north from Bemidji the next morning was almost deserted. Not raining but gray and raw. Desolate country. A few really hardscrabble farms. Some raw towns, no signs of tourism. Signs for Indian casinos. Gambling is the hope of many an Indian nation. Perhaps a false hope, perhaps not. Who knows? Meyer Lansky said, "Gambling pulls at the core of a man." He would have known. And, I think, pulls us all down. Gambling attracts those too interested in money, greedy. Criminals are attracted to the gambling syndrome.

Not far from the Canadian border I headed east toward Ely. The land rose slightly and became more rocky, less thickly forested. I stopped in the no-nonsense town of Tower for a plain but hearty lunch. There was a large man talking loudly on the telephone in what was an almost "stage" Minnesota accent, full of

Scandinavian inflections. The patrons were older, plain people, without anima-
tion. Then, on toward Ely, a former logging and mining town, now given over to
being the headquarters of "the canoeing industry," as recreation is now called.
Entry point to the Boundary Waters wilderness region. Nearing the town was
evidence of the former mining days, slag piles and headframes. Off to the south
was the Iron Range, the Mesabi Range. Tough, hard country. Today Ely is a bit
fussy, with sporting goods shops, gift shops, art galleries. But beneath that lies the
old town, with boarded up buildings, many bars, working men's cafés, they are
still there. I took a room for two nights just out of town in a perfectly decent
knotty pine motel. In the Iron Range phone directory many Slavic or Jugoslav
names, some Italian and Irish. But lots of Slavic ones, ending in "ic."

As I drove downtown in search of a "working man's café" I passed two young
girls who waved at me and shouted "Hi!" I heard one of them say, about me, "He
looks familiar." Bored locals. I suppose that during the summer all sorts of young
men from elsewhere turn up to canoe or find some related employment. The
usual summer resort syndrome. Having no desire for teenage company I found
the sort of dining establishment that I was searching for. A plain bar/restaurant.
At the bar were some older men, retired miners I thought. The atmosphere
reminded me of Cripple Creek. The meal was hearty and satisfying.

Back in the motel I listened to an "Indian Nation radio station," reflecting
that up there the Indians seemed to have their own license plates. Lots of Pride.
But the radio station was filled with all sorts cultural BS to make them angry/
proud/frustrated—lots of incendiary and revolutionary implication. To what
purpose? Yes, the Indians identify with persecuted minorities, understandably.
But stoking anger and having people living with it seems counter productive. On
the other side of the coin, the young white people I saw in Minnesota seemed
clean-cut and attractive. Nordic, is a term that comes to mind. The young man in
the gas station in Ely was very helpful. He said that it was hard to make a living in
the North Country. I would guess so, if one did not have a good union job in the
Iron Range.

The next day there seemed to be a slight break in the weather, and I wanted to
spend time outside poking about. There were still lowering clouds and the temperature was about 50°. The leaves were beginning to turn, and above the firs and
birches one could see here and there a towering white pine, remnant of the vast
forest of such that were mowed down. They are coming back, however, slowly. I
drove out to the area where people start out for the Boundary Waters wilderness.
The path from the parking area to the Woods Lake launching area was one half
mile, rather a long distance I thought to trundle canoes and supplies. I thought of

those wheeled contraptions and wondered if they were used. The parking lot was surprisingly full, mostly cars with Minnesota license plates, but a few from Michigan, Wisconsin and Michigan. One Texas. Although far from optimum weather, there seemed to be quite a few people out on various expeditions. Canoeists, I think, are prepared to paddle and camp in all sorts of weather, days of mist and rain. A fairly rugged crowd. Not effete recreationalists. More down to earth. There was a large map of the Boundary Waters, a very expansive region. I could see that quite a few portages were necessary in the wilderness, some of considerable length. The portages seemed to be measured in "rods," a length given as 15 feet, or a canoe length. (The Maine Oldtowns were 18 feet. So?) There were notices for "canoe towing services," evidently to get on into the area between Canada and the USA with minimum strain. How that works I am not sure. (President Clinton) had the good sense to forbid motors of any kind in the Boundary Waters wilderness. While I was taking all this in a party of "hi tech" kayakers was setting forth.

I spent a couple of hours following a trail into the woods, along some small lakes with faintly rippled surfaces. It was perfectly quiet, and moss and damp smells reminded me very much of Maine. The woods were mixed birch and conifer, with, as I said, occasional large white pines. Somehow I did not have the feeling of remoteness and primitiveness that I expected. Perhaps far into the wilderness, where one can hear the wolves howling. But the scene around Ely seemed very much too organized and recreational. Not the ruthless seriousness of older days, when there were not so many people all doing the same thing. I imagined that during the summer months Ely got quite crowded. Unpleasantly so. I would prefer seeing the region in the fall, even under conditions like that day. A bit uncomfortable, perhaps, but with the right equipment quite tolerable. All those portages might be something of a nuisance, though. I would want to float and paddle only. If I came back to Ely it would be to stay in a cabin and take short canoe trips. I would have to know a great deal more about how everything works.

The next day was gray and drizzly. Ely seemed to have sunk a bit into its former self, a bit depressing. Perhaps the night before I should have gone into one of those old bars, had a few beers and soaked up some atmosphere. Talked to some of the old men, asked how cold it gets during the winter. But, I was glad that I had not done so. Breakfast in the working man's place. Hearty and good. A few canoers, and some old men staring morosely into their coffee cups. Retired miners. Thinking about Ely, it rose in my mind as a pretty pure place, the canoeing types good people; they would have to be, to make all that effort to enjoy wilderness and solitude. I could see myself venturing into the Boundary Waters Wilderness.

An early start southeast toward Lake Superior and Duluth. Road bumpy and the air windy. Rather cool. Region thickly forested, with small lakes and ramshackle resorts here and there. Nothing fancy. I stopped at one lake and had a bit of a walk in the woods. Then on to Lake Superior, which surprisingly was a great disappointment in the gray weather. Lots of traffic on the road bordering the lake. If they were excursionists I don't where they were headed. At Two Harbours was a huge industrial complex, evidently taconite (iron ore) processing plant, docks for loading ships, etc. Unsightly but providing needed and good paying (one hopes) jobs, which seem in short supply in the North Country.

Driving south Lake Superior seemed forbidding, cold and raw. Coming into Duluth there were substantial stone mansions with iron gates along the lake. The homes of the elite. There must have been money in Duluth, from the Iron Range, railroads and shipping. The city seems larger than 90,000. Lots of substantial buildings in the big downtown, with interesting Victorian architecture. Quite a few buildings on the side streets boarded up. Many businesses closed on a Sunday. I saw a scruffy looking black man entering a marginal bar, one or two others lounging nearby. After all the North Country they looked somewhat out of place. The large harbor area was all fancied up, for tourism and other visitations. Rather nice and quite interesting. The largest grain elevator in the world sits ready to load ships with wheat and corn from the Dakotas, Montana, etc. Also large facilities for shipping iron ore and taconite pellets, in those wonderful Great Lakes ore boats (the Edmund Fitzgerald!). The Corps of Engineers Museum was very well done and quite interesting. There were lots of Sunday visitors, families. I saw a large ship's sign board, "Percival Roberts, Jr." From an ore boat, no doubt. Ted Roberts' great grandfather, President of the Pennsylvania Railroad and board member of U.S. Steel. A staff member very kindly provided me with a copy of a photograph of the vessel and some pertinent information, which I will present to Ted. The whole Duluth Harbor syndrome was most interesting.

Superior, Wisconsin was not interesting. Rather drab and down at the heels. From there I headed across the southern portion of the Upper Michigan Peninsula on Route 2. Mostly thick forest with occasional towns that had nice old downtowns (not thriving) and very ugly outskirts, gas stations, car lots, fast food places, all that stuff. As my mother said, "A century of ugliness." The Upper Peninsula poured forth copper in the 19th century, but most of the riches went to Boston and New York, Detroit, too. The miners, mostly Finns and Irish, were ill paid and not well treated. Industrial accidents were common. Today the Peninsula is hunting and fishing, some retirement in spite of the extreme cold. Not much in the way of earning a living. The towns showed that. I think that the Peninsula, or U.P. as I think it is called, was a more interesting place before the Mackinac bridge made it accessible. Those who live there may think differently, though.

On to Escanaba, which I remembered from 1957 as a pleasant and prosperous town on the lake. Along the way were many signs for Indian gambling, which sort of depressed me. In the towns were long haired, tough looking young white men, many in camo outfits (was it bow hunting season?) I saw several trucks loaded with cardboard cartons containing snowmobiles, perhaps headed to Duluth or Marquette, Michigan, and towns in between. These are considered a nuisance by environmentalists, but a source of great recreation to many in Snow Country. About the only sign of any economy was a very large Champion plant in Iron Mountain on the Wisconsin border. On the outskirts of Escanaba I chose the Hiawatha Motel, thinking the name suitable. The clerk asked, suspiciously I thought, and looking out at the truck, "One person only?" Used to being cheated, I guess. The motel was OK, but not in an area where one would want to walk around (safe but dull). At the motel I perused the U.P. telephone book. Almost NO non-European names. One or two Hispanic, two Chinese restaurants, of the doctors one Indian, and of the dentists, all European names. White man's country. Except for the Indians, of course, of whom I gathered there were quite a few. The usual Nordic and Slavic names, with numerous Irish. I noticed a fair number of listings for "supper clubs," a Detroit syndrome (gangsters.) And of course, many gun and sporting goods stores. One can learn a lot from the telephone book.

On the way into town there had been a sign reading "Downtown Escanaba—150 businesses await you!" Well, that was where I was headed the next day to find that local café where a good breakfast would be served and there would be some local color. I found just the right place, across from the court house. There was what I took to be a table of attorneys and prosecutors, other functionaries, local business men, and in the booth behind me a sporting goods store owner was exhorting his staff to "move snow mobiles out!" All very small town American, and satisfying. Good breakfast and coffee, too. The downtown seemed to be fairly healthy, in spite of big box stores on the outskirts of town. There seemed to be a good spirit trying to hold it together. Before leaving town I drove to the nice residential section of substantial house looking out over the lake, something I remembered from that long ago visit. I wondered what life is like in Escanaba, Michigan.

The drive over to the Mackinac Bridge is quite pretty. Nice vistas of the lake, sandy coves with pines. A good, clean environment, nature not compromised. The bridge over the Straits of Mackinac is an impressive piece of engineering, and no doubt deeply satisfying to most if not all the residents of the U.P. I imagine there are those who would prefer things without the bridge and all the people it brings. But, there it is, and over it I went. I have always wanted to stay at the hotel on Mackinac Island, on which are permitted no automobiles. But now I will not, and for a rather unusual reason. That hotel, and the others like it back East, have always been staffed in the summer by nice college students, young women in uniforms as waitresses, etc. But at the hotel on Mackinac, no longer. The management has hired Haitians, the cheapest possible help they could find. I resent and dislike this intensely. Not that I am blaming the Haitians. No, it is the fault of the management. The island and the hotel I think certainly would have been better without the giant bridge looming over it.

I stayed to the west shore, or the Lake Michigan side as my destinations were the resort towns of Petoskey and Charlevoix, which I had heard about for many years. The first I came to was Petoskey, a charming collection of Victorian structures with a handsome and vibrant downtown. Very much a place of money. Leland Feitz had told me that I was going to like Petoskey. "An all white town," he said, meaning the buildings and architecture, not the people. But there was that, too. There was a certain style of architecture that I think has come to be associated with Petoskey, having its origin in the mansions constructed at the turn of the 20th century by the lumber barons of the U.P. Gas lights downtown. But, overall my impression was that the place was just a bit "fussy." Sort of like La Jolla, California. Along the shore to Charlevoix were some gated communities, in the "Petoskey style" and looking very, very exclusive and expensive. There was not the settled New England feel to any of this. Too much new Chicago wealth.

Charlevoix was another matter. Much more of a real town feel, quite low key. Nice old, well kept houses. Unpretentious downtown with stores carrying useful things. I had lunch in a very nice, simple café with wholesome good food. There were two thin blond women lunching—they had that urban, rich look—who ate about half of what was on their plates. The waitress was attractive and friendly—she might have been the owner. I liked Charlevoix. There were some handsome yachts in the harbor, which was connected to a large lake that extended inland. There were some nice homes in pine forests on bluffs along this lake. As I drove inland there were well tended farms and apple orchards. Lots of burly men in pickup trucks with camo outfits. Definitely bow hunting season. A distinct redneck feel. A reaction, I presume, to social conditions in the Michigan cities to the south. I would imagine more people drifting north for a "more wholesome atmosphere."

As I got on the interstate and headed south the radio forecast rain for that night. My destination was Toledo. Almost all the cars were large American makes. Bumper stickers reading, "WAKE UP AMERICA—BUY AMERICAN!" Naturally. As I grew closer and skirted the industrial, or perhaps former industrial, centers, there was more traffic and I suffered a growing sense of unease to be entering urban America.

I fetched up at an Indian run motel in a nondescript area of interchanges and low rent housing in the south part of Toledo. It was just a convenient place off the interstate to crash. I had a sort of dinner in a Mongolian barbecue. It was not good. The patrons looked marginal. After all the good clean air of the north country, the greasy cooking smells, the curry, the exhaust and traffic noise, was hard to take. I slept fitfully and when returning the key in the morning stumbled upon an angry black man shouting at the Indian clerk/owner. There was a welfare syndrome to all that, unsettling. Rain was forecast for later that day, but I would be on turnpikes and figured I would be in St. David's by 5 or 6 P.M.

The truck ran smoothly, and had been comfortable for long stretches of driving. The Ohio Turnpike is boring, the Pennsylvania somewhat less so because of the variety of the country. In the mountains of central Pennsylvania the leaves were definitely turning, but as I approached the east summer was very much still holding on. Green and humid. A lot of traffic as I exited at King of Prussia, but a relieving of pressure as I drove up the narrow roads to St. David's. The dark cloud at the beginning of my trip had lifted somewhat, but not entirely.

◆   ◆   ◆

EASTERN EUROPE

People these days in England look for the most part like Americans—that is, informally and poorly dressed. Here and there, just, one might see someone of the more formal and I should say genteel world of times past. All of Europe is that way, France perhaps less so. The cell phone is more in evidence in Europe than it is here. Seems to be some compulsion to be talking on one all the time.

Eastern Europe, particularly Slovakia, is a very different world, strange, wild and somewhat primitive. Intriguing. Prague was a disappointment—too many tourists, even at the end of October. I much preferred Budapest, a real and beautiful place. Some of the Czech countryside greatly appealed to me, rolling hills with stands of dark fir, tight little villages, Quite pleasant. The food was "peasant style" for the most part, especially in the provincial towns. The people are friendly and "unspoiled," whatever that means. There were no tourists about in the smaller towns. People seem fixated on Prague, which is party town numero uno. For young people—Mecca of decadence, if that makes any sense. If we were under 30 we would probably have loved it. Paris is Paris, but parts of the Right Bank are showing signs of wear, that is excessive tourism of a not particularly elevating type. Around the Pompidou Centre especially. The Left Bank, where we stayed in an eccentric hotel, still maintains its "Frenchness"—very much so. All sorts of odd little shops, antiquarian and otherwise, cafés and good restaurants, and people who actually LOOK French rather than some melange from all over the world. Then it was on to Southampton and the vessel to bring us to New York Harbor. Yes, the Statue of Liberty is a sight!

We flew Chicago-London-Prague. Picked up rental car at the airport and immediately got out of town. Headed to our first destination, Olomouc, a provincial Czech university small city of 200,000 to the NE of Prague. First part of the trip was on the "freeway" that runs to Budapest and seems to be carrying a great deal of Europe's motor truck traffic. And cars speeding at 90 mph, or more. Meredith commented on the graying sky, the ridges of small mountains, the isolated towns and villages, what she called "those pointed trees" (meaning firs), and thought the countryside "looked kind of medieval." It did not look modern. We reached Olomouc about four o'clock, and found the place to be quite fascinating, the inner parts of the town a maze of narrow streets and ancient, Eastern European architecture. Some had said that Olomouc is a miniature Prague without tourism. That it did turn out to be, but initially we could not find the hotel. It was on the map clearly, but one way streets, pedestrian only streets, all sorts of stuff frustrated us. No one spoke English (odd for a University town) and there were no street signs. And of course, the Czech language is to English speakers incomprehensible. Finally we found a central square where we could park, and set out on foot to find the hotel. It was in the old city, which was not that big but a warren of small streets. Finally I found a young student who did speak English, and his directions got us to the hotel. Then we found that the car could get no closer than a block away, so we dragged out heavy bags (I had to take the car to a garage four blocks away.) The hotel, "best in town," was small and rather plain. There was a cute girl at the reception desk, and she informed us there was no lift. We had to drag our bags to the room on the second (European first) floor. We wondered if we had been infirm how we could have managed. Probably would have gotten a student off the street and paid him. The room was OK, nothing fancy.

I went out for a walk. It was rather cool, almost cold, and gray. Northern. The townspeople and the students all seemed rather Teutonic looking. I could see immediately that this was a "real" place, not set up for tourism. The main square was most interesting. It even had a clock similar to the famous one in Prague. It was on the town hall, and all the buildings on the square had that distinct Eastern European look. There were some restaurants and a few coffee houses. I got back to the hotel and found Meredith napping. I went downstairs and discovered in the back of the hotel a rather lively bar, with a tall straw-haired waiter out of some existential film busy serving up foaming steins of beer on a tray which he balanced most dexterously. There was a dining area and I asked to "see menu."

It was all incomprehensible, more or less, but I sort of got the gist of it. I went to retrieve Meredith who said she was tired and not hungry. I explained that it was real interesting, and that she could have a small salad and some tea. She relented and joined me. I got a beer and she a red wine, without difficulty. The menu was another matter. She finally, with some help from the waiter who spoke a bit of halting English, ordered a small salad. I decided that in honor of our first night in Olomouc (we were to spend two) I would have "The Special." We would share a plate of potatoes. We found that all the menus would have potatoes, prepared many various ways. The Special turned out to be rather odd. A sort of breaded pork roll wrapped around prunes. It was quite filling and, I thought, appropriately "cuisine de la region." I should mention that there were no "fast food" places, or anything of that sort, in the old town, which had evidently been carefully cared for. We slept soundly, being of course quite exhausted from the long airplane journey. The hotel was quiet, since there were no cars passing outside.

The next morning I went down for breakfast, which was a little strange but filling. The same waiter from the night before was on duty, and he served me a "café au lait" as if he had been doing it every morning for the last thirty years. I then left Meredith to do her yoga while I took my camera to walk around and take photographs. It was still gray and rather cool. There were those narrow street cars running on some streets just outside the historic pedestrian area, and they always seemed quite full. The clock "did its thing" in the main square before a small crowd. I checked out a few restaurants, and returned to the hotel to meet Meredith. She and I found a wonderfully ornate Baroque church not far from the hotel—really a marvel! We then proceeded to restaurant on a narrow side street that I had seen early in my strolling about, but it did not seem to be open for lunch. We settled for a plain but nice café down the street. The patrons seemed to be "professional types," whatever that might amount to in Olomouc. The menu was again incomprehensible, but Meredith knew how to order salad. I ordered soup, and evidently what turned out to be TWO main courses. The young waitress did not seem to understand what the problem was, and summoned a young man who spoke some English. He remedied the problem by removing the dish I pointed to shaking my head. He realized that the foreigner had made some sort of mistake.

After lunch we strolled about some more, and Meredith agreed that Olomouc was a most interesting place. We stopped in a couple of shops, including a gallery where the young woman spoke good English and had some really unusual glass pieces. I told Meredith to wait, that Prague would be filled with that stuff (To her great regret, I was wrong—there was nothing like the things in that provincial gallery, which we were told were made in the remote mountains near the Slovak border.)

We checked out several restaurants for dinner, without much enthusiasm, but walking in a park near a cathedral late in the afternoon we came upon a U-shaped brick building with a courtyard fenced off with massive iron gates. Very Germanic looking, it gave the feel of a place where during WW II the Gestapo took people in who did not emerge alive. Sort of spooky, really. There were some galleries and studios on the side of this building, and on the ground floor a restaurant called GOURMET. We went in and found it most attractive. A pretty waitress—it was too early for dinner—showed us a menu which was in Czech, German and ENGLISH! It looked good and we booked a table for later in the evening.

When we arrived for dinner there was only one other party present, in another room. We were shown to a large table, and were able to order recognizable items, which when they came were of immense proportions. The two nice waitresses were friendly and attentive, but their English was quite limited. We wondered why no other patrons? The place was attractive, the food was good—perhaps the citizens of Olomouc did not eat out that much. Who knows?

Back to the hotel, a few drinks in the lively bar, served by the same lanky, straw-haired man, and early to bed. We would be off to Slovakia in the morning and I was looking forward to venturing farther Eastward. (I am going to have to speed things along here, or I will get bogged down in endless detail …)

The next day seemed to be clearing and warmer. We headed eastward into rolling agricultural country, quite pleasant. A few industrial towns of medium size, where the infrastructure seemed rather, shall we say, not quite up to date. One had a museum of an old Moravian village under groves of firs. We could see it from the road, and I thought it looked quite Scandinavian. Approaching the range of low mountains that seems to form a natural barrier between the richer Czech and the poorer Slovak halves of the former country of Czechoslovakia, the country grew more forested, especially the mountain ranges to the north. Descending the east side of this range we came to the Slovak border station, where we were waved through after a cursory glance at our passports. Coming down a long valley one could immediately sense Eastern Europe, the influences now from the East and the South. Slovakia used to be known as "Little Hungary" when it was part of the Austro-Hungarian Empire. The villages looked poorer, more ramshackle, there were old women walking with babushkas, men pushing hand carts laden with firewood. Not dirt poor, just poorer. We progressed along a wide river valley to Zilnia, the site of the castle and the tinkers exhibit that had been recommended so highly to Meredith. But that would have to wait for a day or so. We wanted to reach our destination of Banska Bystriaka and get settled. Leaving Zilnia I mentioned to Meredith that the trucks on the road seemed to have Polish names, seemed to be headed north. We found we were on the wrong road, and turned around at what appeared to be a restaurant of some substance. One can usually find the word "pasta" on those menus, along with salad and a few other words that seemed to indicate something we were familiar with. The meal was filling and cheap, and soon we were back on our way to Banska, down long rather rural valley, and up over a very wild mountain range on a twisting road that was quite adequate. It began to mist and rain, and the temperature was at 5° C. as measured by the car thermometer. Coming into Banska was quite confusing, and the rain did not help. Once again we could not find the hotel, and realized that it faced a pedestrian only open space. I got out and found a man who spoke some English. He looked at my map, nodded and indicated a passage way and said something about "on right." I found the town square, a café with the name of the hotel, and finally the hotel through another passage way and up some stairs. The reception was on the second floor, the car would have to be parked quite a way off and our suitcases dragged through a muddy lot where dubious characters were standing around out of the rain. I reported back to Meredith and she said that place simply would not do. We decided to try the "high-rise" Lux Hotel south of town, described by Lonely Planet as "a communist era intrusion." We found it to be quite nice, and took a room facing north overlooking a park and the medieval spires of the town beyond. I returned to the other hotel and explained that "my wife was not well, and could not climb these stairs, etc., etc.," The young woman was most understanding and said, "Go to Hotel Lux, it best." After settling in at the Hotel Lux, with our view out into the rain and mist, we decided on an obligatory look around the town.

The rain was not heavy, so we proceeded with umbrellas through the park. Veering to our right and climbing amongst some stone ruins (which I learned from the guidebook were the remains of fortifications built around 1500 to repel the Turks—who seem to have been up to much mischief in that part of the world.) Nearing the buildings of the old town we came upon a collection of WWII armored vehicles, both German and Russian, preserved in some sort of memorial to the War. And, around the corner, an astounding sight—a large two-engined aircraft, painted camouflage with a large red star on the tail! All rather odd.

Because of the weather the main square was rather deserted, but lined with interesting old buildings. There was quite a bit of graffiti, which surprised me because the Czech Republic had been very clean and graffiti free. I gathered that there was less stability here in Slovakia. The atmosphere in the rain was not encouraging, so we returned to the hotel, to rest a bit and then have a drink in the lobby bar before dinner.

I have to comment that while modern and spacious, everything about Hotel Lux was just a bit odd. The lobby bar had only a few patrons, and there was a somewhat depressed aura pertaining. The dining room was extremely spacious, but only a few tables were occupied. There were two mildly attractive but stern girls in "peasant costume" as waitresses. The menu, thankfully, was in English and German as well as Czech. As we ordered, a jolly man in a tuxedo sat down at the piano and began to play rather out of date or perhaps Eastern European songs. A little girl from a nearby table joined him and together they played a bit of this and that. Then the little girl rejoined her family. The waitress, in her colorful outfit, was efficient and surprisingly good.

The next day it was still damp, misting and drizzling. I went down to breakfast and found an amazing array of peculiar items on the buffet—pickled pigs feet, herring in cream, stuff like that. Fortunately there was more normal fare, also. Meredith spent the morning doing yoga, while I read and went out for another walk. This time I explored further, inspecting in the medieval town square a peculiar smooth black obelisk—a monument to "the heroic Soviet Liberators in 1944." (Lonely Planet mentioned that this was to be taken down.) Some of the side streets were really Eastern looking, and a bit shabby. Of course the people were bundled up against the rain and coolness, so there was a determined atmosphere. Back to the hotel to get Meredith and venture forth for lunch. We found a place on the old square that called itself "Indian Summer," and whose menu had scenes of what appeared to be of the American West. The meal was quite uninspired. We went back to the hotel, and later I went for another walk with my camera. Took various pictures, and wandered aimlessly.

Dinner at the hotel again, this time without the piano player and the costumes on the waitresses. Very few patrons. One thing that we had run across that was different was the Slovak National Boxing Team, who were staying at the hotel. Meredith thought them "very tough looking, a bit scary." Like Russian gangsters.

That morning as I was preparing to go out for my walk I saw at the front desk a short older couple, and a taller younger man who was saying in English, "Dad, it's raining out there—I'll bring the car right out front." Hearing this I stepped up and said, "Are you folks from Pennsylvania?" They looked at me with some astonishment. The young man said, "Yeah, my folks are. Pittsburgh area. They live with me in Hawaii now." I told him it was an informed guess on my part, since so many Slovaks inhabit Pennsylvania, or did. He asked me where I was from in Pennsylvania, and I said near Philadelphia. He asked me, "You move back here?" thinking, I guess, that I was Slovak. I told him that I was just a tourist, and we parted.

The day was fairly clear, and Meredith insisted that we drive north to Zilinia and visit the castle where the tinkers exhibit was. So, we retraced our route through the mountains and north and west to Zilinia. We could see the large white castle on the other side of the railroad, but as usual had trouble finding a route to it. When we did reach it it was deserted. "Open 2–4 P.M." it said. So we retreated to the town square, found a restaurant and had a very strange lunch. My "spinach soup" had an ingredient that definitely was not spinach, and which stuck annoyingly between my teeth in long strings.

The castle, presided over by two plump, friendly girls, was indeed open when we returned. We were the only visitors in the rather chilly atmosphere. The tinkers exhibit was quite fantastic, and the other exhibits pertained largely to the noble family that had owned the castle up to WW II. There was the air of a "forgotten corner of Europe." On the way back we detoured into the low, forested mountains to visit the wooden village of Cicimany, where the log houses are decorated with fantastic white painted designs. This was a very interesting spot, rather remote and from photographs taken in winter, rather deeply covered in snow in winter. I bought a wild boar pin for my hat, and asked the girl (in some sort of sign language) if there were wild boar in the forests. She nodded enthusiastically, and laughed when I pantomimed pulling back an arrow and bow string. We found an interesting mountain route back toward Banska, and made a side trip in dark gloomy forest and winding road to a small town mentioned by Meredith's friend who had lived in Slovakia as being where he had seen women making lace. The place was an old mining town, quite isolated and deserted. There was a sign board in the park with photographs of a brown bear, a wolf and what appeared to be a lynx. I surmised that these animals were still to be found in those wild mountains, and that interested me.

That night we ventured from Hotel Lux to have dinner in the town, and ended up at a pizza restaurant that was uninspired. Some young people came in and out, and that was interesting, to see how they looked like young people anywhere. Pizza.

The next day we set off to Budapest, with a side trip to visit the older and smaller medieval mining town of Banska Stiavnica, which is a World Heritage site. This turned out to be a most interesting place, with wonderful architecture and winding streets. We toured the old castle, which had many exhibits pertaining to repulsing the Turks, seemingly a preoccupation in that part of the world. There was evidence of mining on the hills around, and several buildings devoted of museums or institutes of mining. Had we more time it would have been interesting to spend a night there, in one of the quiet old hotels like the one where we had lunch. First impressions always tend to leave one with notions of places that one would like to return to and spend more time.

Heading south toward Hungary the land grew flatter, richer, and the air warmer. I could see that "Upper Hungary" would have been looked upon from the South as a wild, primitive and hostile place. And perhaps still was … The Hungarian border guards took a bit longer with us that I thought necessary, but soon enough we were rolling through pleasant agricultural country toward Budapest.

I liked the feel of Budapest, the spacious parks, elegant if a bit faded mansions, the grand boulevard that we took toward the river and the bridge to Pest that would take us to the Hotel Carleton. We found the hotel this time with relatively little trouble, although again it was not quite as nice as we had been led to believe. Thoroughly comfortable and efficient, though, and in a good location. The vehicle went in a garage at the bottom of a slight hill, and we took an elevator to our rooms. That evening we climbed up the pathways and stairs to the Castle District and looked for a restaurant we had chosen. We finally found it on a dark side street, and as we were approaching a phalanx of what appeared to be body guards or security men swept out surrounding men in dark suits. All these got into a caravan of Mercedes and sped away with flashing lights. All rather intriguing. We figured that if the restaurant was good enough for those chaps it would surely do for us. And it did. Good food and a small band with a "gypsy violinist." The other patrons were interesting looking, citizens of Budapest rather than tourists. Descent in the dark but not fearfully to the redoubt of the Carleton Hotel, Swiss owned and quite efficient.

Breakfast the next morning was bountiful and good. The other guests seemed to be mostly German, with some Brits. Older folks. While Meredith did yoga I climbed walked north along a residential street. It was turning out to be a fine day, and I enjoyed the elegant old buildings with the occasional view across the river to the city of Buda, the heart of things. Two large American owned hotels were a blot on the otherwise lovely vista. Walking along I came to the large Hilton Hotel, supposedly constructed to blend with its older neighbors, But in this I felt, and Meredith later agreed, that it rather failed. One could see the attempt, but alas … I took a long walk around winding streets and returned by way of an elegant street once occupied by nobles, and still by fashionable people I surmised. I liked the feel of the Castle District. A few tour buses, but not all that many. One had the feeling that real people lived there and went about their business.

Meredith and I boarded one of those wonderful street cars that ran near the hotel and along the river. Earlier that morning I had an interesting experience as I rode that line to the north end and then back. I had not noticed the riders buying tickets, or any conductor collecting anything. I figured there was some procedure but it did not matter to me as I had the three-day pass from the hotel that was part of our "package." There were two burly young men in black leather coats who caught my attention, because they seemed to be getting off and then on again. When I got off at the stop near the hotel they followed me off, saying something in Hungarian. When I did not seem to understand, one said, "Ticket?" I showed my pass and they seemed satisfied. I surmised that they were plain clothes agents to catch people riding without proper paid fare. Interesting.

We went as far as the Gellert Hotel, a magnificent pile of architecture. Intriguing, but I felt we were better off at the Carleton. Better located.

Back to the Carleton, we decided on a motorbus tour of Budapest, something our hotel package gave us a discount on. We walked across the bridge and through a commercial area and a park with a grand cathedral until we found the office of the tour company, where we purchased tickets. Since there was some time we decided to try a wine bar that was on Meredith's "list" and happened to be nearby. It was a rather sophisticated little place, indeed for tasting or sampling various wines, but they did serve up an adequate and tasty lunch. There were three men with several bottles of wine at a table nearby, the types that one might say "had an enjoyment of life not previously possible under the dour Communists." Perhaps.

The two-hour tour was quite good, and covered all the interesting and important parts of the city. After the tour we walked over to the main shopping district and perused items in the store windows along a pedestrian only street. Meredith commented that Budapest was not "a fashion center," not at all up to date. I thought some things looked a little strange myself. Then some hot chocolate/coffee and pastries in a wonderful old café—very "MittleEurope." And back across the Chain Bridge—so called for the design by some late 19th century English engineer—to the hotel. That night a taxi back across the river to some restaurant "on Meredith's list." Modern, in an old building, obviously sophisticated, but not many patrons. We had a very good "continental dinner," and then fell into conversation with two young men at the next table. One was a young American, Harvard graduate, living in Budapest in order "to introduce and promote Hungarian wines in the U.S." He was being interviewed, as MANY wines were being sampled, by a young English chap who wrote for BUDAPEST BUSINESS, an English language publication. Meredith was most impressed by the young American, and the English fellow who thought I was English—from London? How odd! Taxi back to the hotel and early to bed, full of wine!

The next day—warm and pleasant—I once again walked in the castle district, along some streets I had not walked on before. Then went back, collected Meredith and we again made the rather steep climb up to the castle district. This time Meredith wanted to browse in what I shall call "A gypsy market"—a warren of stalls with all sorts of stuff for sale, some interesting and some not so. Meredith was entranced for reasons not entirely clear by a stuffed fox in a Hungarian hunting costume. The expression on its little face, she said. I advised that it was the sort of thing one soon tires of. She purchased paprika instead, several colorful tins. Then we looked at some Herren figurines in a rather fancy store. The idea was to buy something for our friend in New Jersey, Janet Hughes, whose house was recently robbed and we feared her extensive collection of Herren figurines was gone. As is often is the case, Meredith felt that we should cross the river to the main shopping district and find something "better" in the Herren main store. So we descended to the river trolley line and road north a restaurant on MY list, a rather modern place with a view across the river to the wonderful parliament building. Then we crossed the river and made our way through narrow and interesting streets to the shopping district and located the Herren store. To Meredith's dismay she found that the cat-like figurine we had first looked at was a much better piece than anything in the main store. So we rushed back across the Chain Bridge, climbed again up the many stairs and purchased the cat-like figurine just as the store was closing. Phew! The "gypsy market" was still open, and Meredith stopped by to see the little fox again. I was anxious for a café au lait in a nearby fin-de-siecle café with a view of the castle. Then down the stairs in the approaching dusk to the hotel.

That night again a taxi to another restaurant on "Meredith's list." This turned out to be TOM-GEORGE, a very hip and crowded establishment with good food, a good wine list, and excellent people watching, always an important ingredient of the dining experience for me. A pleasant evening, so we decided to walk back. Near our hotel we stopped in a very pleasant local pub, where we felt quite "at home." The bartender asked me, "English?" I nodded. Why not? Then, right across from our hotel, Meredith suggested we stop in another place "for a nightcap." This turned out to be two or three, as I fell into an animated conversation with a Japanese business man who spoke nothing I spoke. We had a wonderful time—he was quite drunk—and Meredith laughed wildly. Quite the international scene. Even the bartender seemed amused. Then, across the street and relatively early to bed. Which was a good thing because we had to leave early the next morning and drive over to the medieval village of Telc in Moravia.

We drove west out of Budapest under lowering sky, along the plains that seemed quite agricultural. We were on the "autobahn" that eventually led to Prague, but somehow we missed the turn and drove into Austria. We took secondary roads toward Brataslava to get back on the right road. Being in Austria was very apparent because the little villages and towns we passed through were simply immaculate. Quite a contrast. At the border we were waved through and were soon cruising along in a sort of mist toward Brno in The Czech Republic, where we would turn onto a secondary road to Telc. We came upon some sort of inspection on the autobahn, and were waved over by a very stern cop. I was driving and was concerned. He kept pointing at the front of the car and saying something like "problem." Were the headlights broken? No! They were not on, as must be the law in rainy or gray weather. Or perhaps all the time. Taking my passport he conferred with another office, then returned it and waved me on, after making sure that I had turned the lights on. Well, at Brno, or just beyond, we got terribly confused and seemed to be heading west, the right direction, but on roads other than the one we wanted. Close study of the map, however, remedied the problem and we were soon cruising along through very pleasant country under a lightening sky. Telc, when we came to it, was a rather small but quite stunning collection of fantastic—there is no other word—row houses around a medieval square. Picturesque does not do justice to this, perhaps the most attractive and interesting village in Eastern Europe. Of course, finding our way to the hotel was a bit of the usual problem. It had to be approached from the rear, through a maze of alleys, but it proved to be quite adequate if a bit odd. The beds were head-to-toe along the wall—an arrangement neither of us had ever seen in any hotel. Well—Eastern Europe has its odd charms. We wandered about in the late afternoon. There were two ponds or lagoons on each side of the village, and some other attractive buildings. Somewhere people seemed to be attending some sort of concert. There was faint music. Back in the square we happened to run into the only other people who looked like visitors. They turned out to be a couple from Los Angeles who were filming some sort of worldwide "project." (I never did figure out exactly what it was.) And a woman who lived part time in LA and Budapest, who was a sort of guide for this couple. We made arrangements to meet for dinner at a restaurant a little way up the road that had been "recommended" to them. A bit later we wandered up that way in the dark, found the restaurant which had no patrons but was run by a nice young man who spoke pretty good English. Meredith had a glass of red wine, and I a Pilsner Urquel, while waiting for "our new friends." We thought we saw them walking by outside, and wondered if we were in the wrong place. But, no, after a bit they joined us. The evening passed pleasantly but without any great moment. The walk back to the village was pleasant in the quiet Czech evening, touched with a bit of wood smoke. The village square and the hotel were absolutely quiet. In the morning I had a simple but adequate breakfast. The only other patron was what appeared to be a young Japanese man, who paid no attention to me. And then—no yoga for Meredith—on the road early for the fairly long drive to Karlovy Vary, the former Karlsbad, where the Grand Hotel Pupp was awaiting us.

The ring road around Prague was the sort of traffic nightmare that one wishes to avoid but cannot. It was a great relief to turn west toward the Bohemian Forest and the spa town. An hour and a half later we were there, lost in a maze of streets and unable to find the hotel. The usual routine. Finally I spotted a grand structure on a forested hill above the town and thought it might be the Grand Hotel Pupp. After several tries we reached this edifice and the doorman rushed out to greet us. I simply held out the map and said, "Wo ist der Grand Hotel Pupp?" He stared at the map, then pointed to the right and indicated down the hill. I caught the word "serpentine," or something like it. We descended into a small valley, and there at the head of the once elegant town of Karlovy Vary was the vast, quite elegant and splendiferous Hotel Pupp, where we were to spend three nights. We had been offered a very good deal, so while not cheap our stay was not outrageously expensive. Now, I say "once elegant" because while most of the 19th century buildings were well preserved, the shops at street level were filled with rather dubious, tourist-oriented material. And the people—well, they seemed to be largely Russian, seemingly on some sorts of package tours. Of course, Karlsbad was famously popular with the wives of the Stalin crowd, so perhaps some of this appeal lingers. We had been told that the Grand Hotel Pupp was "owned by Russians"—a hint of mafia there. The rest of the crowds on the main street seemed of German peasant stock. I was somewhat surprised. At the hotel, which was not at all crowded, things were on a higher plane. We ate, quite well, two nights in the grand dining room, as called for with our "package," and verified that it was the best place in Karlovy to dine. One night we went to the delightful small 18th century opera house to see "Marriage of Figaro," put on by I think an amateur company from Prague. Quite good, however. The opera was poorly attended—I suppose the Russians had no interest, or had no extra funds for the $40 tickets. The patrons looked like the old aristocracy of Karlovy. Quite an interesting assortment. One evening, when Meredith and I were exploring a side street we came upon what appeared to be a group of vagrants drinking. We stared them down, But Meredith said that she did not like their looks. On the next day that Meredith took the treatment—the full works—at the hotel spa, I took the funicular up into the wooded hills behind the hotel and had a long hike in the Bohemian Forest. It was indeed the sort of forest I like. Many coniferous trees and lots of beech. Very appealing. Finally, on a maze of trails I made my way down to the little valley that the town sits in, and back to the hotel. In time to join Meredith and go out to one of the old fashioned coffee houses that hung on. Hot chocolate and cakes. The next day we drove over to the other spa town on Marienbad. Very pretty drive through forests and one lovely town with a large castle that one could tour. Marienbad seemed, in places, somewhat run down, or rather not restored from decades of Communist neglect—if indeed that was what it was. Still, there were some pleasant old fashioned hotels, a nice restaurant where we had a pleasant lunch. But, on the whole, as they say, "The place needed work." I think the best thing about our stay in Karlovy was the very well run, elegant old world Grand Hotel Pupp. First rate, and well worth it.

The drive back to Prague was routine, on a pleasant warm day, but of course once we entered the heart of the city we could not find our way to the Hotel Pariz. There it was, right on the map, but this street was one way, that one did not go through. It was awful. Meredith was driving and getting very stressed. When we ventured down a street strangely devoid of traffic a police car sped after us and waved us over. The usual language barrier, but they had a young woman in the car who spoke English—was she an official interpreter in a city full of strange foreigners? I think so. We had ventured onto a passageway for trams only, but this was overlooked and she gave very explicit directions to the hotel. We finally got there, and were so stressed by the traffic and maze of confusing streets that we simply called the rental agency and asked that they send a man for the car. The extra cost was worth it. The Hotel Pariz was a wonderful if a bit faded pile of Art Deco, of which Prague abounds. The room was small but adequate—and at least it was quiet. We rested up a bit, and then went out exploring. It was a warm late afternoon.

The hotel was on the eastern edge of the Old Quarter, or tourist section. As we left the hotel and headed west toward the main square on a pedestrian only street I was immediately aware of excessive tourism. All the people on the crowded street seemed to be tourists, and the shops were definitely oriented toward tourism, that is, not distinguished but somewhat tacky. Reaching the main square, the one where the famous clock is, we found ourselves surrounded by groups of tourists of various nations. It was rather a disappointment, and not a pleasant syndrome in spite of the wonderful architecture and coffee shops. We found a main street that seemed more in tune with a normal city and looked for a restaurant on Meredith's "list" in order to make reservations for dinner. PRAVDA was definitely "hip and interesting," but they were full for dinner. Perhaps tomorrow night? Yes, at 8 P.M. So it was back to the hotel for dinner, which turned out to be surprisingly good and well presented. We were pleased. A coffee and aperitif in the cosy little bar after dinner. The other patrons, or guests, seemed to be some older Brits, a few Germans, and who knows? Decent looking people.

The next morning a fair breakfast was served. I went out for a walk while Meredith did some yoga. The tourists were out in hordes. There were many advertisements for sex clubs of all sorts, which I had not noticed in Budapest although Meredith reminded me that we had seen some. On some of the narrow, side streets away from the main square, there was some of that wonderful medieval atmosphere that I had been expecting. I checked out some restaurants that seemed to be more oriented toward "locals," and made mental notes. Then I came upon the wonderful Spanish Synagogue, and saw that there was to be a concert that evening. A very polished older woman was seated at a table in front selling tickets. She told me in very good English that it was a somewhat informal concert, with performers "on the way up." I told her that it sounded intriguing and would consult with my wife, but felt that we would come. Later that afternoon when Meredith and I showed up to purchase our tickets she was overjoyed. We had spent the day wandering about, browsing in shops, trying to avoid the tourists as much as possible. We found that the tourists tend to stay on rather predictable trajectories, mostly looking for things to buy. Anyway, when we showed up for the concert we found the Spanish Synagogue interior to be just marvelous in its intricate eighteenth century decor. Beyond description, really. Our fellow concert goers were of all ages and quite serious. Definitely not tourists. I was pleased. The concert was quite good. One had the feeling of the real culture of Prague and its music lovers. We got out just in time to walk a few blocks to PRAVDA, where we had an excellent continental dinner at fairly reasonable prices. Good wine, too. An interesting place, a good choice. After dinner we wandered around. There seemed to be many small bars packed with young people. And the crowds on the streets seemed to be people mostly under thirty, laughing and exclaiming as they went from one bar to another. Lots of pretty girls! Party town for the young set. I had heard that. Someone said that Prague in 2000 was like Paris in the 1920s. I don't know about that. Someone else said that there were gangs of British hooligans that flew in on cheap charter flights for "bachelor parties" and the like, and swaggered drunkenly through the streets, pushing people aside and occasionally engaging in "punch ups." The downside of all this international tourism.

The next day we walked quite a distance to have lunch at the sleek restaurant in the well known Frank Gehry building, the one that is all twisted around and leans over the street at a crazy angle. Quite unusual. The restaurant was rather sophisticated and expensive, and we were given a nice table by the window, looking over the river and up to the Castle District. Very pleasant. We lingered over lunch, and then made our way back to the hotel through a shopping district that was definitely "for locals." Meredith was not impressed with the articles in the shop windows. She perhaps had expected a bit more from Prague. Well, comparing anything to Paris is an exercise in realizing that nothing can compare. In the late afternoon we walked across the river to the Castle District, strolled about amongst the quarter of "little houses" that once housed the castle guards and families, but which are now given over to tourist shops and cafés. Not a real place anymore. We then came back on the famous Charles Bridge. Which was quite wonderful, the vistas and everything, except for the throngs of tourists and all the stalls selling postcards and other stuff. Meredith did buy a packet of small photographs from a young fellow who was himself the photographer. They were quite good. Somewhere later I saw a photographs of the Charles Bridge taken in the 1970s. There were only a few people, going somewhere.

We had checked out a few restaurants in our strolls, and had chosen for that night one that looked rather "bohemian"—that is, that it might have been in Greenwich Village or North Beach. Waitresses in black. That sort of thing. It was just about what we had expected. I think Meredith had looked at the menu in the afternoon and seen that they could provide a decent vegetarian dinner. Which they did, after a fashion. Part of the establishment was a lively bar, with the usual young people coming and going. Pretty girls. I was looking for "my friend," the saucy Czech girl I had met on the train from Venice to Vienna in 1972. I did not find HER, but there were enough "interesting pieces" that I could have reconstructed her, so to speak, out of all those pretty, young Czech girls. Well, back to the hotel, a nightcap in the little bar, and early to bed because we had a taxi coming at 5 A.M. to take us to the airport. We had to fly to London, change planes and fly to Paris. All because British Air does not fly direct from Prague to Paris. So once again we had to struggle through Heathrow airport along with what seemed to be people from every country in the world.

We arrived at DeGaulle aerodrome at about 11 A.M., and were shortly thereafter in a taxi on our way to the Hotel Universitie on the Left Bank in Paris, a fifty dollar ride. The outskirts of Paris seemed to go on and on, modern apartment buildings, and modern commercial and office space. All very moderne, and not very interesting. Then the "real" Paris began, the old buildings, the wide boulevards. We were deposited at the hotel, which was more funky than we had anticipated. The elevator, or lift, could barely accommodate two personas. We had to send it back down for the desk clerk to place our luggage in it. The room was small but did look out over a sort of courtyard. The price was OK, but not at all cheap. Paris is VERY expensive these days, and the fall of the dollar against the euro did not help. After getting settled we went out for a walk.

The Left Bank is, to me, the heart of Paris, and the people "real" French. It does not seem too touristy, and many of the cafés seem to cater to the residents of the area. We managed to locate a restaurant on Meredith's list, but were too late for lunch. We made a reservation for dinner at eight. A hip and trendy place, from the look of it. We managed a sort of late lunch at an outdoor café bistro down the street, where the theatrical waiter sort of took a liking to me because of my moustache. Perusing the shops Meredith saw MANY interesting things to buy! The clothes particularly interested her. We are NOT in Eastern Europe! she exclaimed. Dinner was quite good and well served. Modern cuisine. Good vegetarian stuff for Meredith. After dinner a stroll about the Left Bank, always busy and thronged with people coming and going from many restaurants and café/ bars. One evening we were amazed by what seemed like an endless swarm of bicyclists flowing along the Boulevard, a real spectacle.

The next day Meredith had an appointment to have her hair fashionably and "a la Parisienne" attended to. Something for the QM2, I think. I arranged to meet her and then we took the bus to view the very interesting and archaic museum of paleontology exhibits. Bizarre, but interesting. Then a lunch at a Vietnamese restaurant nearby, which was very much the sort of place for students. Filling, not too expensive, but rather basic. It was a warm Saturday afternoon. Meredith had some things she wanted to do, so I wandered over to the Right Bank. I was in for a surprise. The area around the Pompidou Centre has been more or less been blocked off for pedestrians, and the streets were packed by not very impressive looking people "from all over the world," Arabs and Africans predominantly. And sort of degenerate French punks. Plus a lot of bourgeoise looking tourists. I wanted to get away from there fast! Back to the calm "Frenchness" of the Left Bank. So that is what I did. Stopped in the café where the day before we had had lunch. The waiter greeted me as if I had been stopping in for the last ten years. "Where is the wife?" he asked. "Shopping," I replied. He shook his head, commiserating. "Oui, très dangerous," I said. He smiled at my French. Restored by the good coffee and the excellent people watching, I left to wander back to the hotel. The waiter called out a cheery, "Bonjour, monsieur." I made a mental note to stop in the next day if possible. Made me feel part of the scene, sort of.

We dined that night, rather late, at another of the restaurants on Meredith's list. L'Editeur was very French and very bustling. The food was traditional Paris, rich and bountiful. Not an especially good vegetarian choice for Meredith, but as she said, the French can always put forth a good plate of vegetables. And so they did. Strolling about after dinner, we stopped in the café Deux Magots for a nightcap and some people watching. I think in that atmosphere one can feel more of the traditional Paris than in that rather distressing scene around the Pompidou Center. Long lines at the Louvre, so Meredith opted for a lesser museum the next day, the Musee D'Orsay, which she said was most interesting. I did not join her there because there were lines sufficiently long to discourage me. I opted for walking in the Luxembourg Gardens. We were lucky to have fine warm weather the entire three days we were in Paris. It was strange that we had progressed from the cold grayness of Olomouc through progressively warmer environments, but in this we had no complaint.

Meredith took me to dinner on our last night in Paris since it was my birthday. We went to the rather showy restaurant Zinc, which was a bit of a mistake because of its theatrical nature. I found it passable, though. But not as "French" as Brasserie Lipp, where we had lunch that final day. Meredith thought we were being treated with some disrespect because of the "bad" table we were placed at, but I am not sure. I had Steak Tartare, which I was curious to see how it would be. Delicious, with a glass of house red wine—très forte!

A taxi was at the hotel at 9 A.M. the next morning, and got us to the airport in plenty of time. The flight across the English Channel was routine, except for the White Cliffs of Dover which interested me. Also, circling around Heathrow Aerodrome, I was interested in the landscape below. The housing was in clusters, with quite a bit of open space all around. Good planning, I think. At the aerodrome reception area there was a representative from Cunard as promised. A problem, though. Not enough room on the bus they had contracted for. A slight delay, and Meredith and I had our own private bus. On the way to Southampton I was impressed by the amount of open space we passed through. It was a nice day, a few clouds. It seems that England, and most European countries, control sprawl far better than we in the U.S. do. Right up to the outskirts of Southampton were expanses of rolling, chalky hills, quite a few groves of fir trees.

The town of Southampton seemed to be doing pretty well. The harbor area especially. The one thing that can be said about the QM2 is that it is BIG! REAL BIG! The procedure for getting aboard was not exactly elegant, but it was fairly efficient. ID photo cards had to be issued, which we were told would act as credit cards aboard the ship. The Cunard representatives were most polite and we were given a diagram to our suite on deck 5. Yes, a suite. We were traveling first class, and would be dining in The Queen's Grill, where evening clothes were required. Our suite was lavishly appointed. No port hole, but a sliding door to a sitting area. It was always too cold and windy to spend more than a short time out there. Champagne, wine and flowers were in our quarters, and shortly two young Asian men introduced themselves as the porters in charge of our little section. Anything we wished would be gotten or done, they assured us. This proved to be true. We polished off the bottle of champagne just before sailing time. When we heard the might blast of the ship's horn—from the original QM—we joined the other passengers on the many decks to observe our departure. It was just past dusk on Halloween, so there were fireworks on shore that added to the drama as we rather silently and smoothly glided seaward. Then back to the suite to prepare for dinner. The first night of six, the formal clothes were not required, but we still had to dress in what I think is called these days "business casual." Something like that. At our table in the rather elegant Queen's Grill were three other men. Les Atwood, a computer programer from Toronto, something of a nerd who had for some reason "been up-graded." Sid Griffin, a real charming 75 year old who was from Palm Springs and among other things had been a physical assistant to some famous Hollywood people, Gene Autry among them. He was a real ladies' man, and charmed Meredith. Our third table mate was Bob Murphy, a rather prim and reserved chap from Staten Island, who took offense when I asked if he "ever got into Manhattan." I apologized profusely and he graciously accepted. Bob was taking something like his 35th voyage on a Cunard liner in 12 years. He and Sid had left New York 30 days previously, had cruised the Mediterranean, and now were headed to home. These three proved to be courteous and interesting table mates, though Bob talked of little else than affairs concerning Cunard, the ships and various captains. Sid confided to us that after almost 30 days at the same table 3 times a day he "knew nothing about Bob and his personal life." Meredith was not able to pry much out of him, though she thought he was mysterious and interesting. Rather good looking and VERY well dressed. The meals in the Queen's Grill were as good as anything in Paris or New York, really outstanding. We had two waiters assigned to our table. Elizabeth, rather proper and very efficient young English woman. And Brian, an equally efficient Irishman. The service was quite formal, except that we were addressed by our first names. But not Bob. He was called "Mr. Murphy." Meredith thought he had told them to do so. I agree. Bob said that the proper English preferred the QE2, and rather looked upon the new QM2 as "The American vessel." Bob had sailed on the QE2 and said that it was totally formal. I think that he was simply checking out this new vessel. It took quite a bit of checking out, from the nightclubs to the fine library in the bow, to the health clubs including a Canyon Spa facility, and even a planetarium in the auditorium where various scholars from Oxford put forth some rather fine programs. One certainly did not lack for things to do on that floating palace, which cruised at sea at about a steady 21 knots. Fuel consumption? 29 feet per gallon! A couple of days out the ship began to creak and roll. The weather turned quite dramatic, and the seas rose to a category 4 (out of 5) with 50 knot winds. There was quite a bit of movement. At lunch one day there was a loud crash, and a serving cart went careering away. Meredith had some sort of "magic strip" on her wrist that prevented seasickness, and it worked. We noticed fewer of our fellow diners in the Grill, and surmised that perhaps they were not feeling quite up to the wonderful offerings. We ate heartily, however, and suffered little effect from the movement of the ship, which at times was considerable. Someone said that this was the worst weather they had ever encountered. Perhaps the Captain. We did several turns around the ship on deck each day and the wind and waves were most impressive.

The Captain's party was quite festive. By invitation only. Meredith looked quite smashing in her gown. My tuxedo—of mysterious provenance—passed muster. Later, at the dinner table Bob Murphy gave us a rundown on all the Cunard captains, their skills, personalities, etc. Our present Captain on the QM2 was a thorough professional and quite gregarious. The previous Captain, son of the original QM Captain, was more formal and aloof. One does not quite see a Cunard captain as a "pop figure."

Several lectures by Oxford professors, and an excellent presentation by Scotland's leading environmentalist, were very much appreciated. Meredith enjoyed the planetarium presentation, although I found such a facility a bit over the top. I enjoyed sitting in the library of the ship, with an excellent view of the waves and troughs that the ship was plowing through.

The weather cleared, then eased off as we neared New York. We began to sight vessels steaming in the same direction, although we invariably overtook them and left them in our wake, so to speak. I think we must have caused some excitement on those vessels, seeing the mighty QM2 steaming at 21 knots toward the port of New York. Almost like Titanic—although that might be "an unlucky" comparison to make.

We had been informed that we would be passing under the Verrezano Bridge at 5 A.M., and sure enough we did. It was not quite light, and the sight of the bridge with its strings of lights was most impressive. It seems that the QM2 was constructed so to pass under that bridge, barely. Staten Island, and then in the early morning light from our port side suite the sight of the Statue of Liberty brought a lump in my throat, or something like that. A sight never to be forgotten!

The Hudson River was quite impressive on a bright clear morning. Large buildings on the New Jersey side. There were helicopters overhead, and Coast Guard boats circling around. Tight security! The vessels seemed to almost dock itself. There were a few tugs hovering, but they did not seem to do much.

Breakfast had lost its elan. Bare minimum. Everybody was looking ahead to disembarking. The staff perhaps had time for a bit of Manhattan. But not much, since the vessel was due to said on its next excursion that evening. No languishing in port. Time is money, I guess.

The procedure for disembarking involved a bit of waiting, but soon enough we were on the dock to collect our large bags which we had placed outside the suite the night before. Bags were in position by suite number, and we soon had ours. We were in New York, after 5 days and six nights of luxury at sea.

One footnote: on the dock were porters to get the luggage out to where the taxis were waiting. These men were older, Irish—looking guys, with flat bed, four wheeled carts that looked about 100 years old. We hailed one of these guys, who piled our stuff on his cart and pushed it out to the line of cabs. $10 for this, and a $5 tip because we had been on the great vessel. These men were definitely an anachronism Some union thing, I figured.

As Bugs Bunny used to say, "That's all, folks."

◆   ◆   ◆

17.8.06
St. David's, PA

Lambertville, New Jersey, where I had a fine lunch with my old Haverford and Yale classmate, Dr. James Hughes, and his wife. Why Lambertville and not Princeton? Well, there is a very fine restaurant along the river and canal, Lambertville Station. Indeed in the old railroad building. With plenty of parking space, which cannot be said for crowded and somewhat tacky New Hope across the river. Or for Princeton, either, where one has to worry about time when parking in a rather out-of-the-way spot. One of course enjoys strolling on the Princeton campus, but not in the brutal heat of August. So, Lambertville it was.

Yesterday in town to see the excellent documentary on the songwriter/poet Leonard Cohen. After steak frites at the very French Caribou Café. A bit of an indulgence. I asked the waitress (pardon, the server) who very much resembled a Parisian waif all in black, "Will we be speaking French today?" She laughed and replied, "Most definitely not." "But we will," I told her—"Steak frites." Her cheerfulness only went so far, but some of it resumed as the meal progressed. Leonard Cohen I cannot comment on, since it is all too complex. Perhaps you know something of the man and his work ... I enjoyed the film immensely, along with the few others in the theatre.

In the meantime my current book "When Earl was King Neptune" is being published/printed at this very moment, and should be ready in about ten days. I believe I have mentioned my local scenes for the book, as indeed it is much focused on this locale and at least some of its people, past and present. I do not pretend that these efforts are anything much beyond personal indulgence, but I think that to some degree there is "redeeming social importance." Is that not what they say to elevate something above pure pornography?

As far as visits to Colorado are concerned, the "modest dwelling" in Victor was not mine, but belonged to Mr. Moore. So, with his demise I am bereft of both reason to visit Victor and a place to stay. Which, 1 should say, pretty much reduces the equation to zero. My cousin has offered me his place in Colorado as an exchange, but it is a former vacation cabin in the woods, in a location somewhat distant from either Manitou Springs or Colorado Springs, "Where the action is." So, each September, since the demise of Mr. Moore I have journeyed north to stay at the Foothill Lodge in Manitou Springs, situated on the bountiful creek which issues from the mountains above. This establishment is in the central business district, so I can walk to the Mountain Café in the mornings for the paper, coffee and a healthful bran muffin. I stay three or four days, as the cost is not great. The establishment is run by a Polish couple, the wife of which is of that attractive, Nordic Polish type that one sees in native costume adorning travel posters for that country. I am sorry to say that her two daughters appear to have succumbed to the obesity that seems to be attacking our culture. I catch up with some old friends in the region, forgo a visit to Cripple Creek as something from the past that does not have to be revisited. Then it is time to head south. Going north I take the scenic route through the mountains, but on the return it is the interstate that runs along the eastern edge of the mountains, over the plains which are here and there dotted with antelope. Not an unpleasant drive, if one keeps from thinking about the increased cost of fuel these days.

Yesterday, walking back from the station after my visit to town, I came upon two young boys selling lemonade at the entrance to a drive leading to the largest house in this area—an English style mansion owned by a popular Philadelphia TV sports broadcaster. It is usually young girls selling lemonade, a very American thing. These two lads were supervised by a very attractive young woman who I felt was not the mother, who perhaps had "more important things to do." As it turned out I was right—she was the "nanny" (a word I instinctively dislike.) She spoke excellent English with a slight accent. I asked where she was from and she answered, "Russia." Then, "Georgia, actually," probably thinking, correctly, that most Americans know little if anything about Georgia, the former Soviet territory. I am sure that has been her experience, so she was surprised when I said, "Georgia, the soft and temperate birthplace of Joseph Stalin. Known for its fine wines." I went on, as her eyes widened somewhat. "Of course, Stalin's problem was that he never got over being a Georgian. Toward the end he used to get drunk with his cronies in the Kremlin and sing Georgian folk songs." She, her name was "Tamari," wanted to know how I knew such things. I told her it was my business to know things. I told her to look me up on the internet, and gave her one of my cards advertising *Captain Midnight*. Which, incidentally, my friend Pam, the information librarian at the Radnor Library is reading "with intense interest," she says. She is the type of intelligent young woman who takes an "intense interest" in many things. She rows in a "dragon boat" with other women on the Schuylkill River. You will have to Google "dragon boat" if you want to know what that is ...

The *Philadelphia Inquirer* has recently been full of articles about the proprietor of Geno's House of Cheese Steaks in south Philadelphia, the son of Italian immigrants, refusing to serve people in any language other than English. Directed at the growing number of Mexicans in that neighborhood, who, evidently, cannot or will not make the effort to learn the few words of English necessary to place an order for a cheese steak. A somewhat widespread and resented phenomenon here in Pennsylvania, I might add. When in Mexico I can muster enough Spanish to order in a restaurant. Even in the Czech Republic I learned enough to order a meal. Most travelers do. So what is it about these Mexicans in South Philadelphia who cannot or will not make the effort to placate the owner of Geno's by using a few words of English to place an order? Why is this a problem? He says they do it deliberately, to create a problem and make the shop's employees speak THEIR language. I have heard this theory advanced before. Years ago Ted in Berkeley told me one time that he thought everybody in California "should be FORCED" to speak Spanish. "Whatever on earth for?" I inquired. His answer was so that we could communicate with the Mexicans. I told him that I thought it should be the other way around, that he was suffering from his immense load of white liberal guilt. I wonder if he came back to his nice home in the Berkeley Hills and found thirty Mexicans living in it, eating his food and so forth, if he would just shrug his shoulders and say that they were only poor people looking for a better way of life?

Los Angeles is a great example of diversity in the extreme. I have in my files an op ed piece from the *Los Angeles Times* a few years back written by Father Cliff Marquis, a well known and respected social activist in central/downtown Los Angeles. The piece in essence said (I almost quote exactly) "We must all shed our ethnic identities or this city will become uninhabitable." I believe that one can well imagine what the rest of it was about. Something that is not happening …

Having said all this, I am well aware of the role of Charles F. Lummis in advancing Spanish culture, etc. emphasize SPANISH, because that is significant. I wonder what his position would be today? Something to think about, and I imagine there are those who would say that he would be all for the wave of Mexicans entering the United States. Perhaps not illegally. On the other hand, he might have a few misgivings about the syndrome. He seemed more oriented toward what and who were already here (if you will forgive that awkward construction.)

I am off to take my old friend Jean Jarrett out for some ice cream. She is a bit older than I and is in declining health, She has sold her house in Strafford, built just up the road from that of my grandparents by her mother in 1940. Jean told me on the telephone that the people buying the house plan to tear it down and construct a monster house—a common phenomenon these days. She said that thought greatly depresses her, and I can understand very well why. Because I would feel the same way about someone buying this house in St. David's and tearing it down, as they very well might want to. They would be fools, because somewhere in the future a small house will be a great asset. But by that time these fools may have dragged us all down and under with them.

Took Jack on a tour of the Amish country to get him out and about. He is pretty much a city fellow, and was amazed at how much I knew about that country, its ways and people. Of course I had learned all that from Mr. Hoffman over the years. We stopped at the country store in Strasburg for ice cream, and on the way back swung by Mr. Hoffman's old place to see what if anything had happened to it. Found it looking better than he ever kept it. His old car was in the drive, along with a new van by the barn. But it did not appear that anyone was living there. On the way out I stopped at the farmhouse a half mile away, occupied by two young men, and learned that the children are hanging on to the place, for whatever reason unknown, and keeping it up. Mr. Hoffman's cousin from a neighboring farm, Gunnar Zorn—how's that for a Pennsylvania name?—checks on the place every couple of days. I think that the nearby Chester County Airport will eventually acquire the thirty acres—and that will be that. As we drove the back roads Jack kept commenting on the many fields of corn, how lush they seemed. Mr. Hoffman would have been pleased. He always said that all good things follow a good corn year ...

When I went to pick up my friend Jean for ice cream I found her much depressed, as indeed she had indicated over the telephone, Sitting in a darkened room, speaking so softly that I could hardly hear her. When I mentioned ice cream, she said that she would rather have a drink, perhaps several. That is not what I had in mind—but what could I do? So we found ourselves at the large and rather well set up bar of the restaurant George's, an off-shoot of the very posh Le Bec Fin in Philadelphia. Jean had two Gibson's, a rather dated concoction, looked at the other patrons and pronounced the atmosphere "cheap." I had to agree—East Hampton it was not ...

◆   ◆   ◆

Saturday, 12 August 2006
St. David's, PA

Here is a very vivid dream that I had last night:

We, me in one car and Meredith in another following, were driving north across what I took to be Oklahoma. The land was flat, the sky overcast, gray and greenish. I saw a tornado to the left, or west, a very clearly defined funnel, with a helicopter hovering front of it, at some distance, as if to monitor the tornado's path and to warn people. Meredith and I stopped our cars to watch this storm, then got out and conferred, talking about waiting for the tornado to pass in front of us and on to our right, or east. So that is what we did, waited, and then got back in our cars and continued north. There were other cars on the narrow road also headed north.

Suddenly I saw before us a large, brightly illuminated (by the sun), very colorful large bluff running at a right angle to us, or west to east. I thought this formation odd for Oklahoma, more like North Dakota or some other western state. As we approached this bluff the road began to descend to a very green canyon or valley. Part way into this valley I, Meredith, and the other cars suddenly came to a spot where water was flowing over the road. It seemed too deep and dangerous to pass through, and I put on my brakes sharply. My car slithered around and came to a halt facing up the hill toward Meredith and the other cars. No damage was done. We all got out to survey this scene of the water flowing over the road, and to confer about what we should do. We decided to wait to see if the water might recede to a point where we could get through.

While I was looking around, I noticed that at a point about a half a mile farther on the road was perfectly dry. I told the others that perhaps we could make it through to that point and then be able to continue (to what destination I did not know.) They agreed, but wanted to wait for the water to go down to a point where they felt safe to make an attempt to drive through. While we were waiting I began to look around, down into the valley or canyon. There were large, old Victorian houses along the road farther along, almost to the bottom of the valley. They were damaged, leaning at odd angles with broken windows, and had "For Sale" signs on them. It seemed quite odd—who would want to purchase such vulnerable and badly damaged structures? Looking at this scene I felt that the whole place looked ruined, doomed.

Then I heard Meredith calling that the water had gone down, that we could/should continue.

End of dream. Very vivid!

What does this mean? if anything ...

◆   ◆   ◆

22.9.06
St. David's, PA

Penn's Woods, where there is a touch of fall in the air—although a warming trend is predicted for next week. I have been here just under a week and have thoroughly settled in, as they say. I have outlined plans, museum visits, lunches, meetings with a very few select friends, films to see—all that sort of thing. (I was going to say "stuff," but remembering my grandfather's revulsion at the term decided not to.)

I have gone about my new book, *When Earl Was King Neptune*, promotion in local style. I have scheduled for January a program at the Radnor Library, co-sponsored by the Historical Society. I am to be interviewed by the "culture editor" of the local paper. And today I will be taking copies of the book to the bookstore in Wayne, "Readers' Forum," a most charmingly cluttered and disordered place but one that nonetheless has promised me space in the window with the notation "Local Author." Barnes & Noble was amenable to some sort of appearance, but I decided that between them and the library it would have to be "one or the other." So, I decided the library would be the best place. Mr. Dunk, who produces the internet syndrome "Global Province" (you would have to take a look at it to understand) indicates some sort of promotion/publicity, for whatever good it might do. So, that is the story as of now.

Yesterday was an exceptionally fine day, and finding that I had some mild business down Bryn Mawr way I decided to take one of my one and one half hour "strolls" about the lovely campus of Haverford College. Indeed, if I were producing some sort of major motion picture with a college theme I would choose the Haverford Campus. Less "busy" than the lovely Princeton affair. So, after passing by lake and woodland, I came out upon the expanse very lush and green athletic fields. A cross country running meet was being held, amongst the many colleges in this region, and the majority of the contestants seemed to be female—sprightly lasses all, even the Bryn Mawr "women," as they insist on being called. It was a sparkling, cool day, and dozens of these (white) college girls were running and gliding across and through the green fields, a "visual symphony" of mostly blonde ponytails twirling and pale legs flashing in the sun. Very American. Lost America.

I visit the Radnor Library to use the computer for email and sundry matters that can be accomplished on that machine. Like making reservations for the holiday period at a hostelry in St. Michael's, MD, a place of some interest and appeal on the Eastern Shore, which was, when I was growing up, known for its isolation, rustic charm and colonial towns. The Chesapeake Bay Bridge changed all that. But not completely. A strong preservation milieu has kept pressure to develop all and everything to a mild minimum. Still, there are occasional disasters here and there. One seeks to avoid them. As do I, having some knowledge of how to navigate that country. Mr. Hoffman and I made visits there to sample various crab and seafood luncheons. We also once stopped in a boatyard where he engaged several people in rather lengthy conversations about various nautical matters. Including reference to a rather rare species of wooden yacht that he had sailed on with a long past female acquaintance. Her father was the commodore of said vessel, and made Hoffman handy in tying off lines and the like. A slimmer Hoffman, with a shock of Germanic red hair, bronzed and hardened by salt sea spray. Well, Meredith I hope will enjoy a visit by the Bay, perhaps a short cruise if the weather is not too cold, and a sumptuous meal at the Inn at Perry Cabin, an antebellum mansion now given over to excess for the wealthy of the Washington, DC, area—and other places, one presumes, such as Philadelphia. She is still pining for a few days in New York—at the Yale Club of course, which she "just loves!" And which I greatly appreciate for is various amenities, including a wonderful and very restful library which I repair to while Meredith applies herself to yoga. There is no longer the crush at the bar in the evenings, wreathed in cigarette smoke, a la John Cheever, and the presence of women is definitively modern. Still, there is a lingering air of exclusiveness—which unnerved poor Dr. Avis with his complex of feeling that he does not quite "belong," at the Club. When arriving to have lunch with me and Meredith he complained that upon entering the establishment the doorman "rushed" at him, saying, rather rudely, he thought, "May I help YOU, Sir?" Ah, the old complexes die hard, if they die at all. John O'Hara suffered thus. I remember that when living in Princeton, rich and famous, he asked a friend to gather up some matches from the New York Athletic Club (where he was not a member) so he could have them lying about his house. A lovely young woman in Princeton who gave me directions did not, I think, suffer from any such sense of not belonging. Well, I am afraid that I shall have to humor Meredith with a day or two at the Big Apple. Dr. Hughes can arrange accommodations at the Yale Club.

Of course, all of the above involves considerable effort and planning. Already I worry about the train back to Philadelphia. Actually, it is cheaper for two or more to rent a compact vehicle and drop it off in Philadelphia. Followed, of course, by an expensive dinner. Meredith's "favorite," Le Bec Fin is now prix fixe of $138, but there is a "light meal" for $39. I fear Meredith will complain, "I don' wanna light meal!" We shall see. There is always the Olde City Tavern, where one can dine "a la Colonial." Chicken pot pie does not lighten one's billfold unduly. It is also a goodly and pleasant atmosphere. Of course, just a half block away is the newly refurbished Bookbinder's, which seems to be making quite a success of itself, particularly the sumptuous oyster bar manned by very serious looking older black men in immaculately starched white jackets. Worlds away from the City Different! Which is, of course, the point.

A barrage of noise outside. Men cutting and trimming the lawn. They spend ten minutes max doing it, once every two weeks. A bargain. One of the benefits, I suppose, of this flood of cheap Mexican labor—a benefit with a vast (delayed) price that one day not too far off will come due. But Americans live for today, and what matters most is the lowest possible price. Reference here to a book about the effects of Wal-Mart, "The High Cost of Cheap Prices."

Now, a break in this chronicle, to gather up my books for delivery, and then, down the street, a free lunch at Christopher's. I say free because I have accumulated enough "credits" with lunches past. Does keep me coming back, especially on Fridays when one is awarded "double credits." I don't think the Parisian restaurateurs go in for these sorts of "games." So, the temporary closing down of this machine, and off to other matters. Not sure when I shall get back to it. Spell of rain predicted for tomorrow morning, so perhaps then it shall be. I have correspondence from a friend in San Francisco. I cannot comment on his doings, but can only imagine them. I can visualize his neighborhood, but seem to have in my mind affixed it to the Castro (homosexual) District, which is quite "lively" in its own peculiar way. Farther east on Market I remember some interesting restaurants, a "revolutionist" bookstore where I would buy Marxist-Leninist tomes as presents to my father who had quite an academic interest in those things for reasons I was never sure of. He was a firm believer in Marxist conspiracies, Hollywood in his mind being a hotbed of them.

Am continuing this after lunch. The chap at the bookstore seemed rather vapid, but did say that the book would be in the window. Molly at the restaurant assures me that she will buy one. She can afford it—she owns the restaurant, which does a great business, especially on Friday evenings as it fills with slim, blonde young women—of which Molly is decidedly one, if a bit older. Lots of that in Wayne. Perhaps my friend Maurice the architect will purchase a book. People are always saying that but I have ways of finding out that they never have.

Checking email I find that my cousin Rich, from Novato, California, has sold his business of 20 years and has taken to the wilds of the shores of British Columbia to photograph grizzly bears and other wildlife. And also "to find" himself. He has established a blog, which Pam at the library assisted me in calling up. Actually, I found it rather interesting—his adventures in driving to Bella Coola on the coast of the Inland Passage to Alaska. Winter will be acomin' on soon—loud sing goddamn!—and I wonder what his plans are? As a young hippie he hitch-hiked all over the country, living by the advice contained in the—was it Abbie Hoffman or Jerry Rubin?—book "Steal This Book!" He said it worked, but did not comment on the ethics or lack thereof. More power to him. He made a success of his business and sold out to a large corporation when the American dollar could still buy something—except respect.

Will break my afternoon walk with a visit to the Anthony Wayne Theatre to see the Brazilian film "House of Sand." Well reviewed but will not be attracting much of an audience out here. That sort of thing usually plays at one of the Ritz theatres in Society Hill. Or at the Bryn Mawr Film Institute, which rose phoenix-like from the ruins of the old Bryn Mawr Theatre, born of the inspirations of a young film enthusiast, Barbara Goldman. She brings an almost "LA-like" enthusiasm for film to placid Bryn Mawr. But, with the proper enticements one is surprised how many intellectuals crawl out of the shadows on the Main Line. The "Main Line matron" type who was taking tickets the other day (a volunteer, no doubt) when I saw *The Black Dahlia*, was very literate and au currant. Refreshingly so. And, after the show a young, intellectual-looking black man, who works at the theatre, and I had quite a long conversation about the Black Dahlia case and the various books written on the subject. One never knows … Attached to the theatre, in a space that formerly sold comic books, is the rather sophisticated Café Seville, a coffee house. One can enjoy the accoutrements of Santa Fe without the posturing and pretense. Even Villanova University these days offers classical music, jazz and theatre. My immediate neighbor, Eastern University, a Baptist institution, shows signs of joining the modern intellectual world.

The City of Philadelphia has just been named "most violent" of America's ten largest cities. That is a real shame, because so much is happening to pull the city up. But, sadly, there is another Philadelphia, the violent one that is pulling the city down and apart. The Chamber of Commerce was wondering, "Who wants to move a business to a city designated "Most violent?" But, as the Police Commissioner points out, and so does the paper with detailed maps, the violence is far removed from the parts of the city that are being resuscitated.

Not too many years ago when I was in New York, I walked over to 310, East 75th Street, the address of my "first home." The building is still there, and the neighborhood did not strike me as "upscale Upper East Side." 310 was a brand new luxury building in 1939. Today it looks rather ordinary. Not a high rise, no doorman. I would say that my visit was perhaps 10 years ago. Perhaps things have changed. No doubt they have. The building in New York is phenomenal. Frightening, almost. I suppose one gets used to living in a box high up off the street. The energy of the city.

I have "reconnected" with Dr. Avis, by telephone. He complained that his "silence" was a combination of being rather hurt by the tone of my correspondence, and by him suffering from health and financial problems, as well as some "emotional problem"—a heavy psychic tri-partite. He did not go into much detail, except for his health, which seemed to me an accumulation of relatively minor and somewhat psychosomatic matters. We brushed aside a previous miscommunication and had a pleasant conversation about the world "falling to pieces." I mentioned that I would be in New Haven a day early. He suggested that he might come down for lunch. That would be nice. I shall be at the Hotel Duncan.

When I spoke of the threat to Moosehead Lake in Maine, he said that he did "not want to hear about it." Wanted always to remember the place as he had known it. Well, why not? Alexander, when confronted with a minor Turkish fortress that seemed "unassailable," waved his army on Eastward, saying, "Forget it—greater things await ..."

◆   ◆   ◆

18.11.06
St. David's, PA

Just got in from an invigorating walk of about one hour and a half. Quite well past dark when I strode up to the house. Annoyed, as always by my neighbor's very unnecessary and intrusive lights. Only house around here with such. Shine into my back yard. Such is life.

Last weekend in New Haven. All went about as expected, except that Henry Powell and I spent more time than anticipated in the Owl Bar, an offshoot of the old Owl Tobacconist Shop in which bar cigars may be enjoyed. Since Henry is something of a cigar aficionado … Well, the lively Irish lasses present added to our downfall.

Have not seen a Yale/Princeton game in 50 years, and had forgotten the spirit and spectacle, the elaborate tailgate parties, all that. There were sufficient "old grads" with style to bring alive the F Scott Fitzgerald sort of syndrome.

Drove up a day early to get situated at the old Hotel Duncan on Chapel Street in New Haven. $50 a night! A bit funky—could use a good going over—but rather European in its down at the heels charm. Don't think Meredith would take to it, but I found it quite adequate. Took the Merritt Parkway up for old times sake. Still quite a bit of color on the trees, and with a fine clear day it was a nice trip if a bit crowded with machines. On Friday drove up to Watertown to lunch with Dr. Avis, who it seems does not venture far from home these days, for reasons I cannot fathom. We proceeded to lunch at the Curtis Inn, oldest in Connecticut, where we were probably the youngest patrons. Lunch was surprisingly good—the old yankee pot roast syndrome has been laid to rest. Then back to Watertown and New Haven in time for a stroll about the campus before the cocktail party preceding our banquet. Noticed that the students appear somewhat more scruffy than a few years ago. Must be in reaction to some move away from materialism perhaps, and the $40,000 a year that it now costs to attend Yale. At least for those who are charged the full rate. If one's family is impoverished and you are admitted, then Yale will pick up the complete tab. Article in Yale Daily News indicated that Yale now has 9% black freshmen. Perhaps—but what about subsequent classes? I saw lots of Asians but not that many blacks …

For a small and supposedly poor city, New Haven has a surprising amount of energy. Lots of urban renewal, downtown condo projects, tall buildings. And a huge (black) angry under-class that is an immense source of many social problems. To a certain extent Yale is an island in the midst of this angry underclass, and the contrast is not always pleasant. It is also a great source of employment and other benefits that are not always appreciated. Well, so be it. Not the tranquil environment of the Princeton Tiger.

Back in St. David's things are peaceful. Some torrential tropical rain last week. Good chance to see how the basement waterproofing held up. Good. I had a feeling those men knew what they were doing. More so, perhaps, than "Dr. Desert Dry," whose advertising fills the air waves. Flooded basements are much a problem with the older houses around here. As are falling trees.

In town for some seafood and cinema. And strolls around Old City, Society Hill and Queen Village. Rather quaint sounding, and the fringes are indeed gentrifying. A friend's son-in-law bought two South Philadelphia row houses and joined them together into one townhouse now worth well in excess of 1/2 (mill that is!) In an area of former mansions of garment manufacturers that are being rehabilitated. I walked the street and found it quite gentile (I mean genteel! Pardon my crude, Hoffman-like humor.) A new and quite lavish seafood restaurant in the old Philadelphia Savings Funds Society building, a wonderful 1882 structure. Very elegant oyster bar, and extensive menu of fish. Equal to anything in New York. Almost anything!

Speaking of New York, Meredith wants to take the train up to New York Christmas Day for an elegant meal. Why this when she is both vegetarian and on a diet, I question. I have reservations at the Fountain in Philadelphia, one of 10 best restaurants in the country according to something or other. But it is a groaning buffet, and when examining the menu on line Meredith became quite nervous. When I suggested The Olde City Tavern, where we dined on Christmas Day some years ago, serenaded by musicians playing "authentic colonial era music," she seemed unenthusiastic. I see Amtrak and the spires of The Big Apple looming. Will we end up in the dated, quiet elegance of Café Pierre? Or the more exuberant atmosphere of Gramercy Tavern? God only knows …

Ran into the owner of the local bookstore at lunch the other day, and he informed me that all my books that I dropped off in October have sold. So another order for 10 more has been placed, to be delivered here in 7 to 10 days. Which is pretty good service. The Radnor Historical Society is now a cosponsor of my event at the library in January, and barring a snowstorm I think that event might go fairly well. Dr. Avis is about half way through my book and reports that he finds it an important social history of a dying if not dead way of "upper middle class Ango-American life." Perhaps. That sort of thought has occurred to me as well. More applicable to my mother and grandparents than to me. Again, perhaps … Parts of the book, my personal observations and reactions strike me as somewhat more "stuffy sounding" than might jibe with reality, but, then, at times I was deliberately aiming to come off as such. Perhaps to counterbalance Mr. Hoffman's crudeness.

(Continued Sunday evening) Just as I was starting to type, an electronic message appeared asking if it was ok to start cleaning the printing head. Oh, the marvels of electronics. A man in the library told me that since he has been "unemployed," evidently a period of several years, he had put his "whole life" on the computer. Good god! Outdid "Earl," the chap did. I told him that was great, the computer and all—if the electricity is on. Well, he said, "There is that ..." Just finished Tom Friedman's *The Earth Is Flat*. Saw it at the library and decided I had better read this book that "explains" the 21st century. Most interesting, and amazing, this interconnected world and what gets done. Not so applicable to me, as I am always trying to simplify. Did a little research on NYC restaurants, in case Meredith wears me down. And tried to find an article that I read somewhere in the 1970s about an uptight small town police chief in Idaho who went on a rampage and was shot dead by state troopers. "The Rage of Chief Simpson" was, I think, the article by, I also think, Joe Esterhaz, and might have been in *Rolling Stone*. None of that turned up anything for me.

Another cold and dark day. English, or Northern Europe, weather. I do not mind it. Gives a touch of mystique to the twilight as I walked through North Wayne, an area that Dr. Avis described as "being only in America." The only jarring note on my walk was the intrusive and annoying sound of leaf blowers being employed by various residents to clear their spacious lawns of annoying leaves. An article in the paper a few years ago advised leaving the leaves lie where they fell as they are part of nature's ongoing process. I did so one year, and found that the grass was poorly served by acidic leakage from the leaves. Here and there some were using a rake, and the rhythmic sound of that instrument was far more pleasing than the nasty whine of the leaf blowers. As darkness fell the residents put aside their machines, and a quietness fell over the streets. I could hear church bells from downtown Wayne. It was all most peaceful and satisfactory. Here and there a hint of wood smoke as perhaps some family was settling down before a fire. That seems a rare image these days, but indeed at Strafford we would gather before the fire sipping tea or hot chocolate, waiting for dinner to be announced. For a while my mother had trained me to stand at the top of the two steps of the raised dining room and say, "Le diner est servé ..." Where she got that notion, I am not sure. The Alliance Francaise, I guess ...

Am currently reading a book by John Katzenbach about obsession and all that psychotic syndrome. Reminds me of a strange episode at the Santa Fe Library years ago. I used to take the papers into the Southwest Room to read, and there for a while was a man, not badly dressed, standing and seemly staring out the window. Every day. Odd. One day I positioned myself behind him and could see that he was staring at an office building across the street. Probably watching for somebody to come out. I examined this man more carefully, surreptitiously of course. He had a certain look one would recognize from having seen it on the streets of San Francisco, perhaps most likely on Market Street or around North Beach, "Psychotic" would be my perhaps not very clinical term. "Disturbed," "obsessed," variations thereof. I reported the man to the ladies behind the info desk. "Oh, we know all about him. He's harmless …" I was informed. I started to explain that I was familiar with that syndrome, and the man was seriously disturbed, watching for someone who might be in some sort of danger. Every day! I was blown off by the "He's harmless" thing. Well, OK. I do not run the library, and evidently the man was not breaking any laws. Still, I was concerned …

A few weeks later there was in the local paper a very sad story that verified my sense of concern. The chap who had been looking out of the library window confronted a young woman as she came out of Albertson's Market, shot her dead, then shot himself dead. He had had a very brief friendship with the young woman, who had not encouraged him. Flowers, notes, candy, letters, telephone calls—the whole bit. She got a restraining order, but the police always say they cannot do anything until the man "does something." Then, of course, it is always too late—as it was in that sad case. When I saw that man staring out that window, I knew that look. I reported him. That was all I could do. I asked Meredith what she would do. "Take him out!" was her answer. The book I am reading goes into all the ramifications of obsession, stalking, all that. Along with other things, one wonders how people go so very much off the rails.

The current controversy in Philadelphia is the intended sale of the painting, "The Clinic of Dr. Gross," by Thomas Eakins, for the immense sum of $68 million, to a consortium put together by the National Gallery of Art and Mrs. Alice Walton of Wal-Mart, whose personal worth is given as $18 billion. She evidently wants the painting for a museum she is putting together in Bentonville, Arkansas, of all places. Philadelphia is given 45 days to match the sum or away goes the painting. A sense of outrage has gripped the city—or at least certain portions of it—but the likelihood of coming up with the $68 million is almost nonexistent. But we shall see.

And now, downstairs to read a bit more of the NYT …

◆   ◆   ◆

POSTSCRIPT

I should have included above that the Eakins painting is owned, having been acquired in 1882 for $200, by Thomas Jefferson Medical College (now University.) The expected $68 million is to be the "kick start" of a $400 million campaign of improvements to what is currently a very important contributor to the City of Philadelphia.

The latest development is a proposal by the Mayor to have the painting declared "an historical attribute," thus making it ineligible to be removed from the City of Philadelphia. How that would affect the expected $68 million I cannot say, and I would imagine there might be some interesting legal aspects. We shall see ...

◆   ◆   ◆

3.12.06
St. David's, PA

There was, this past week, a notice in the paper of an art exhibition to be held at "Salon des Amis" of paintings of Chester County barns. I was tempted to attend, but my last visitation there did not exactly inspire. A summer day it was, and the patrons did not seem of a particularly elevated type. The proprietress was drunk, as was the featured artist, whose subject matter was old trailers of Chester County. I did admire his work, but failed to connect verbally with him about his subject matter, which interests me somewhat from observations in travels with Mr. Hoffman. So, this time I decided to pass on Salon des Amis, which is on a handsome farm out toward Chester Springs, where the Pennsylvania Academy of Fine Arts had its summer quarters and which still consists of a fine collection of old buildings and a rather good restaurant. Worth a visit, and Meredith might enjoy such a country excursion during her visit here. I used to know a chap, years ago, who lived in an old unrestored farmhouse out that way, rather primitive. But he was an art student and the somewhat bohemian atmosphere suited. Derek Warner by name, he had frequent parties always with charming young ladies in attendance. Derek was from a sophisticated world, and knew people far and wide. When I went out to California I lost touch. Now, on occasional drives out to Chester Springs I pass that house and remember. It is fully restored now, rather "gentrified" one might say, and there are expensive automobiles parked. No longer a bohemian haunt, with parties far into the soft and languid Chester County summer nights.

This afternoon I shall be attending a concert at Roberts Hall on the Haverford College campus, of the American Brass Ensemble. Not, perhaps, a suitable substitute for those tuxedoed gentlemen outside Shreve's in San Francisco at the Christmas season, who are so firmly imprinted on my mind, but it will have to do. It has been unseasonably warm all this week, until last night, if gray and damp. On my walk on the Haverford College campus in the late afternoon last week I was consistently reminded of the English countryside, Surrey or Kent, but without the oaks and rolling hills. But the mist was just so, and the campus lamps slightly reminiscent of gas. A very pleasant walk it was, and after I repaired to the Seville Café at the newly restored Bryn Mawr Theatre (originally The Seville) which now functions as the Bryn Mawr Film Institute, a very worthy enterprise that would be at home in Berkeley. The young woman who served up my latté did not have a bolt through her nose, for which I was grateful.

Several of my books sold at the Station Café in Wayne, now under the new proprietorship of Eddie, an energetic young man from Queens, and his attractive wife. They have installed a deli and serve up soup and sandwiches. I would prefer something "more sophisticated," so when I stop by I limit myself to a latté, for which Eddie charges me only one dollar (creating good will, word of mouth, etc ...) Mr. Hoffman and I used to patronize the place under a previous ownership. He was always energized by the trains passing by, particularly the fast expresses of the Keystone Service.

Speaking of trains, reservations have been made on Amtrak for me and Meredith to and from the Big Apple on Christmas Day. Up on the Acela from Philadelphia, and return on Keystone to Ardmore (actually an Irish town, not Welsh.) Even with senior discount the fares are rather expensive. But not as much as the meal for which Meredith has made reservations. L'Atelier de Joel Roberchon (Google it if you wish). Why I have allowed this to happen I am not sure. Something to do with Meredith's accusation of me "being in a rut." Or guilt about wriggling out of a trip to Buenos Aires and Rio. Well, if the weather is OK, the excursion might be somewhat better than tolerable. The tree and rink at Rockefeller Centre—an early childhood memory.

Friday past I accepted an invitation from my friend Maurice Weintraub, an architect and very savvy chap with an office in Wayne with whom I occasionally lunch. He wanted me to see his house in the country—actually not far, in Malvern, but sufficiently rustic. A very interesting place. Très moderne, but built in 1957 by an architect named Baringer, who evidently was under the perhaps Bauhaus spell popular in the '50s but not much if at all in evidence on the Main Line. Well, there are a few of that period hidden here and there. Mature landscaping and some slight improvements by Maurice and his wife, a landscape architect, have rendered a very sophisticated and comfortable living space. Craftsman furnishings seem quite appropriate to the almost Japanese interior. Hi tech electronic equipment, with a large stereo TV to entertain his two teenage girls. His wife was at the office they share in Wayne, and Maurice explained that Friday was his day home alone to work and have friends in. I felt honored to be included in the latter. He keeps saying that he is going to purchase the book but so far seems not to have to gotten around to it. I have placed a new batch with The Readers Forum, perhaps America's most cluttered and disorderly bookshop. They are lucky to have a loyal clientele who are dedicated to patronizing the locally owned business, of which there are a fair number left in Wayne.

One of my favorites is Pat, the barber. Pat Shea, with his fast talking Philly accent. A man of great political incorrectness—i.e. "Where all these fuckin' Mexicans come from? They're everywhere, like cockroaches …" I think that says it. So a man of great charm, in a rough way. His shop also must rank high on the disordered and ill-maintained scale—there are great amounts of hair accumulated on the floor which he only occasionally sweeps up. He has an old fashioned brass cash register which opens with a mighty clang. Sometimes, to make change he retrieves crumpled dollar bills that are stuffed into a plastic supermarket bag which he keeps in the closet. He also has a loyal clientele, I among it, who appreciate his salty wit, his reasonable price and his quick, efficient if not stylish haircuts. A solid Wayne character. Not a reading man, so no mention of the book. Plus, I don't want him knowing all my secrets—which are revealed in the book. Well, some of them …

Money is being raised to try to keep the Eakins painting in Philadelphia. One third of the 68 million so far. But I do not think enough will be raised by the 26 December Deadline. What I do think will happen is what the Mayor seems to be planning. And that is, to have the City Historical Commission declare the painting "an historical object," rendering it ineligible to be removed from the city. Thus, legal wrangling would begin, perhaps lasting for a suitable time for the rest of the 68 million to be raised, allowing Jefferson University to recoup money expected from the sale of the painting. Then, presumably, everyone would be happy. Except probably Ms Walton, who seems set on having "great art" in the wilds of Arkansas. A worthy cause, perhaps. On the other hand, perhaps not …

The Barnes Collection seems well on its way to a location in a structure to be built on the Parkway, not far from the esteemed Philadelphia Museum of Art. There are still problems—lingering lawsuits, lack of sufficient funds, things like that. But, I believe they will be overcome. In New Haven Henry Powell and I had coffee with a friend of his, an Englishman who is curator at the Mellon Centre for British Art and who is acquainted with Derek Gilmore, another Englishman who has just been appointed new Director of the Barnes. "Rather a challenging job," said Henry's friend, with typical British understatement. And, speaking of things cultural, Meredith and I will be attending the annual New Year's Eve concert of the Philadelphia Orchestra. Wherein quite a few Strauss waltzes are played, along with other energetic pieces. We will have a light supper before, perhaps a few drinks after, but no carousing on the Eve. Safe and sound back in St. David's. By train if that is convenient. As Maurice says, "We'll train to the city …" That sounds somewhat New Yorkerish. Do they not say things like, "I'll cab up there?" Or as they say in LA, "We went surface …" meaning not on the over-crowded freeways. Ah, the ever evolving lingo of urban America. Which term I presume to be a crude variety of "lingua."

On Wednesday, after "training to town," I was headed to Philadelphia Fish and Company, to sample the very excellent bargain the Executive Lunch; soup, salad, drink and a very excellently prepared and presented fish for $12. All in "an atmosphere agreeable ..." But, some inner voice diverted me to Ludvig's Bavarian Garten, where some time ago I had, as one might expect, a rather filling buffet of Germanic items. Unfortunately—or perhaps fortunately?—that is no longer available, "Not since four years ago," the elderly waiter sadly informed me. I commented that they probably lost money with Philadelphians packing the buffet food away. He nodded and turned to get me a menu, but I was already out the door and headed for the nearby McGillin's Olde Ale House on Drury Lane, founded in 1865, and today managed by the ever cheerful Mary Ellen Mullen and where the clientele is very traditional Philadelphia and the waitresses are older women who call you "Hon." The food is traditional fare and not expensive. No gourmet awards, but quite adequate. After the communal soup crock pot (that day corned beef and cabbage soup—ugh!) I had the Shepherd's Pie, these days almost universally made with ground beef, about which I always comment negatively saying "Who ever heard of a shepherd pushing cows around?" Mary Ellen is the daughter of Henry, the owner and bartender when Ted Roberts and I were patrons so long ago, struggling with trying to establish some rapport with the Irish shop girls who swarmed into the place on Friday nights. Finally we settled for Carol and Stevie, nice Protestant young women from the Quaker community of Moorestown, NJ. They shared a small house on narrow South Delhi Street in what was to become "olde City," where many young people lived and there were frequent "block parties." A great deal of all that is in the book *Earl* ...

For many years, perhaps since this house was built by my mother in 1961, there has been in the attic an "antique" dollhouse that amused my mother when she was a child at Shadowild in Strafford, a few miles away. Perhaps I should say "almost antique," since the item is less than 100 years of age and is somewhat crude in its construction. It was built by my grandfather, who was no carpenter but did know how to do things, and furnished with dollhouse things of the 1920s. I always admired it in the attic and thought it was "going to waste" up there where no one ever saw it. So I concocted a scheme of getting it down to the upstairs hall and displaying it on a low table I purchased at the unpainted furniture place in Wayne. Last week, with some struggle I got the thing, which is rather large and heavy, being constructed out of fairly thick wood, down the narrow attic stairs into place. Now I am wondering if my idea was such a good one after all. Because the dollhouse is rather over-large and not in scale with the hallway. I shall wait to see what Meredith's reaction is. In the meantime it needs a thorough cleaning and restoration of many of the interior pieces. The thing does have a certain charm, but I am not sure that where it is now is the right place. I could never get it back up to the attic myself, so the only onward path would have to be down—and then where who knows?

While walking in Independence National Park in town I notice that pedestrians have disfigured the grass by "cutting corners" from the paved walks. I remember that the students at Yale used to do that, and it annoyed me. Then small chain partitions were placed at the corners to discourage the "cutting." These were mostly successful, because evidently the same urge to cut the corner made the effort of stepping over the small barriers not worth it. There is something about people that is unable to keep them on the path, either in the Park or in Life. Social disorder in Philadelphia indeed drags the city down. I gather that London these days is experiencing severe social disorder. Not so when I was there for several months in 1958 and 1959. One felt perfectly safe in London. A woman I know who lives there, quite well off, calls herself "a champagne socialist," tells me that one is safer in New York now than in London. Astonishing ...

I think about the person and plays of August Wilson, who studied at the Yale School of Dramatic Art. I have seen several of his plays, which were popularly reviewed, and wondered about them. There was something a bit off. It seemed to me that he was really pushing the "black culture thing." Pushing it in the audience's collective face. Then, as I read a bit of Mr. Wilson biography I began to see a certain pattern. First, one has to look twice at his photograph to discern that he is (or was, since he is deceased) "black." The son of a black father and an Italian mother, as a child he was rather light in color. I have read how this can cause an "identity problem," with the child not being accepted by either blacks or whites. I am presuming that to overcome this, Mr. Wilson devoted his life to proclaiming his "blackness." Indeed, I read that he was a fervent supporter of, and contributor to, black causes. I would say that all this, his plays and everything, adds up to a vast effort to "prove his blackness." Not that any of that diminishes his value as a playwright and/or social critic. It is just interesting, to me if to no one else. And as Meredith frequently reminds me, many things that interest me do not other people and they would prefer that they not be subjected to some of my peculiar interests. I understand. Mea culpa ...

Lunch last week at the Indian buffet over toward Valley Forge, where I used to dine with Mr. Hoffman so he could "load up." And where after I often feel that I have made something of a mistake and that my money might have been better spent some other place. As I entered I noticed a "help wanted" sign in the window, which I find odd since there always appeared to be no shortage of Indian waiters. On this occasion there was only one Indian man circulating in the fairly large room. As it is a buffet, he was mostly bringing drinks and filling glasses. I notice now that not only kitchen help is Mexican, but there was a rather Mayan looking, short woman clearing and resetting the tables, quite solemnly—for her Indian overlords. The place is usually quite full of Indians from the high tech establishments in the area, so I presume that is a testament to the authenticity of the offerings.

A bite to eat before the concert, and a stroll on the Haverford College campus after. The NYT reading will be a bit behind schedule, but that cannot be helped. A brief ten days back in Santa Fe, then back here to get ready for Meredith. Must have her room immaculately clean. She complained the last time. My standards are no where near as high as hers. I always wonder how she fares in India …

◆   ◆   ◆

16 January 2007
St. David's, PA

The New Year. It is hoped that it will be a good one, but one cannot helping wondering, "In what way?"

I am still, as of this date, in Penn's Woods, having just last Thursday evening given my talk and book signing at the Radnor Memorial Library. The event went tolerably well, although I feel that it might have been better attended. It was co-sponsored by The Radnor Historical Society and promoted throughout the membership. One has to face the reality that quite often what one is presenting is simply not of much interest to all that many people. Of course, today the media has the power to CREATE interest, and it does. Reference Oprah and her "book club"—guarantees a half million in sales! What power! Anyway, at the event I sold seven copies. Next to deal with is my book *Dust Devils*, currently in production by Sunstone Press in Santa Fe. They recently over-nighted me the manuscript and cover art to "proof" for the final time. There is inconsistency, which I previously pointed out, with the word café—sometimes with the "acute" slash, and sometimes without. I don't know what their reasoning is, if any. Seems a simple matter to deal with, but what they do seems beyond me. The cover art is about as bad as I can imagine, but I did not offer any comment as I am tired of these people and how they do things. I would think that this awful cover would discourage people from buying the book. We shall see. I don't think the Sunstone people care very much about my book, something I have felt from the beginning.

Now, to reverse gears and return to the pre-holiday period. I arrived at the PHL aerodrome Tuesday 19 December on time at 4:40 P.M. Since Jack no longer drives at night he does not come to pick me up at that hour. I schedule my arrival midweek to avail myself of the frequent train connections between the aerodrome, 30th Street Station and the line out to St. David's. It is relatively quick and enjoyable, the train being a welcome respite from the confines of the flying machine. The brisk ten minute walk from the St. David's station to the house is restorative. I have only a very small carry-on, so there is no impediment of that nature to trundle along.

On Saturday Meredith arrived on the same Southwest flight. We repaired to the city (Not capitalized as is that west coast center of pretentiousness.) to dine at Bistro Seven, one of the many small storefront BYOL restaurants that seem to be springing up in Society Hill and Olde (Yes, unfortunately with the "e.") City. An excellent meal, prepared by a hands-on chef from local and organic ingredients, which Meredith pronounced equal to anything in Santa Fe—if that be a compliment or not.

The next day, Sunday, "The New York Times," of course, seeing a film, and generally getting organized to take the Acela up to The Big Apple on Christmas Day for our holiday fashionably late lunch at L'Atelier de Joel Robishon. The train was more crowded than I would have thought, and neither as luxurious nor speedy as I had been led to believe. Not worth the extra fare in this man's opinion. I was glad that our return accommodations had been booked on a conventional train.

We arrived in a Penn Station that was startlingly different from what I remembered, having been "refurbished" in questionable manner. Still an underground warren. Many indigent persons waving paper cups, but the hard hearts of the impatient travelers did not open for these entreaties, even on Christmas Day.

We had plenty of time before our meal, so we took the bus north on Madison from Penn Station (#34, senior fare one dollar in change only—I had done my research!) We chatted amiably with the only other passenger, a woman who had come in from Long Island to share a holiday meal with friends. Then off at 57th, to stroll around and perhaps have a pre-luncheon drink at the Oak Room Bar of the Plaza Hotel, where my father always said his cousin Claude DuHaine "drank himself to death," which I always rather doubted but something did bring on a premature death to that unfortunate chap. The taxi driver (Meredith had a walking problem because of fancy shoes.) told us that the Plaza was closed, and indeed it was—being made into condominiums, or "condemniums," as John Galey referred to them. The size and energy of Manhattan never cease to amaze and awe. One wonders what keeps it all going, and what it means? Along Fifth Avenue there seemed to be an unusual number of those very dark, non-English speaking Africans selling all sorts of "fake" or duplicate merchandise for out of town suckers thinking they are getting a bargain. I have noticed that these fellows are "run" by Arabs lurking nearby and who appear to collect money before any tempting amount accumulates. A modern form of slavery, one might think. The crowds around Rockefeller Center were immense, made up it seemed of bridge and tunnel people from all over the world. Many different languages and faces. All, it seemed, in good Christmas cheer. The decorations were, as always, lavish, and the skaters whirled with abandon on the ice. I remembered that several times my father and I had struggled on that ice, I less than he, because I had practice at the Ardmore rink at home. Before we left the plaza and the carriages, where once my father had donated a very fine overcoat to the best-looking driver and conveyance (something that perchance had belonged to his father's "coachman" long before?), I checked my change to verify that I had enough for the bus ride back to the station later that afternoon. To my great chagrin I found that somehow I had only one ninety-five—a nickel short! How had that happened? What to do? Buy some expensive, unwanted item just to get change? Meredith had no change at all. Then—a solution! Right in before us, in front of the former General Motors building, now taken over by Apple, perhaps the new corporate giant, one might say, was a large reflecting pool into which the superstitious and hopeful had hurled all manner of coins. On my knees, in hat and dark overcoat, I fished out first a quarter, then a nickel to be safe, while Meredith photographed this odd and, she commented, "rather sad" spectacle with her marvelous little digital camera. Whatever—I had the necessary change for the bus, and would not have to brood about that matter during our Christmas lunch.

The meal was elegant, as were the surroundings, minimalist and quite delicious. Served by very professional waiters, all of whom seemed to be from Bangladesh. Perhaps doctors and lawyers in that country of limited opportunity. All spoke excellent English. How all that is arranged would be interesting to know. At the next table sat a man whom I took to be "a Russian gangster," alone except for a tough-looking young man who perhaps was a body-guard. He was treated with great deference, and several people stopped at this table "to pay respect." As he got up to leave, when passing our table Meredith said brightly, "Merry Christmas." He paused, smiled and said "Thank you." The modern elegance of L'Atelier, and of the Four Seasons, is rather over the top, unsettling to one used to the "down home funkiness" of Philadelphia. Quite unnecessary, in my humble opinion, which is most often mine and mine alone. As is the case in such places, everyone is most deferential and helpful, no doubt expecting to be rewarded momentarily as the patrons of such places are generally known to distribute tips in a lavish manner thereby achieving an aura of power and respect whether or not they are so entitled. Not so with this Philadelphia Quaker, if I may harken back to my early heritage. I am sure that they look upon the parsimoniousness of my sort with contempt and scorn, the almighty dollar being the prime energy that motivates The Big Apple. After our meal, which was most decidedly not over-filling, as are so many holiday repasts, there was a bit of time for window shopping on Madison, then over to Fifth Avenue just as a light rain was beginning to fall, and a wait on church steps for the #34 bus back to Penn Station. A family of dark skinned foreigners, not at all poor looking, attempted to board the bus but were told they could not ride unless they had "correct change." They were having difficulty understanding what the black driver was telling them, only that they could not board the bus, so the driver just closed the door in their collective face, leaving them in the rain (and perhaps mad at America?) The driver did, I think, the only thing he could do. Hey—this is Noo Yawk! Then the train, rattling across dark, familiar flatland New Jersey, New Brunswick, Trenton (the bridge across the Delaware still reads "Trenton makes, the world takes.") and the car parked at 30th Street Station, for a hefty fee. And finally St. David's. It was still early. Meredith went alone to a movie. I read quietly.

The next day, the day after Christmas, we got a late start in the machine for the Eastern Shore (of Maryland.) I had planned lunch at the Kitty Knight house on the Sassafras River, but we were just south of Wilmington when Meredith inquired about lunch. She does not eat breakfast, substituting yoga which I am not sure is nutritionally responsible. So we detoured, slightly, to the wonderful colonial town of New Castle, Delaware, one of America's rather undiscovered treasures. After a short stroll about I found "The Arsenal," where Meredith and I had dined on a June day a few years before. Alas, it was closed for the winter. A sign directed us to Jessup's Tavern, seemingly the only place open. It was full, and there was an interminable wait for our meals to appear. I began to get quite agitated, not wanting to arrive in St. Michael's in the dark. No fear, however, because when we were back on the road it was a quick two hours to our destination. Meredith was interested in how the atmosphere of Maryland began to look "Southern." Plantation houses, large flat fields, stands of yellow leaf pine, meandering tidal streams and bogs. As one approaches St. Michael's, on a peninsula jutting into Chesapeake Bay, one notices a very mellow harmony of land, water and sky. And, the architecture of the earlier colonial period blends nicely into all that. Rain showers erupted as we drove into town. I was hoping they would be brief. It was not quite dark as we found our lodging, "The Harborside Inn," which had offered a mid-week and mid-winter price break, so our suite overlooking the harbor and moored boats was comparatively reasonable. I had been to St. Michael's a few years earlier with Mr. Hoffman, accompanying him on some errand to a boat building concern of considerable seriousness. The whole of the Eastern Shore was, and still is to some extent, tied to the water, Fishing, clamming, oystering. Moving agricultural commodities and people to towns by steamship and ferry. Other forms of maritime commerce. Today it is yachting, a pastime mostly for the wealthy and not much of character building. Quite a heritage of wooden vessel construction. A wonderful maritime museum in St. Michael's captures the heritage of all this, for those interested, as I am, in that sort of thing. For those not interested, well, they might be better off at the Metropolitan Opera in Lincoln Center. I had spent a couple of hours there while Mr. Hoffman visited with the boat builders. Maritime architects, rather. Others did the actual building. When he took me there before we left, I learned that his errand had something to do with a distinguished wooden yacht owned by the family of a young woman he had formerly paid attentions to. What all that was about I had no idea. I remembered that I enjoyed the atmosphere of St. Michael's and the crab lunch we had at an establishment where they pulled tubs of struggling crabs right out of the water so they could be boiled and prepared for the lunch and dinner crowds. Called "The Crab Claw," rather tritely. Probably better that than "Davey Jones' Boudoir ..." On this visit with Meredith it was closed for the winter.

After getting settled at The Harborside, we went for a short walk in the twilight. It was unseasonably warm. Quite still. The showers had let up. The back streets of the town held very many quite attractive houses, once perhaps the residences of "watermen," as those making a living from the sea are called in those parts. But now quite obviously the (summer) homes of wealthy persons from "afar," probably Washington and New York. Quite a bit of skilled restoration was going on, and there were lovely Christmas decorations and lights. I got the impression that increasing numbers of those from "afar" were opting for year round—or nearly year round—residence. Talking to a few people I did get the feeling that some found it "too quiet," too removed ... That happens in Santa Fe, too.

The only place we found open for dinner was a fairly rough tavern for locals, with a dining area where Meredith was sure we would be served a frozen then micro-waved meal of little or no charm, or taste. So, back to the hotel it was, where in the upstairs dining room over looking the lights of the harbor we were served a surprisingly delicious and very sophisticated meal. Quelle surprise! A few drinks in the lounge, where I was eyed (suspiciously?) by a German speaking bunch—perhaps because of my moustache, then a restful night with waves lapping against the harborside and buoys clanging in the straits.

The next day dawned bright and clear. While Meredith applied herself to yoga, I took a paper, coffee and croissant at the hotel, and then walked through the charming streets to the maritime museum. Though familiar with it there is always something new to see, particularly among the working wooden boat collection. When I was there before they had been engaged in the actual construction of a wooden schooner, the last wooden boat of its size to be built on the east coast, perhaps in America. The subject of a *New York Times* article a few weeks before my previous visit. I had read that the mast of eighty feet had to be imported from Oregon. On this visit there were virtually no other visitors so I was able to spend quite a bit of time with two docents, a very well informed chap and his chipper wife. They had retired to St. Michael's from Seattle, the reason being evidently that he was originally from Baltimore and had summered on the Eastern Shore in his youth. My visit consumed about two hours. When I returned to the hotel Meredith was ready for lunch and the afternoon we had planned for a drive out to Tilghman Island off the very end of our peninsula. A place of serious watermen, I had been informed in my guidebook. Lunch at the Chesapeake House was a mistake, in spite of the visual charm of the establishment. Long, long wait for tasteless food, served by a cheerful but inept teenaged waitress. Once more a late start but not that many miles to cover. The ride out to the Island was through agricultural, tidewater plantation country. Long driveways going to large houses on the water. These are now being bought up by the rich from afar, the longtime local owners not being able to afford them any more. We were informed that Donald Rumsfeld and Dick Cheney are buying property in the area. Ugh! There were some interesting villages with various types of watermen's vessels in harbors. It did look serious. One vessel was flying a Confederate flag. I guess that might be some sort of indicator. We heard one fellow on his cell phone, talking rather loudly. I told Meredith to get a good earful of his accent, with was as unique as any to be found in America these days. Out at the very tip of the island is an establishment very much of the 19th century called Black Walnut Inn. Now owned by the State, it was open during the winter. Indeed, as we were poking around some guests arrived, perhaps thinking what they had probably arranged for on the internet had not seemed quite as isolated and rough as this place. Well, not actually rough—spare would be more like it. Run by a rather dour middle aged woman who said she was glad for some guests, that "It would be good to have somebody to talk with." So much for long winter nights at the Black Walnut Inn, with Chesapeake winds and clanging buoys. With no one to talk to. She gave us a long spiel about hurricane Irene some years back and the havoc it wreaked. Nearby we took a stroll through one of the charming small villages. A man working in his yard did not look up as we passed. Two fellows that I took to be watermen were drinking beer on a bench outside the local store. They regarded us rather coldly, I thought. I surmised that the watermen did not think much of outsiders, that they would prefer to be left alone. I don't blame them—who does like "outsiders?" Only those who are dancing like monkeys for their money, I suppose.

Dinner that night had been planned for the elegant Inn at Perry Cabin, an establishment that has grown in size and opulence beyond what I think might be in keeping with the more rustic heritage of St. Michael's. Nonetheless, the restaurant was very highly rated, and other options seemed few. The dining room was hardly full, and it was definitely the sort of place where you might look around and see Rummy and his gang at a nearby table. An unsettling thought. The food and wine were excellent, the service most professional, and the crabcakes pronounced by Meredith the best she had ever eaten—just superb! After dinner we were shown around by a charming young man, the assistant manager, and informed that if we chose to return to stay a few days, or longer, with them every need and desire would be attended to. The place was part of a chain of exclusive establishments in this country and Europe. Rather over the top for my taste … Back at the hotel a "night cap" in the lounge before retiring. No staring Germans this time.

Pleasant weather the next morning, still warm. The agenda was Oxford and lunch in Easton, perhaps not quite in that order. I strolled a bit farther afield while Meredith attended to yoga, finding more attractive corners of St. Michael's, wondering just how crowded it got in the warm months. Rather too much was my impression. I was glad to be there in the quiet off season. The annual wooden, boat festival might be interesting, however. In the fall, I think.

We went to Oxford first, and found it an utterly charming place, with a long main street leading to the water, lined with attractive houses. One of the first "gateways" to the colony of Maryland, there had been wealth enough to construct substantial houses. Nothing more than a small grocery store was open—we had been informed that there were no commercial establishments in Oxford so to not lure "day trippers" and other tourists who seek only to buy things. Common sense, I thought. So, for food we beat a retreat to Easton, the county seat of Tolbert County, a town of some size with all the requisite commercial establishments and some colonial charm. We ate at the Tidewater Inn, which was adequate, barely. A walk about town after. To the east I noticed a few Mexican establishments, evidence of the influx of those people to the chicken industry of the Eastern Shore, wherein they have replaced at low wages long time black employees. Another matter …

Back in Oxford we took a lengthy walk around the place. At the foot of the main street, by the water, is the old Morris Inn, where James Michener stayed for almost two years while he wrote his massive (eight hundred pages!) book *Chesapeake*. I have a paperback edition but as yet have not been able to get started on it, led astray by such things as a book on the history of the AK-47 assault weapon—"the gun that changed the world." There was a lowering sky that added a sense of loneliness to the remote and seemingly deserted town. There were some serious boatworks with vessels in drydock or up on rails. Expensive looking, the boats and the work. I have been told that the upkeep on a wooden vessel is punishing. When I told Meredith that I had thought of buying such a vessel, she snorted, "Fine—and then you can live on it, alone!" It was into twilight when we started back to St. Michael's, and I must say that I thought Oxford one of the most charming and alluring places I have seen. I think of it still. There was certainly nothing in that sublime environment to make one reflect on the ugly social/racial disorder that had taken place in the early 1970s just to the south in Cambridge, Maryland.

Last night at St. Michael's and we had only one option left for dinner—the Crab and Steak House, which was crowded and quite good. The diners did not seem an affluent crowd, more local and middle class. Very American, which is, I think, one of the subtle appeals of places like St. Michael's. We had lunch there the next day before leaving, and that also was a satisfactory meal. Meredith wanted some crabcakes from the Inn at Perry Cabin to go—they were so delicious. When she opened the container, as we sat in the car by the harbor before our "regular lunch," she was dismayed to find that they had given her one order cut into two, for twice the price of one order. Some serious failure of communication. Plus, as I suspected would be the case, eating them in the car would not prove as satisfying as the night before at a well appointed table in an elegant dining room. No ...

Three hours later we were back in St. David's. Enough time for me to take a walk, and for us to prepare for our 9:30 P.M. reservation for dinner at Le Bec Fin, Philadelphia's most elegant (and expensive) restaurant. The drive into town was without complication, and I found a parking spot on Walnut Street not TOO far from the restaurant, thus saving the $18 valet fee plus $5 tip. Always the thrifty Quaker, I am—when I have the chance, that is.

Monsieur Perrier has regained his fifth star from Mobil Travel Guide for Le Bec Fin, although I am not sure just how much of an honor that really is. It seems important to some, however. I have dined numerous times at this fine restaurant, and my reaction is always the same—that it is reaching very high and just barely does not make the goal it has set for itself. That does not mean that it is not a very fine restaurant, especially for Philadelphia. And therein lies the point, which may be somewhat psychological. It is not in New York or Paris! The food is of the very highest quality, and immaculately presented, although I sometimes feel that the waiters are not quite as sophisticated as they would be in the afore-mentioned cities. And the patrons—well, quite often I have observed them to definitely not be of the character that one would expect in New York and Paris. These are not complaints—merely observations. The once high and overwhelming dessert cart has been down-sized, though still laden with the most wonderful tarts and sweets, several of which are always placed in a small bag to be taken home. With the late hour of our meal it was almost midnight when we emerged on a nearly deserted Walnut Street. Light traffic on the way out to St. David's and dreams of the dessert cart lurching out of control.

Must fast forward here, as things are bogging down in too much detail. A Sunday lunch with Meredith and my neighbor and Radnor Historical Society president at the relatively new Margaret Kuo's in Wayne. A great disappointment. I would not return, nor would I recommend the place. This in spite of quite favorable reviews. Then train to town and the annual New Year's Eve concert by the Philadelphia Orchestra, in the new and very handsome Kimmel Center. Rousing music, followed by a drink and a jazz ensemble on a mezzanine. Uncrowded train out, before the witching hour, and the conductor thrust my money back in a gesture of good will. Much appreciated.

New Year's Day found us at the annual party at The Merion Cricket Club. Sumptuous buffets, two jazz bands playing and "Miss Justine" a very good vocalist. A thoroughly pleasant affair, and a nice way to tie a last bow on the Holiday Season. Meredith enjoyed it immensely.

Next day delivering Meredith to her Southwest flight at the Philadelphia aerodrome, back to a New Mexico and Santa Fe buried under two feet of snow and frigid temperatures. The East Coast remained unseasonably warm. As I drove back to St. David's from the aerodrome, I found myself thinking, not kindly, "Free at last! Free at last! God almighty, free at last!" One may read into that what one will …

Well, the whole thing WAS cheaper than Buenos Aires and Rio. Of that I keep reminding myself. Today, at lunch at Christopher's in Wayne there was a new server. A tall, blonde, gray-eyed young woman with the interesting name of "Lenka." From what Eastern European country? I wondered. I did not ask, being pre-occupied with the task of finishing the proofing of the "Dust Devils" ms and sending it back to Santa Fe.

2007—another "new year," and we shall see what it brings …

◆   ◆   ◆

FINIS

(Poem by Walter Savage Landor, 1775–1864)

"I strove with none, for none was worth my strife.
Nature I loved and, next to nature Art:
I warmed both hands before the fire of life;
It sinks, and I am ready to depart."

(New Oxford BOOK OF ENGLISH VERSE 1250–1916, 1955
    Edition)

Sitting in the old farmhouse, in a chair by the kitchen table, a warm wind rustling the beech tree outside in the dark, Hornbeck read the short Landor poem over and over. It had come, mysteriously, in the mail. From whom? Hornbeck did not know. Ready to depart? Ready, perhaps. But to depart, well, not quite yet. A few more years.

It had all been a wonderful, magnificent joke—he and the other man, the author. They had pursued parallel lines, lives even, and had become as one. Perhaps had always been one. Who could tell? Some sage perhaps, with mystical powers. But the ordinary person, no. It was all so artfully, supremely constructed, intertwined and dissolving.

Hornbeck smiled to himself, and put the poem and the *Oxford Book of English Verse* he had consulted aside. No more need of that stuff. He took a quaff of Irish ale, and a puff on his seegar. The smoke wreathed around the lamp on the table, then was pulled out through the windows by the warm wind outside. The night was deep and quiet, but Hornbeck reflected that in the deserts on the other side of the world the martyrs were restless. He understood fanatics, and deserts, the purity and timelessness of deserts. But, there in the quiet farmhouse kitchen Hornbeck was far from deserts.

He got up and went to the fridge for another beer. Passing the wall mirror he glanced at himself in it. He seemed to be disappearing down and into a hall of mirrors, growing smaller and smaller, until—nothing. I am reflecting, he thought, reflecting into nothingness ...

◆   ◆   ◆

FINAL NOTE

Has the reader "put it all together?" Understood *Constructing Hornbeck*? Or has it all been one "baffling mess"? Think, reader, think! Do the fogs and mists dissolve? And the bright clarity of sun and daylight illuminate?

◆   ◆   ◆

Or do the fogs and mists remain, obscuring, confusing things, leaving one groping and stumbling in a wilderness?

◆   ◆   ◆

(A troubling and often recurring dream …)

A freight train is rumbling through the thick forests and canyons of Northern California, its air horn reverberating in the mountains. A man stands on a bank above the tracks, watching the train. Suddenly the earth of the bank, saturated by many recent heavy rains, starts to crumble. The man begins to slide down in a cascade of earth, toward the tracks, toward the rumbling train. He reaches for a fir branch in an attempt to stop his downward slide, to save himself …

(A careful reading in January 2007 of the perhaps parochial and somewhat boring suburban Philadelphia newspapers might have brought the reader's attention to the following article, which Hornbeck read with great amusement. He read it several times, laughing quietly to himself in the farmhouse kitchen.)

From the Wayne, PA, *Suburban*

Dayton Lummis
Main Line memories

By Ryan Richards

An imposing figure in a wide-brimmed green-felt hat, blue kerchief around the neck and dressed in a blue plaid shirt, jeans and brown hiking shoes. Dayton Lummis seems out of place amid the trendy boutiques and restaurants of Wayne. His handlebar mustache completes the picture of a man more at home at his cottage, called a casita, in Santa Fe.

But the author is here to talk about the East, about growing up on the Main Line, experiences—good and bad—here. His latest book, *When Earl Was King Neptune*, captures his youth in Strafford and St. David's. On the cover of the book is a painting of his grandparents' home on Homestead Road in Strafford.

The 69-year-old writer, a resident of both St. David's and New Mexico, says during the interview that the Main Line of his youth was "more uptight" than it is today. And unlike today, Democrats were a rare sighting in public.

New York-born, Lummis was brought to live at his grandparents' Strafford home in 1940. His grandfather, Paul Lewis, a newspaper man and then Philadelphia advertising whiz, was one of the cofounders of Tredyffrin Township's Martin's Dam swim club, where he learned to swim.

The young Lummis attended the former Booth School in Devon, Valley Meeting and The Haverford School, where he participated in football and track. His idle time was spent in the Anthony Wayne Theater hooked on cowboy and war-film matinees.

His mother, Dorothy Lewis Lummis, "a divorced woman with a small child," made ends meet by opening up a women's clothing shop, Country Cousin, where the Paisley Shop is now on East Lancaster Avenue, Wayne, in 1950. She ran a tidy shop where "the cookie jar was always full of cookies" from a local bakery.

"My mother had a real feeling for clothing and fashion," he explained. The shop was successful, so much so that she opened a similar shop in Bryn Mawr.

Lummis' book includes a chapter, "Crime and Punishment," which recounts his run-ins with the law as a youth in 1952. "Mild by today's standards," he writes, "nonetheless troublesome and a grave disappointment to my family and others."

"It was rather unfortunate," he said during the interview. "But it taught me a lesson."

His book includes his frank modern-day observations of the Main Line. He says the area has retained many of its hometown charms, such as families taking evening strolls and youth involved in organized sports. He says Santa Fe, on the other hand, has become touristy.

"I have traveled all over the country and this is as healthy as it comes," he said of the Main Line.

As for the title, *When Earl Was King Neptune*, it refers to Earl, one of his favorite summer-camp counselors, a "cheerful, older country fellow," who was "King Neptune" during a water carnival.

Lummis, a Yale grad and retired director of various cultural history museums in Western states, previously wrote a book of "cowboy poetry," and one about California, where his father worked as an actor. He is now in the final stages of completing a book on the people and places of the "Inter Mountain West," as he calls it, the region between the Rockies and the West Coast.

Lummis' new book is available at Reader's Forum and the Station Café, both in Wayne, as well as Amazon.com, and he will do a local book signing in January. In the meantime, you may see the writer, whose biography states that he has never owned a television, moseying about town, greeting Pat the barber, Georgette the *Suburban* receptionist and other town folk. He says he plans to spend more time on the Main Line—just don't expect him to swap his blue kerchief and plaid shirt for tweed and an ascot anytime soon.

978-0-595-44306-2
0-595-44306-0